The Princeton Review®

Cracking the

AP®

ENGLISH LANGUAGE AND COMPOSITION EXAM

2019 Edition

The Staff of The Princeton Review

PrincetonReview.com

Penguin
Random
House

The Princeton Review
110 East 42nd St, 7th Floor
New York, NY 10017
Email: editorialsupport@review.com

ISBN: 978-1-5247-5803-5
eBook ISBN: 978-1-5247-5836-3
ISSN: 1558-9676

Editor: Orion McBean
Production Editors: Kathy Carter and Jim Melloan
Production Artist: Gabriel Berlin
Content Contributor: Linda Kelley

Printed in the United States of America on partially recycled paper.

10 9 8 7 6 5 4 3 2 1

2019 Edition

Editorial

Rob Franek, Editor-in-Chief
Casey Cornelius, Chief Product Officer
Mary Beth Garrick, Executive Director of Production
Craig Patches, Production Design Manager
Selena Coppock, Managing Editor
Meave Shelton, Senior Editor
Colleen Day, Editor
Sarah Litt, Editor
Aaron Riccio, Editor
Orion McBean, Associate Editor

Penguin Random House Publishing Team

Tom Russell, VP, Publisher
Alison Stoltzfus, Publishing Director
Amanda Yee, Associate Managing Editor
Ellen Reed, Production Manager
Suzanne Lee, Designer

Acknowledgments

The Princeton Review would like to thank Linda Kelley for her thorough review of this title and useful updates to the 2019 edition.

Contents

Get More (Free) Content

1 Go to <u>PrincetonReview.com/cracking</u>.

2 Enter the following ISBN for your book: 9781524758035.

3 Answer a few simple questions to set up an exclusive Princeton Review account. (If you already have one, you can just log in.)

4 Click the "Student Tools" button, also found under "My Account" from the top toolbar. You're all set to access your bonus content!

Need to report a potential **content** issue?

Contact **EditorialSupport@review.com**.
Include:

- full title of the book
- ISBN
- page number
- description of the error

Need to report a **technical** issue?

Contact **TPRStudentTech@review.com** and provide:

- your full name
- email address used to register the book
- full book title and ISBN
- computer OS (Mac/PC) and browser (Firefox, Safari, etc.)

The **Princeton Review**®

Once you've registered, you can...

- Take a full-length practice SAT and/or ACT

- Get valuable advice about the college application process, including tips for writing a great essay and where to apply for financial aid

- If you're still choosing between colleges, use our searchable rankings of *The Best 384 Colleges* to find out more information about your dream school

- Access a comprehensive study guide and a variety of printable resources, including: scoring and bubble sheets and a key terms list.

- Check to see if there are any corrections or updates to this edition

Look For These Icons Throughout The Book

 ONLINE ARTICLES

 MORE GREAT BOOKS

 APPLIED STRATEGIES

 PROVEN TECHNIQUES

 COLLEGE ADVISOR APP

Part I
Using This Book
to Improve Your
AP Score

- Preview: Your Knowledge, Your Expectations
- Your Guide to Using This Book
- How to Begin

PREVIEW: YOUR KNOWLEDGE, YOUR EXPECTATIONS

Your route to a high score on the AP English Language and Composition Exam depends a lot on how you plan to use this book. Respond to the following questions.

1. Rate your level of confidence about your knowledge of the content tested by the AP English Language and Composition Exam.

    A. Very confident—I know it all
    B. I'm pretty confident, but there are topics for which I could use help
    C. Not confident—I need quite a bit of support
    D. I'm not sure

2. Circle your goal score for the AP English Language and Composition Exam.

    5   4   3   2   1   I'm not sure yet

3. What do you expect to learn from this book? Circle all that apply to you.

    A. A general overview of the test and what to expect
    B. Strategies for how to approach the test
    C. The content tested by this exam
    D. I'm not sure yet

Not Sure Yet?

If you answered these three questions with "I'm not sure," you may need more time before you take the AP exam. But don't be discouraged! Review the content chapters before you take the practice tests in this book and you'll see improvement in your confidence and even your test scores.

YOUR GUIDE TO USING THIS BOOK

This book is organized to provide as much—or as little—support as you need, so you can use this book in whatever way will be most helpful to improving your score on the AP English Language and Composition Exam.

- The remainder of **Part I** provides guidance on how to use this book and helps you determine your strengths and weaknesses.

- **Part II** contains Practice Test 1, its answers and explanations, and a scoring guide. (Bubble sheets can be found in the very back of the book for easy tear-out.) We strongly recommend that you take this test before going any further, in order to realistically determine:
    - your starting point right now
    - which question types you're ready for and which you might need to practice
    - which content topics you are familiar with and which you will want to carefully review

    Once you have nailed down your strengths and weaknesses with regard to this exam, you can focus your test preparation, build a study plan, and be efficient with your time.

- **Part III** of this book:
    - provides information about the structure, scoring, and content of the AP English Language and Composition Exam
    - will help you to make a study plan
    - points you toward additional resources

- **Part IV** explores various strategies, including:
  - how to attack multiple-choice questions
  - how to write effective essays
  - how to manage your time to maximize the number of points available to you

- **Part V** of this book is a review of the terms and rhetorical modes that will give you an edge on the AP English Language and Composition Exam.

- **Part VI** contains Practice Test 2, its answers and explanations, and a scoring guide. (Bubble sheets can be found in the very back of the book for easy tear-out.) If you skipped Practice Test 1, we recommend that you do both (with at least a day or two between them) so that you can compare your progress between the two. Additionally, this will help to identify any external issues: if you get a certain type of question wrong both times, you probably need to review it. If you got it wrong only once, you may have run out of time or been distracted by something. In either case, this will allow you to focus on the factors that caused the discrepancy in scores and to be as prepared as possible on the day of the test.

- **Online Resources** contain a study guide and useful key terms. Follow the study guide based on the amount of time you have to study for the 2019 exam. Use the key terms to improve your vocabulary by creating flashcards to help you learn words you might see on the test.

You may choose to use some parts of this book over others, or you may work through the entire book. Your approach will depend on your needs and how much time you have. Let's now look at how to make this determination.

HOW TO BEGIN

1. **Take a Test**

   Before you can decide how to use this book, you need to take a practice test. Doing so will give you insight into your strengths and weaknesses, and the test will also help you create an effective study plan. If you're feeling test-phobic, remind yourself that a practice test is a tool for diagnosing yourself—it's not how well you do that matters but how you use information gleaned from your performance to guide your preparation.

   So, before you read further, take Practice Test 1 starting at page 8 of this book. Be sure to do so in one sitting, following the instructions that appear before the test.

2. **Check Your Answers**

   Using the answer key on page 34, count thenumber of multiple-choice questions you answered correctly and how many you missed. Don't worry about the explanations for now, and don't worry about why you missed questions. We'll get to that soon.

Once you register your book online, you can print the bubble sheets and scoring worksheets for both practice tests!

Scoring Worksheets
We've included a scoring worksheet for the practice tests in this book at the end of each Answers and Explanations chapter. Remember that these worksheets are meant to serve as a rough guideline only. AP exam scores are weighted according to a statistical process that varies slightly every year based on how students perform on the exam, but you can use the worksheets to approximate your score.

3. **Reflect on the Test**

   After you take your first test, respond to the following questions:
   - How much time did you spend on the multiple-choice questions?
   - How much time did you spend on each essay?
   - How many multiple-choice questions did you miss?
   - Do you feel you had the knowledge to address the subject matter of the essays?
   - Do you feel you wrote well-organized, thoughtful essays?

4. **Read Part III and Complete the Self-Evaluation**

   Part III provides information on how the test is structured and scored. As you read Part III, re-evaluate your answers to the questions above. At the end of Part III, you will revisit and refine the questions you answered above. You will then be able to make a study plan, based on your needs and time available, that will allow you to use this book most effectively.

5. **Engage with Parts IV and V as Needed**

   Notice the word *engage*. You'll get more out of this book if you use it intentionally than if you read it passively, hoping for an improved score through osmosis.

   The Strategy chapters will help you think about your approach to the question types on this exam. Part IV opens with a reminder to think about how you approach questions now and then closes with a reflection section asking you to think about how or whether you will change your approach in the future.

   The Terms and Modes chapters in Part V are designed to provide a review of the terminology you are likely to encounter on the exam, and will help you to identify the rhetorical fallacies and modes used in both test passages and student essays. You will have the opportunity to assess your mastery of the content of each chapter through test-appropriate questions and a reflection section.

6. **Take Practice Test 2 and Assess Your Performance**

   Once you feel you have developed the strategies you need and gained the knowledge you lacked, you should take Practice Test 2, which starts at page 206. You should do so in one sitting, following the instructions at the beginning of the test.

   When you complete the test, check your answers to the multiple-choice sections against the answer key on page 232. If possible, find a teacher to read your essays and provide feedback.

   Once you have taken the test, reflect on what areas you still need to work on, and revisit the chapters in this book that address those deficiencies. Through this type of reflection and engagement, you will continue to improve.

7. **Keep Working**

   As we will discuss in Part III, there are other resources available to you, including a wealth of information on **AP Students:** apstudent.collegeboard .org/apcourse/ap-english-language-and-composition. You can continue to explore and engage in areas needing improvement right up to the day of the test.

Part II
Practice Test 1

Practice Test 1

AP® English Language and Composition Exam

SECTION I: Multiple-Choice Questions

DO NOT OPEN THIS BOOKLET UNTIL YOU ARE TOLD TO DO SO.

At a Glance

Total Time
1 hour

Number of Questions
54

Percent of Total Grade
45%

Writing Instrument
Pencil required

Instructions

Section I of this examination contains 54 multiple-choice questions. Fill in only the ovals for numbers 1 through 54 on your answer sheet.

Indicate all of your answers to the multiple-choice questions on the answer sheet. No credit will be given for anything written in this exam booklet, but you may use the booklet for notes or scratch work. After you have decided which of the suggested answers is best, completely fill in the corresponding oval on the answer sheet. Give only one answer to each question. If you change an answer, be sure that the previous mark is erased completely. Here is a sample question and answer.

Sample Question   Sample Answer

Chicago is a
(A) state
(B) city
(C) country
(D) continent
(E) village

Use your time effectively, working as quickly as you can without losing accuracy. Do not spend too much time on any one question. Go on to other questions and come back to the ones you have not answered if you have time. It is not expected that everyone will know the answers to all the multiple-choice questions.

About Guessing

Many candidates wonder whether or not to guess the answers to questions about which they are not certain. Multiple-choice scores are based on the number of questions answered correctly. Points are not deducted for incorrect answers, and no points are awarded for unanswered questions. Because points are not deducted for incorrect answers, you are encouraged to answer all multiple-choice questions. On any questions you do not know the answer to, you should eliminate as many choices as you can, and then select the best answer among the remaining choices.

GO ON TO THE NEXT PAGE.

This page intentionally left blank.

ENGLISH LANGUAGE AND COMPOSITION
SECTION I
Time—1 hour

Directions: This part consists of selections from prose works and questions on their content, form, and style. After reading each passage, choose the best answer to each question and completely fill in the corresponding oval on the answer sheet.

Note: Pay particular attention to the requirement of questions that contain the words NOT, LEAST, or EXCEPT.

Questions 1–10. Read the following passage carefully before you choose your answers.

This passage is an excerpt from an essay published in 1729.

There only remains one hundred and twenty thousand children of poor parents annually born. The question therefore is, how this number shall be reared and provided
Line for, which, as I have already said, under the present situation
5 of affairs, is utterly impossible by all the methods hitherto proposed. For we can neither employ them in handicraft or agriculture; we neither build houses (I mean in the country) nor cultivate land: they can very seldom pick up a livelihood by stealing, till they arrive at six years old, except where
10 they are of towardly parts, although I confess they learn the rudiments much earlier, during which time, they can however be properly looked upon only as probationers, as I have been informed by a principal gentleman in the county of Cavan, who protested to me that he never knew above one or two
15 instances under the age of six, even in a part of the kingdom so renowned for the quickest proficiency in that art.

I am assured by our merchants, that a boy or a girl before twelve years old is no salable commodity; and even when they come to this age they will not yield above three
20 pounds, or three pounds and half-a-crown at most on the exchange; which cannot turn to account either to the parents or kingdom, the charge of nutriment and rags having been at least four times that value.

I shall now therefore humbly propose my own thoughts,
25 which I hope will not be liable to the least objection.

I have been assured by a very knowing American of my acquaintance in London, that a young healthy child well nursed is at a year old a most delicious, nourishing, and wholesome food, whether stewed, roasted, baked, or boiled;
30 and I make no doubt that it will equally serve in a fricassee or a ragout.

I do therefore humbly offer it to public consideration that of the hundred and twenty thousand children already computed, twenty thousand may be reserved for breed,
35 whereof only one-fourth part to be males; which is more than we allow to sheep, black cattle or swine; and my reason is, that these children are seldom the fruits of marriage, a circumstance not much regarded by our savages, therefore one male will be sufficient to serve four females. That the
40 remaining hundred thousand may, at a year old, be offered

in the sale to the persons of quality and fortune through the kingdom; always advising the mother to let them suck plentifully in the last month, so as to render them plump and fat for a good table. A child will make two dishes at an
45 entertainment for friends; and when the family dines alone, the fore or hind quarter will make a reasonable dish, and seasoned with a little pepper or salt will be very good boiled on the fourth day, especially in winter.

I have reckoned upon a medium that a child just born
50 will weigh 12 pounds, and in a solar year, if tolerably nursed, increaseth to 28 pounds.

I grant this food will be somewhat dear, and therefore very proper for landlords, who, as they have already devoured most of the parents, seem to have the best title to
55 the children.

1. This text can best be described as

   (A) scientific
   (B) satirical
   (C) forthright
   (D) humanitarian
   (E) sadistic

2. In the first, second, and fourth paragraphs the author relies on dubious

   (A) similes
   (B) *ad hominem* arguments
   (C) extended metaphors
   (D) arguments from authority
   (E) appeals to ignorance

GO ON TO THE NEXT PAGE.

3. It can be inferred that the "merchants" (line 17) and the "American" (line 26) represent

   (A) cannibals who routinely eat children
   (B) the author's fictional acquaintances
   (C) aristocrats who exploit the poor
   (D) businessmen well-versed in commerce
   (E) typical Londoners

4. The phrase "the charge of nutriment and rags having been at least four times that value" (lines 22–23) is ironic chiefly because

   (A) food was relatively cheap at that time
   (B) "four times" is a mere approximation
   (C) twelve pounds is a very small sum of money
   (D) the parents could not support their children without the aid of the kingdom
   (E) there is no evidence that the children were wearing rags

5. The word "fricassee" (line 30) is best interpreted to mean

   (A) animal
   (B) child
   (C) dish
   (D) place
   (E) master

6. Which of the following rhetorical devices does the author employ in lines 32–39?

   (A) Process analysis
   (B) Example
   (C) Cause and effect
   (D) Deductive reasoning
   (E) Analogy

7. The phrase "always advising the mother to let them suck plentifully in the last month" (lines 42–43) extends the comparison between the children and

   (A) properly nourished mammals
   (B) poor and ruthless parents
   (C) savages
   (D) animals raised for slaughter
   (E) the poor treatment of animals

8. In line 52, "dear" means

   (A) expensive
   (B) sweet
   (C) cherished
   (D) unforgettable
   (E) unhealthy

9. In context, "devoured" (line 54) is an effective word choice because

   (A) it fits both figuratively and literally
   (B) it is appropriate only literally
   (C) it is indicative of the landlords' plight
   (D) it works as a sentimental appeal
   (E) it reveals the author's point of view

10. The author mentions "sheep, black cattle or swine" (line 36) in order to convey which of the following ideas?

   (A) Animals are often treated more humanely than are children.
   (B) Large numbers of animals should be kept for breeding purposes.
   (C) Male animals are often more effective for breeding than female animals.
   (D) The poor are often used as commodities to profit their owners.
   (E) Marriage is not universally valued in all cultures.

GO ON TO THE NEXT PAGE.

Questions 11–22. Read the following passage carefully before you choose your answers.

This passage is excerpted from a contemporary article in a scholarly journal.

The most obvious joke in the title of Swift's *Travels into Several Remote Nations of the World* is that what purports to be a chronicle of several excursions to remote nations
Line turns out to be a satiric anatomy of specifically English
5 attitudes and values. But there is a second joke. Many of the…supposedly unfamiliar and exotic sights Gulliver sees in his sixteen years and seven months of wandering in remote nations, and even the radically altered perspectives from which he sees them (as diminutive landscapes, giant
10 people, intelligent animals, etc.), could have been seen or experienced in a few days by anyone at the tourists' sights, public entertainments, shows, spectacles, and exhibitions in the streets and at the fairs of London.

It is not surprising that *Gulliver's Travels* should be
15 filled with the shows and diversions of London. All the Scriblerians were fascinated with popular entertainments; collectively and individually, they satirized them in many of their works. Swift shared this fascination with his fellow Scriblerians, and he transforms the sights and shows of
20 London into an imaginative center of *Gulliver's Travels*.

1

Gulliver himself senses that the wonders he sees in remote nations resemble popular entertainments back home in England when he notes that the capital city of Lilliput "looked like the painted Scene of a City in a Theatre."[1] And
25 other popular entertainments would allow Londoners to see many of the same sights Gulliver saw in Lilliput. A Londoner could experience what a miniature city looked like to the giant Gulliver by going to see the papier-mâché and clay architectural and topographical models displayed at fairs and
30 in inns, some of which were extraordinarily elaborate and detailed, such as the model of Amsterdam exhibited in 1710, which was twenty feet wide and twenty to thirty feet long, "with all the Churches, Chappels, Stadt house, Hospitals, noble Buildings, Streets, Trees, Walks, Avenues, with the
35 Sea, Shipping, Sluices, Rivers, Canals &c., most exactly built to admiration."[2]

Miniature people, as well as miniature landscapes, could be seen in one of the most popular diversions in London, the peepshows, which were enclosed boxes containing scenes
40 made out of painted board, paper flats, and glass panels and given the illusion of depth by mirrors and magnifying glasses. All of this was seen through a hole bored in one side. Among the most popular scenes were interiors, particularly palace interiors of European royalty, and so there is a direct
45 analogy between peering in the hole of a peepshow and

Gulliver's looking into the palace in Lilliput: "I applied my Face to the Windows of the middle Stories, and discovered the most splendid Apartments that can be imagined. There I saw the Empress, and the young Princes in their several
50 Lodgings. Her Imperial Majesty was pleased to smile very graciously upon me, and gave me out the window her Hand to kiss." The queen's movements could have been seen in the peepshows, too, for clockwork animating the figures was introduced early in the century. And much the same illusion
55 of a living, miniature world could be found in another popular diversion, the "moving picture," a device in which cutout figures were placed within a frame and activated by jacks and wheels. This curiosity fascinated contemporary Londoners: "The landscape looks as an ordinary picture till
60 the clock-work behind the curtain be set at work, and then the ships move and sail distinctly upon the sea till out of sight; a coach comes out of town, the motion of the horses and wheels are very distinct, and a gentleman in the coach that salutes the company; a hunter also and his dogs keep
65 their course till out of sight." Swift saw this same moving picture, or one very much like it, and was impressed.

11. The purpose of the passage is most likely to

(A) describe the cultural landscape in *Gulliver's Travels*
(B) draw a comparison between the fictional world Gulliver experienced and the similar imaginative elements of eighteenth-century London
(C) point out the superfluous nature of entertainment in Swift's London
(D) provide evidence that Swift's satire is derived from the natural curiosity of European royalty
(E) discredit the notion that *Gulliver's Travels* is a wholly original work

12. In the passage, the author's overall attitude toward *Gulliver's Travels* can best be described as

(A) cleverly subversive
(B) bitingly sarcastic
(C) generally appreciative
(D) halfheartedly engaged
(E) insistently dismissive

1 *Gulliver's Travels*, in *The Prose Works of Jonathan Swift*, ed. Herbert Davis, 14 vols. (Oxford: B. Blackwell, 1939–68), XI:13

2 Quoted in John Ashton, *Social Life in the Reign of Queen Anne* (New York: Chatto and Windus, 1883), 219–20

GO ON TO THE NEXT PAGE.

13. "Scriblerians" (line 16) refers to

    (A) book craftsmen in London
    (B) characters in Swift's novels
    (C) English politicians and aristocrats
    (D) historians of popular entertainment
    (E) a London-based circle of English authors

14. It can be inferred from the second paragraph that Jonathan Swift was

    (A) a citizen of London
    (B) a producer of public entertainments
    (C) a member of the Scriblerians
    (D) a painter as well as an author
    (E) a traveling salesman

15. The stylistic feature most evident in the first two paragraphs (lines 1–20) is the use of

    (A) repeated syntactical patterns
    (B) shifts in tense and person
    (C) historical allusions
    (D) a series of extended metaphors
    (E) didactic analogies and asides

16. In describing miniature people and landscapes in the final paragraph, the author emphasizes their

    (A) size
    (B) obscurity
    (C) magnificence
    (D) commonness
    (E) transience

17. In the fourth paragraph, the author includes long quotes primarily in order to

    (A) refute the claims of his detractors that *Gulliver's Travels* was purely imaginative
    (B) document the connection between *Gulliver's Travels* and popular entertainments
    (C) challenge the prevailing scholarship on the miniature people and landscapes in *Gulliver's Travels*
    (D) highlight the inconsistencies within *Gulliver's Travels* regarding miniature people and landscapes
    (E) inform the reader of the sources for the study of miniature people and landscapes in *Gulliver's Travels*

18. Which of the following best describes the relationship between the first section (lines 1–20) and the second section (lines 21–66) of the passage?

    (A) The second section answers the series of questions raised in the first section.
    (B) The second section challenges the prevailing picture detailed in in the first section.
    (C) The second section undermines the positions of scholars introduced in the first section.
    (D) The second section expands on a technical definition introduced in the first section.
    (E) The second section provides evidence for the claims introduced in the first section.

19. Footnote 1 in line 24 indicates that

    (A) the article first appeared as an addendum to *Gulliver's Travels*
    (B) *Gulliver's Travels* was first published in 1939
    (C) the quotation "looked like the…Theater" was excerpted from *Gulliver's Travels*, part of a 14-volume set of Swift's works
    (D) the quotation "looked like the…Theater" was originally written by Herbert Davis
    (E) *Gulliver's Travels* was reprinted in its entirety in 1939, and credited to Herbert Davis instead of Swift

GO ON TO THE NEXT PAGE.

20. Footnote 2 in line 36 indicates

  (A) the quotation was taken from a professional journal
  (B) the quotation refers to a 1710 exhibit in Amsterdam
  (C) the quotation originally appeared in *Gulliver's Travels* in 1883
  (D) the quotation, describing a miniature exhibition of Amsterdam, first appeared in a book by John Ashton
  (E) the quotation was originally published in a newspaper

21. The details in lines 46–52 suggest the scene is viewed by which of the following?

  (A) An impartial anthropologist
  (B) An intrigued visitor
  (C) A critical literary scholar
  (D) An argumentative architect
  (E) A struggling writer

22. The speaker's tone might best be described as

  (A) emphatic and insistent
  (B) scholarly and enthusiastic
  (C) dejected but hopeful
  (D) erudite and cynical
  (E) intransigent yet competent

GO ON TO THE NEXT PAGE.

Questions 23–33. Read the following passage carefully before you choose your answers.

This passage is from an eighteenth-century protofeminist work.

My own sex, I hope, will excuse me, if I treat them like
rational creatures, instead of flattering their fascinating
graces, and viewing them as if they were in a state of
Line perpetual childhood, unable to stand alone. I earnestly
5 wish to point out in what true dignity and human happiness
consists—I wish to persuade women to endeavour to acquire
strength, both of mind and body, and to convince them
that the soft phrases, susceptibility of heart, delicacy of
sentiment, and refinement of taste, are almost synonymous
10 with epithets of weakness, and that those beings who are
only the objects of pity and that kind of love, which has been
termed its sister, will soon become objects of contempt.

Dismissing then those pretty feminine phrases, which the
men condescendingly use to soften our slavish dependence,
15 and despising that weak elegancy of mind, exquisite
sensibility, and sweet docility of manners, supposed to be
the sexual characteristics of the weaker vessel, I wish to
show that elegance is inferior to virtue, that the first object of
laudable ambition is to obtain a character as a human being,
20 regardless of the distinction of sex; and that secondary views
should be brought to this simple touchstone.

This is a rough sketch of my plan; and should I express
my conviction with the energetic emotions that I feel
whenever I think of the subject, the dictates of experience
25 and reflection will be felt by some of my readers. Animated
by this important object, I shall disdain to cull my phrases
or polish my style;—I aim at being useful, and sincerity will
render me unaffected; for, wishing rather to persuade by the
force of my arguments, than dazzle by the elegance of my
30 language, I shall not waste my time in rounding periods,
nor in fabricating the turgid bombast of artificial feelings,
which, coming from the head, never reach the heart—I
shall be employed about things, not words!—and, anxious
to render my sex more respectable to members of society, I
35 shall try to avoid that flowery diction which has slided from
essays into novels, and from novels into familiar letters and
conversation.

These pretty nothings—these caricatures of the real
beauty of sensibility, dropping glibly from the tongue, vitiate
40 the taste, and create a kind of sickly delicacy that turns
away from simple unadorned truth; and a deluge of false
sentiments and overstretched feelings, stifling the natural
emotions of the heart, render the domestic pleasures insipid,
that ought to sweeten the exercise of those severe duties,
45 which educate a rational and immortal being for a nobler
field of action.

The education of women has, of late, been more attended
to than formerly; yet they are still reckoned a frivolous sex,
and ridiculed or pitied by the writers who endeavour by
50 satire or instruction to improve them. It is acknowledged that
they spend many of the first years of their lives in acquiring a
smattering of accomplishments: meanwhile strength of body

and mind are sacrificed to libertine notions of beauty, to the
desire of establishing themselves—the only way women
55 can rise in the world—by marriage. And this desire making
mere animals of them, when they marry they act as such
children may be expected to act—they dress; they paint, and
nickname God's creatures—Surely these weak beings are
only fit for a seraglio!—Can they govern a family, or take
60 care of the poor babes whom they bring into the world?

23. In the initial paragraph, the author employs both

(A) apology and classification
(B) irony and exposition
(C) analogy and extended metaphor
(D) flattery and epithets
(E) induction and persuasion

24. In the initial paragraph, the author decries

(A) traditional feminine attributes
(B) traditional male attributes
(C) modern sexuality
(D) the importance of love
(E) the importance of sentiments

25. In the initial paragraph, the author suggests that

(A) men prefer strong women
(B) a man will never truly love a strong woman
(C) men never respect strong women
(D) women need emotional and physical strength
(E) women need intellectual and physical strength

26. The author ties the second paragraph to the first by using
the words

(A) "vessel" and "touchstone"
(B) "soften" and "inferior"
(C) "laudable" and "sex"
(D) "slavish" and "virtue"
(E) "soften" and "weak"

GO ON TO THE NEXT PAGE.

27. The word "vessel" (line 17) is a metaphor for

    (A) sex
    (B) woman
    (C) man
    (D) phrase
    (E) character

28. The author suggests that a woman's worth may be best judged by

    (A) comparing her with a praiseworthy man
    (B) examining the elegance of her writing
    (C) evaluating the strength of her character
    (D) evaluating her physical beauty
    (E) examining her manners

29. The author proposes to write in a manner that is both

    (A) cogent and emotional
    (B) polished and intellectual
    (C) ornate and rhetorical
    (D) elegant and cerebral
    (E) convincing and flowery

30. The words "pretty nothings" (line 38) are a reprise of

    (A) "letters and conversation" (lines 36–37)
    (B) "essays" and "novels" (line 36)
    (C) "flowery diction" (line 35)
    (D) "rounding periods" (line 30)
    (E) "members of society" (line 34)

31. With the phrase "dropping glibly from the tongue" (line 39) the author begins

    (A) a caricature of women
    (B) a critique of turgid bombast
    (C) a panegyric of sugary writing
    (D) an analysis of sentimental writing
    (E) an extended metaphor

32. One can infer from the passage that to become strong human beings, rather than mere children, young women need

    (A) an education different from that of young men
    (B) more understanding husbands
    (C) obliging husbands
    (D) a good marriage
    (E) the same education as that of young men

33. The tone of the final paragraph is

    (A) sardonic
    (B) lyrical
    (C) condescending
    (D) frivolous
    (E) reserved

GO ON TO THE NEXT PAGE.

Questions 34–44. Read the following passage carefully before you choose your answers.

This passage is excerpted from a nonfiction work about the modern education system.

But it is important to keep in mind that the engineering of learning is very often puffed up, assigned an importance it does not deserve. As an old saying goes, *There are one and*
Line *twenty ways to sing tribal lays, and all of them are correct.*
5 So it is with learning. There is no one who can say that this or that is the best way to know things, to feel things, to see things, to remember things, to apply things, to connect things and that no other will do as well. In fact, to make such a claim is to trivialize learning, to reduce it to a mechanical
10 skill.

Of course, there are many learnings that are little else but a mechanical skill, and in such cases, there well may be a best way. But to become a different person because of something you have learned—to appropriate an insight, a
15 concept, a vision, so that your world is altered—that is a different matter. For that to happen, you need a reason. And this is the metaphysical problem I speak of.

A reason, as I use the word here, is different from a motivation. Within the context of schooling, motivation
20 refers to a temporary psychic event in which curiosity is aroused and attention is focused. I do not mean to disparage it. But it must not be confused with a reason for being in a classroom, for listening to a teacher, for taking an examination, for doing homework, for putting up with school
25 even if you are not motivated.

This kind of reason is somewhat abstract, not always present in one's consciousness, not at all easy to describe. And yet for all that, without it schooling does not work. For school to make sense, the young, their parents, and their
30 teachers must have a god to serve, or, even better, several gods. If they have none, school is pointless. Nietzsche's famous aphorism is relevant here: "He who has a *why* to live can bear with almost any *how*." This applies as much to learning as to living.
35 To put it simply, there is no surer way to bring an end to schooling than for it to have no end.

34. The "engineering of learning" (lines 1-2) most nearly means

(A) development of schools
(B) building of schools
(C) educational methodology
(D) building up of knowledge
(E) study of engineering

35. The "old saying" (line 3) serves as

(A) an analogy to the sentences that follow
(B) a contrast to the sentences that follow
(C) an illustration of the first sentence
(D) a historical interlude
(E) a tribute to tribal lays

36. The series of infinitives in the initial paragraph emphasizes that the learning process is

(A) long and tedious
(B) multifaceted and impersonal
(C) active and varied
(D) difficult and trivial
(E) mechanical and complicated

37. According to the author, motivation is

(A) not important
(B) synonymous with reason
(C) abstract and fleeting
(D) momentary and concrete
(E) psychological and enduring

38. Both the first and third paragraphs contain

(A) aphorisms
(B) ironical statements
(C) syllogistic reasoning
(D) *ad hominem* arguments
(E) notable parallelism

39. In line 30, "god" most nearly means

(A) religion
(B) deity
(C) reason
(D) person
(E) Nietzsche

GO ON TO THE NEXT PAGE.

40. The author employs the argument from authority as

    (A) a contrast to his point of view
    (B) a relevant concrete example
    (C) an apt analogy
    (D) an example of cause and effect
    (E) an illustration of the cruelty in schools

41. The paradox in the final sentence rests on

    (A) different meanings of "end"
    (B) a crass simplification
    (C) the comparison between schooling and learning
    (D) the eternal process of learning
    (E) a new way of bringing schooling to an end

42. The principal contrast employed by the author in the passage is between

    (A) education and wisdom
    (B) theory and practice
    (C) knowledge and literacy
    (D) ignorance and religion
    (E) motivation and purpose

43. Which of the following best states the subject of the passage?

    (A) The historical development of educational institutions
    (B) The necessity of higher purpose in education
    (C) The challenges of educational reform in the United States
    (D) The lack of scientific rigor in educational theory
    (E) The separation of church and state in American education

44. The passage as a whole is best described as

    (A) an objective analysis
    (B) an impassioned plea
    (C) a linear narrative
    (D) a dramatic monologue
    (E) a reasoned argument

GO ON TO THE NEXT PAGE.

Questions 45–54. Read the following passage carefully before you choose your answers.

This passage is excerpted from the 1896 Plessy vs. Ferguson case.

It is one thing for railroad carriers to furnish, or to be required by law to furnish, equal accommodations for all whom they are under a legal duty to carry. It is quite another
Line thing for government to forbid citizens of the white and black
5 races from traveling in the same public conveyance, and to punish officers of railroad companies for permitting persons of the two races to occupy the same passenger coach. If a state can prescribe, as a rule of civil conduct, that whites and blacks shall not travel as passengers in the same railroad
10 coach, why may it not so regulate the use of the streets of its cities and towns as to compel white citizens to keep on one side of a street, and black citizens to keep on the other? Why may it not, upon like grounds, punish whites and blacks who ride together in street cars or in open vehicles on a public road
15 or street? Why may it not require sheriffs to assign whites to one side of a court room, and blacks to the other? And why may it not also prohibit the commingling of the two races in the galleries of legislative halls or in public assemblages convened for the consideration of the political questions of
20 the day? Further, if this statute of Louisiana is consistent with the personal liberty of citizens, why may not the state require the separation in railroad coaches of native and naturalized citizens of the United States, or of Protestants and Roman Catholics?
25   The white race deems itself to be the dominant race in this country. And so it is, in prestige, in achievements, in education, in wealth, and in power. So, I doubt not, it will continue to be for all time, if it remains true to its great heritage, and holds fast to the principles of constitutional
30 liberty. But in view of the constitution, in the eye of the law, there is in this country no superior, dominant, ruling class of citizens. There is no caste here. Our constitution is color-blind, and neither knows nor tolerates classes among citizens. In respect of civil rights, all citizens are
35 equal before the law. The humblest is the peer of the most powerful. The law regards man as man, and takes no account of his surroundings or of his color when his civil rights as guarantied by the supreme law of the land are involved. It is therefore to be regretted that this high tribunal, the final
40 expositor of the fundamental law of the land, has reached the conclusion that it is competent for a state to regulate the enjoyment by citizens of their civil rights solely upon the basis of race.
     In my opinion, the judgment this day rendered will, in
45 time, prove to be quite as pernicious as the decision made by this tribunal in the Dred Scott Case.
     It was adjudged in that case that the descendants of

Africans who were imported into this country, and sold as slaves, were not included nor intended to be included
50 under the word "citizens" in the constitution, and could not claim any of the rights and privileges which that instrument provided for and secured to citizens of the United States; that, at the time of the adoption of the constitution, they were "considered as a subordinate and inferior class of beings,
55 who had been subjugated by the dominant race, and, whether emancipated or not, yet remained subject to their authority, and had no rights or privileges but such as those who held the power and the government might choose to grant them." The recent amendments of the constitution, it was supposed,
60 had eradicated these principles from our institutions.
     I am of opinion that the state of Louisiana is inconsistent with the personal liberty of citizens, white and black, in that state, and hostile to both the spirit and letter of the constitution of the United States. If laws of like character
65 should be enacted in the several states of the Union, the effect would be in the highest degree mischievous. Slavery, as an institution tolerated by law, would, it is true, have disappeared from our country; but there would remain a power in the states, by sinister legislation, to interfere
70 with the full enjoyment of the blessings of freedom, to regulate civil rights, common to all citizens, upon the basis of race, and to place in a condition of legal inferiority a large body of American citizens, now constituting a part of the political community, called the "People of the United
75 States," for whom, and by whom through representatives, our government is administered. Such a system is inconsistent with the guaranty given by the constitution to each state of a republican form of government, and may be stricken down by congressional action, or by the courts in the discharge
80 of their solemn duty to maintain the supreme law of the land, anything in the constitution or laws of any state to the contrary notwithstanding.
     For the reason stated, I am constrained to withhold my assent from the opinion and judgment of the majority.

45. The speaker in this passage is

  (A) delivering a political speech
  (B) rendering a legal judgment
  (C) reminiscing about the past
  (D) a state governor
  (E) involved with the railroad company

GO ON TO THE NEXT PAGE.

46. In the first paragraph, the series of rhetorical questions serves the speaker's strategy of reasoning by

    (A) appeals to authority
    (B) analogy
    (C) description
    (D) induction
    (E) deduction

47. In lines 27-28, "it" refers to

    (A) "white race" (line 25)
    (B) "country" (line 26)
    (C) "prestige" (line 26)
    (D) "power" (line 27)
    (E) "time" (line 28)

48. Which of the following best describes the rhetorical function of the sentence "There is no caste here." (line 32)?

    (A) It reiterates the claim of the previous sentence with a different syntactical structure.
    (B) It clarifies the author's attitude toward the caste system through analogy.
    (C) It specifies the author's preference for the best social system for the United States.
    (D) It refutes the claims of his opponents by using a simple syntactical structure.
    (E) It documents the claims introduced in the first paragraph by appealing to a comparison to the caste system.

49. The passage indicates that the speaker holds that

    (A) racial equality will become a reality in America
    (B) civil equality is guaranteed by the Constitution
    (C) racial equality is guaranteed by the Constitution
    (D) both civil and racial equality are guaranteed by the Constitution
    (E) neither civil nor racial equality is guaranteed by the Constitution

50. In line 45, "pernicious" most nearly means

    (A) just
    (B) unjust
    (C) useful
    (D) propitious
    (E) harmful

51. In the speaker's opinion, the Louisiana law is subject to censure by

    (A) either the United States Congress or the United States Supreme Court
    (B) Louisiana legislation only
    (C) United States legislation only
    (D) the people of Louisiana only
    (E) neither the United States Congress nor the United States Supreme Court

52. In line 66, "mischievous" is best interpreted to mean

    (A) whimsical
    (B) insubordinate
    (C) troublemaking
    (D) pernicious
    (E) disgraceful

53. The final paragraph functions as

    (A) an exception to the rule offered in the first two paragraphs
    (B) a critique of the claims of his political and ideological opponents
    (C) a definitive statement of dissent from the claims of the court
    (D) a contrast to the claims of the previous paragraph
    (E) an acknowledgement of an objection to the author's central thesis

54. The style of the entire passage can be best described as

    (A) ornate and whimsical
    (B) dry and objective
    (C) abstract and legalistic
    (D) terse and opinionated
    (E) probing and subtle

END OF SECTION I

AP® English Language and Composition Exam

DO NOT OPEN THIS BOOKLET UNTIL YOU ARE TOLD TO DO SO.

At a Glance

Total Time
2 hours, plus a 15-minute reading period

Number of Questions
3

Percent of Total Grade
55%

Writing Instrument
Pen required

Instructions

Section II of this examination requires answers in essay form. To help you use your time well, the coordinator will announce the time at which each question should be completed. If you finish any question before time is announced, you may go on to the following question. If you finish the examination in less than the time allotted, you may go back and work on any essay question you want.

Each essay will be judged on its clarity and effectiveness in dealing with the requirements of the topic assigned and on the quality of the writing. After completing each question, you should check your essay for accuracy of punctuation, spelling, and diction; you are advised, however, not to attempt many longer corrections. Remember that quality is far more important than quantity.

Write your essays with a pen, preferably in black or dark blue ink. Be sure to write CLEARLY and LEGIBLY. Cross out any errors you make.

The questions for Section II are printed in the green insert. You are encouraged to use the green insert to make notes and to plan your essays, but be sure to write your answers in the pink booklet. Number each answer as the question is numbered in the examination. Do not skip lines. Begin each answer on a new page in the pink booklet.

GO ON TO THE NEXT PAGE.

ENGLISH LANGUAGE AND COMPOSITION
SECTION II
Total Time—2 hours, 15 minutes

Question 1

Suggested reading and writing time—55 minutes.
It is suggested that you spend 15 minutes reading the question, analyzing and evaluating the sources,
and 40 minutes writing your response.
Note: You may begin writing your response before the reading period is over.

(This question counts for one-third of the total essay section score.)

Throughout much of history, humans have defined themselves as members of their tribe. With the growth of civilization in the Neolithic period, humans began to define themselves by their village or state. By the nineteenth century, humans were defining themselves by their nation. Today, in the twenty-first century, humans are being asked to define themselves as citizens of the world.

Carefully read the following seven sources, including the introductory information for each source. Then synthesize the information from at least three of the sources and incorporate it into a coherent, well-developed essay that argues a clear position on the extent to which people are able to define themselves as global citizens.

Your argument should be the focus of your essay. Use the sources to develop your argument and explain the reasoning for it. Avoid merely summarizing the sources. Indicate clearly which sources you are drawing from, whether through direct quotation, paraphrase, or summary. You may cite the sources as Source A, Source B, and so forth, or by using the descriptions in parentheses.

Source A   (Hassanpour)
Source B   (graph)
Source C   (Symons)
Source D   (Kennedy)
Source E   (Pirie)
Source F   (Yeo)
Source G   (map)

GO ON TO THE NEXT PAGE.

> **Source A**
>
> Hassanpour, Amir. "The Kurdish Experience." *MERIP*
> 189. Middle East Research and Information
> Project. July 1994. Web. 31 Jan. 2017.

The following is excerpted from an article on a Web site that provides analysis and information on the Middle East.

Numbering over 22 million, the Kurds are one of the largest non-state nations in the world. Their homeland, Kurdistan, has been forcibly divided and lies mostly within the present-day borders of Turkey, Iraq and Iran, with smaller parts in Syria, Armenia and Azerbaijan. The greatest number of Kurds today still live in Kurdistan, though a large Kurdish diaspora has developed in this century, especially in the main cities of Turkey and Iran and more recently in Europe as well. Between 10 and 12 million Kurds live in Turkey, where they comprise about 20 percent of the population. Between 5 and 6 million live in Iran, accounting for close to 10 percent of the population. Kurds in Iraq number more than 4 million, and comprise about 23 percent of the population.

In the modern era, the Kurdish nation, with its distinctive society and culture, has had to confront in all of the "host" states centralizing, ethnically-based nationalist regimes—Turkish, Arab and Persian—with little or no tolerance for expressions of national autonomy within their borders. While the modes and scale of oppression have varied in time and by place, the conditions of Kurds share some important features. First, the Kurdish areas overlap nation-state borders: They thus acquire significance for "national security" and are vulnerable to interference and manipulation by regional and international powers. Second, the Kurdish regions of these countries are usually the poorest, least developed areas, systematically marginalized by the centers of economic power. Third, the dynamics of assimilation, repression and Kurdish resistance in each country have affected the direction and outcome of the Kurdish struggles in the neighboring countries. A fourth shared feature is that these Kurdish societies are themselves internally complex, and fraught with differences of politics and ideology, social class, dialect and, still in a few places, clan.

In spite of a long history of struggle, Kurdish nationalism has not succeeded in achieving its goal of independence or even enduring autonomy. Do recent events require us to change this assessment? In 1992, a Regional Government of Iraqi Kurdistan was established, but it is economically besieged and functions very much at the sufferance of a Western military umbrella. In Turkey, a ten-year-old armed struggle has effectively defied the unrestrained efforts of the Turkish state to impose a military solution, but a political solution acceptable to the Kurds does not appear imminent. The Kurdish movement, in contrast to many other national liberation movements, has experienced a persistent contradiction between its traditional leadership and the relatively developed society it seeks to liberate. Only to the extent that this may be changing does the future hold some promise for Kurdish aspirations. Today, about half the population lives in urban centers, and feudal relations of production in rural areas have almost disappeared. Yet the politics and ideology of much of the leadership can hardly be distinguished from the worldview of landed notables of the past.

GO ON TO THE NEXT PAGE.

Source B

Investing.com. Untitled graph. June 2016. Web. 31 Jan. 2017.

The following is a graphic depicting the value of the British pound sterling on June 24, 2016, the day that England voted to leave the European Union.

GO ON TO THE NEXT PAGE.

Source C

Symons, Emma-Kate. "Marine Le Pen's New York
Times op-ed is a knife in the back for France."
Qz.com. 19 Jan. 2015. Web. 31 Jan. 2017.

The following is excerpted from an article taking exception with The New York Times' publication of an op-ed by Marine Le Pen, the leader of the French far-right political party Front National.

Since 17 people were murdered in the Paris terror attacks that started with a massacre of cartoonists, staff, and police at Charlie Hebdo magazine, *The New York Times* has not deemed fit to print even one caricature by the French satirical weekly, citing Muslim sensitivities.

But today the Times opened up her august op-ed pages to France's extreme right Front National (FN) party president, Marine Le Pen, the chief Gallic spokesperson for Islamophobia and racism.

We must explain who Le Pen is here because the Times did not include even a phrase qualifying its op-ed contributor as a far right party boss, nor explaining her movement's long history of Muslim-baiting, incitement to racial hatred, Holocaust denial, and generalized anti-foreigner bile stretching back to the grimmest days of World War II collaborationist Vichy France.

The deliberately divisive FN leader is less Pat Buchanan, the renegade Republican, as she is white supremacist David Duke, and it is highly doubtful the Times would give an op-ed to either, especially on the Martin Luther King Jr. holiday weekend.

The daughter of party founder Jean-Marie Le Pen, an avowed Algerian war-torturer, she appropriated the legacy of Albert Camus and Georges Clemenceau, then purported to speak for "The French people," "French values," and the national value of "laïcité," secularism built upon the strict separation of church and state.

In 2010, to cite one notorious example among many, Le Pen compared Muslims praying in French streets (for lack of mosques) to an "occupying force" akin to the Nazis, though such outrages were airbrushed from her carefully-worded Times screed.

Her op-ed, littered with half-truths and lies, distorts the position of the French government, which strongly condemned the Charlie Hebdo attacks, the murder of police, and the attack on a Kosher market as terrorism, driven by Islamism, and as fundamentally anti-Semitic.

Of course Le Pen did not dare mention anti-Semitism, and she conveniently neglected to detail that her party promises to end all immigration, send migrants "home," strip non-white French people arbitrarily of citizenship, close mosques and prayer halls, deport Roma peoples, close France's borders and Europe's free movement of peoples, leave the euro zone, and install the "national preference" for only "real" French i.e., white, nationals, thus forcing out millions of French people with dual nationality.

Le Pen is hoping to having a real shot at the French presidency in the 2017 elections, and her popularity is soaring, with more than one third of French agreeing with her views. Her success would mean a hijacking of French democracy as we know it.

The FN's DNA is firmly fascist and Le Pen has never renounced the core of her father's ideology; she has just presented a more acceptable face, refocused the hatred on Muslims, and calibrated her incoherent economic "platform" to sound like far-left anti-globalization populism.

But the leopard has not changed its spots. The FN remains what it always has been. It is a fascist-derived front party that capitalizes on hatred of the other, chiefly immigrants, and today, especially Muslims. Its platform espouses a monocultural white France, and its supporters are among France's most virulently anti-Semitic voters.

Le Pen's values are an insult to French values—the Front National abhors the legacy of the French revolution, and the universalist notion of French citizenship, as something that is not tied to race, but tied to republican French values of liberty, equality and fraternity.

GO ON TO THE NEXT PAGE.

GO ON TO THE NEXT PAGE.

Source D

Kennedy, Patrick F. Statement on Sri Lanka Day.
4 Feb. 2016.

*The following are remarks given on Sri Lanka Day in 2016 from the Under Secretary of Management,
Organization of American States, U.S. Department of State.*

Thank you, Ambassador Kariyawasam, for that kind introduction, and the honor of your invitation.
And I must say that I'm incredibly excited to visit your beautiful country later this month and see the
progress already made on our new embassy complex.

68 years ago today, Sri Lanka found itself in good company when it joined the rather exclusive club of
great nations that chose the fourth day of the month to declare independence from the United Kingdom.

Like Sri Lankans are doing today, in a few months Americans will mark our anniversary of
independence, when we will also remember the heroes and patriots of years past, and reflect on how far
we've come in our long quest for a more perfect union.

And like Sri Lankans of today, Americans are still striving to address some of the very challenging
problems that have long bedeviled us. Problems like poverty, discrimination, and injustice.

But Sri Lankans and Americans both understand that these problems can only be solved through the use
of the ballot box, the voice of a free press, the strength of a healthy civil society, and the actions of an
empowered citizenry that is committed to democracy, human rights, and progress for all.

Yes, our nations share many interests in global affairs, and that makes us strong partners. We also have
many of the same core values, and face many of the same hard problems. And that, I believe, makes us
strong friends. For, in the words of the Roman poet Sallust, "to like and dislike the same things, that is
indeed true friendship."

We love to see our friends succeed, and the accomplishments of the Sri Lankan people and their
government over the past year have made all of us rightly proud.

Source E

Pirie, Dr. Madsen. "Ten Very Good Things: 9. Globalization." *AdamSmith.org*. 12 Oct. 2012. Web. 31 Jan. 2017.

The following is excerpted from a blog of a nonprofit organization dedicated to economic policy.

Over the course of decades globalization is turning the world into an integrated economy instead of what it has been for most of its history, a series of relatively isolated economies. The more trading that takes place, the more wealth is created, and global trade across international frontiers has created more wealth than ever before in human history, and has helped lift more people out of mere subsistence than ever before.

To poorer countries, globalization brings the chance to sell their relatively low cost labour onto world markets. It brings the investment that creates jobs, and although those jobs pay less than their counterparts in rich economies, they represent a step up for people in recipient countries because they usually pay more than do the more traditional jobs available there.

To people in richer countries, globalization brings lower cost goods from abroad, which leaves them with spending power to spare and a higher standard of living. It also brings opportunities for productive investment in high growth industries in developing countries.

Those adversely affected by the global exchanges are the people in rich countries whose output is now undercut by the cheaper alternatives from abroad. They often need to find new jobs or to be retrained to do work that adds higher value. The extra wealth generated by globalization has brought an increase in service sector employment, which provides many of the new jobs needed.

Competition from abroad forces firms to become more efficient and to use resources more efficiently. Often they choose to go upmarket, seeking higher added value products that face less competition from relatively unskilled labour. Thus firms which once sold cheap textiles move into fashion and design, and find customers among the rising middle classes in developing countries.

The integration of the world economy has brought with it an interdependence. As countries co-operate in trade with each other, they get to know each other and grow into the habit of resolving disputes by negotiation and agreement instead of by armed conflict. The 19th century French economist Frederic Bastiat expressed this pithily: "Where goods do not cross frontiers, armies will."

GO ON TO THE NEXT PAGE.

Source F

Yeo, Sophie. "China Air Pollution Blankets U.S. West
  Coast." *ClimateChangeNews.com.* 21 Jan. 2014.
  Web. 31 Jan. 2017.

The following is excerpted from an article on a website devoted to matters of climate change.

Air pollution in China is blowing over the Pacific Ocean and settling on the west coast of America, causing at least one extra day of dangerous smog in Los Angeles every year.

This is a case of getting what you pay for, according to a new study led by researchers from Peking University in Beijing.

They have calculated that approximately one quarter of the sulphate pollutants that cross into the US are tied to products created within China but destined for American consumers.

"We've outsourced our manufacturing and much of our pollution, but some of it is blowing back across the Pacific to haunt us," said co-author Steve Davis from the University of California Irvine.

"Given the complaints about how Chinese pollution is corrupting other countries' air, this paper shows that there may be plenty of blame to go around."

One of the drivers of the economic boom in China over the past ten years has been the demand for its exports. Between 2000 and 2007, the volume of Chinese exports grew by 390%.

At the same time, discontent over hazardous levels of air pollution in cities such as Beijing has been growing. Today, the governor of Hebei, the province surrounding Beijing, threatened to fire any officials who add new steel capacity, and thus increase the amount of coal being burnt.

GO ON TO THE NEXT PAGE.

Source G

"International Space Station Operation and
Management." *NASA.gov.* Web. 31 Jan. 2017.

*The following map shows the various international facilities that support the operation and
management of the International Space Station, launched in 1998.*

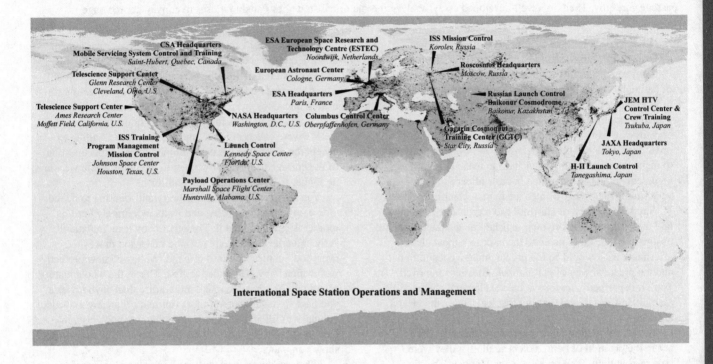

International Space Station Operations and Management

GO ON TO THE NEXT PAGE.

Question 2

Suggested time—40 minutes.

(This question counts for one-third of the total essay section score.)

The passage that follows is an excerpt from Emmeline Pankhurst's "Freedom or Death" speech, delivered in Hartford, Connecticut on November 13, 1913. Pankhurst was a British political activist and leader of the women's suffrage movement in Britain who was widely criticized for her militancy. The following speech addresses her critics and defends the tactics of the suffragettes. Read the passage carefully. Then, in a well-developed essay, analyze the rhetorical strategies Pankhurst uses to convey her message.

Tonight I am not here to advocate woman suffrage. American suffragists can do that very well for themselves.

Line
I am here as a soldier who has temporarily left the field of battle in order to explain—it seems strange it should have

5 to be explained—what civil war is like when civil war is waged by women….Since I am a woman it is necessary to explain why women have adopted revolutionary methods in order to win the rights of citizenship. We women, in trying to make our case clear, always have to make as part of our

10 argument, and urge upon men in our audience the fact—a very simple fact—that women are human beings.

Suppose the men of Hartford had a grievance, and they laid that grievance before their legislature, and the legislature obstinately refused to listen to them, or to remove their

15 grievance, what would be the proper and the constitutional and the practical way of getting their grievance removed? Well, it is perfectly obvious at the next general election the men of Hartford would turn out that legislature and elect a new one.

20 But let the men of Hartford imagine that they were not in the position of being voters at all, that they were governed without their consent being obtained, that the legislature turned an absolutely deaf ear to their demands, what would the men of Hartford do then? They couldn't vote

25 the legislature out. They would have to choose; they would have to make a choice of two evils: they would either have to submit indefinitely to an unjust state of affairs, or they would have to rise up and adopt some of the antiquated means by which men in the past got their grievances remedied.

30 Your forefathers decided that they must have representation for taxation, many, many years ago. When they felt they couldn't wait any longer, when they laid all the arguments before an obstinate British government that they could think of, and when their arguments were absolutely

35 disregarded, when every other means had failed, they began by the tea party at Boston, and they went on until they had won the independence of the United States of America.

It is about eight years since the word *militant* was first used to describe what we were doing. It was not militant at

40 all, except that it provoked militancy on the part of those who were opposed to it. When women asked questions in political meetings and failed to get answers, they were not doing anything militant. In Great Britain it is a custom, a time-

honored one, to ask questions of candidates for parliament

45 and ask questions of members of the government. No man was ever put out of a public meeting for asking a question. The first people who were put out of a political meeting for asking questions were women; they were brutally ill-used; they found themselves in jail before 24 hours had expired.

50 We were called militant, and we were quite willing to accept the name. We were determined to press this question of the enfranchisement of women to the point where we were no longer to be ignored by the politicians.

You have two babies very hungry and wanting to be fed.

55 One baby is a patient baby, and waits indefinitely until its mother is ready to feed it. The other baby is an impatient baby and cries lustily, screams and kicks and makes everybody unpleasant until it is fed. Well, we know perfectly well which baby is attended to first. That is the whole history

60 of politics. You have to make more noise than anybody else, you have to make yourself more obtrusive than anybody else, you have to fill all the papers more than anybody else, in fact you have to be there all the time and see that they do not snow you under.

65 When you have warfare things happen; people suffer; the noncombatants suffer as well as the combatants. And so it happens in civil war. When your forefathers threw the tea into Boston Harbor, a good many women had to go without their tea. It has always seemed to me an

70 extraordinary thing that you did not follow it up by throwing the whiskey overboard; you sacrificed the women; and there is a good deal of warfare for which men take a great deal of glorification which has involved more practical sacrifice on women than it has on any man. It always has been so.

75 The grievances of those who have got power, the influence of those who have got power commands a great deal of attention; but the wrongs and the grievances of those people who have no power at all are apt to be absolutely ignored. That is the history of humanity right from the beginning.

80 Well, in our civil war people have suffered, but you cannot make omelettes without breaking eggs; you cannot have civil war without damage to something. The great thing is to see that no more damage is done than is absolutely necessary, that you do just as much as will arouse enough feeling to

85 bring about peace, to bring about an honorable peace for the combatants; and that is what we have been doing.

GO ON TO THE NEXT PAGE.

We entirely prevented stockbrokers in London from
telegraphing to stockbrokers in Glasgow and vice versa:
for one whole day telegraphic communication was entirely
90 stopped. I am not going to tell you how it was done. I am not
going to tell you how the women got to the mains and cut
the wires; but it was done. It was done, and it was proved to
the authorities that weak women, suffrage women, as we are
supposed to be, had enough ingenuity to create a situation
95 of that kind. Now, I ask you, if women can do that, is there
any limit to what we can do except the limit we put upon
ourselves?

GO ON TO THE NEXT PAGE.

Question 3

Suggested time—40 minutes.

(This question counts for one-third of the total essay section score.)

In response to the issue of racial imbalance, a sociologist argued, "Neutrality in our society is supposed to be the great equalizer because we believe that, if we don't favor any one group, things will work themselves out and become more equal. But the thing is this: neutrality has this effect only if there is no previous social or historical context. But that's not how the real world is. There is, in fact, a social and historical context for every situation. So if I were being "neutral" and viewing everyone as being the same, ignoring personal contexts, I wouldn't be promoting equality because I would be ignoring the differences that exist and allowing the inequalities to continue to exist, given that I wouldn't do anything to help change them. Identifying problems and actively promoting solutions are necessary to effect useful change; being neutral is consenting to the status quo."

In a well-written essay, develop your position on whether a "neutral" stand on race perpetuates racial imbalance today. Use appropriate evidence from your reading, experience, or observations to support your argument.

STOP

END OF EXAM

Practice Test 1:
Answers and
Explanations

PRACTICE TEST 1 ANSWER KEY

1. B	28. C
2. D	29. A
3. B	30. C
4. C	31. E
5. C	32. E
6. A	33. A
7. D	34. C
8. A	35. A
9. A	36. C
10. D	37. D
11. B	38. E
12. C	39. C
13. E	40. C
14. C	41. A
15. A	42. E
16. D	43. B
17. B	44. E
18. E	45. B
19. C	46. B
20. D	47. A
21. B	48. A
22. B	49. B
23. B	50. E
24. A	51. A
25. E	52. D
26. E	53. C
27. A	54. D

Once you have checked your answers, remember to return to page 4 and respond to the Reflect questions.

PRACTICE TEST 1 EXPLANATIONS

Multiple-Choice Questions

1. **B** This first passage, taken from Jonathan Swift's "A Modest Proposal," is a relatively straightforward one. If you take the author's proposal seriously, then (A), (C), (D), and (E) are plausible; the key is to understand that the author is not making a serious proposal, but rather satirizing other so-called scientific studies that, under the guise of humanitarianism, tend to offer cruel (if not sadistic) "solutions" to poverty. Therefore, (B) is the only acceptable answer.

2. **D** Even if you are not familiar with the term "arguments from authority," you should be able to guess the meaning. The authorities cited are "a principal gentleman in the county of Cavan" (paragraph 1), "our merchants" (paragraph 2), and "a very knowing American of my acquaintance in London" (paragraph 4). These are dubious authorities, which is one of the sources of humor in the passage.

    Use Process of Elimination (POE), a strategy we will discuss later on in this book. The easiest and fastest way to use POE in this case is to examine the shortest of the paragraphs, the fourth. There are no similes, (A), or extended metaphors, (C), in the fourth paragraph, so there is no need to check the first or second paragraphs for these rhetorical devices. The other two answers are more esoteric, but logic leads you to eliminate them, even if you do not fully understand them as rhetorical terms. There is no appeal being used in paragraph 4, so eliminate (E). There is also no attempt to argue a point, so get rid of (B).

3. **B** The "merchants" and the "American" both seem to believe the prospect of selling and eating children is feasible. The entire piece is a satire, though, so (A) is too literal. The merchant is not necessarily an aristocrat, so eliminate (C). There is no evidence to suggest that their sentiments are typical of all Londoners, so rule out (E). Since the author is satirizing, the merchants and American are no doubt fictional, so (B) is the best choice.

4. **C** The irony comes from the clever juxtaposition of the phrase "nutriment and rags" with the sum of money, twelve pounds (four times three pounds). Twelve pounds is a paltry sum and indicative of the abject poverty of the children and their families, so (C) most accurately captures the irony of the statement. We have no idea what the price of food was at that time, (A), nor what the children are wearing, (E). Approximation is not ironic, (B), and most likely the parents are NOT being aided by the kingdom, (D), thus their poverty.

5. **C** You may or may not be familiar with the word "fricassee," but when you read it in context, the answer may become apparent—the entire paragraph is about food, and you should understand the other terms (*stewed, roasted, baked, boiled*). Reading the term in context allows you to eliminate the other choices: "animal," "child," "place," and "master."

6. **A** The best approach to this question is to use Process of Elimination. You can eliminate (B) and (C) right away. If you remember that deductive reasoning means starting with a generality and working logically to a specific conclusion, you will know that (D) is also incorrect. Choice (E) may be tempting because of the phrase "which is more than we allow to sheep, black cattle or swine," but this paragraph is not dominated by analogy. Although this comparison is extended, it is not really a pattern. Process analysis, (A), is the best answer; in this paragraph, the author analyzes a problem and proposes a process that will bring about a solution. The proposal describes the process for breeding, fattening, and preparing this very unusual source of protein.

7. **D**   This question is related to the previous one. The proposal is to fatten the children for slaughter, just as if they were livestock (sheep, cattle, or pigs). Choice (D) is the answer.

8. **A**   By using Process of Elimination, you should be able to narrow your choices down to (A) and (C). The author says that the new meat will be expensive, and only the rich landlords will be able to afford it. The correct answer is (A).

9. **A**   By this point, you must have digested (forgive the pun) the satire, so you understand that the landlords have "devoured" the parents by charging unreasonably high rents and that, according to the author, they may as well literally devour (eat) their poor tenants' children. Choice (A) is correct. It is understandable that (E) may tempt you, but the diction in this sentence is hardly a revelation; behind the comical satire is the rage of a man disgusted by the exploitation of the poor by the rich.

10. **D** The reference to farm animals serves to show that the poor and their children are being treated like chattel, similar to the way animals are treated by their owners. Choice (D) captures the point of this analogy. Breeding is not the point, so eliminate (B) and (C). Marriage is also not the point, so eliminate (E). Humane treatment is not mentioned, so rule out (A).

11. **B** To answer this question, think in terms of main idea. This is a fairly straightforward question that asks you to consider the type of material you are reading and what the author is saying within that context. In this piece of literary criticism, the author is making a connection between what Gulliver experienced and what an 18th-century Londoner might have seen exhibited in fairs and inns.

12. **C** The author describes Swift's achievement in *Gulliver's Travels* in generally positive terms, so (C) is correct. If the author were "cleverly subversive," he would have attempted to undercut his generally positive portrayal of Swift in some way, but he never does; eliminate (A). Authors on the AP exam are rarely only "halfheartedly engaged," so (D) can also be eliminated. Both (B) and (E) are wrong and cannot be substantiated in the passage.

13. **E** This is a challenging question because the author provides no explicit definition for the "Scriblerians" in the passage. You know that they were "fascinated with popular entertainments" (line 16) and that they "satirized them in many of their works" (lines 17–18), which means they are authors, not book craftsmen, (A), or literary characters, (B). There is no evidence that they worked as either historians or politicians, so eliminate (C) and (D).

14. **C** In lines 18–19, you learn that Swift "shared this fascination with his fellow Scriblerians," which makes him a member of the circle. Therefore, (C) is correct. While he does have a distinct interest in public entertainments, he is not necessarily a "producer" of one himself, so (B) can be eliminated. There is simply no evidence in the passage for any of the other answer choices.

15. **A** The first two paragraphs maintain a consistent tense and person, so (B) can be eliminated. The author does not invest time in drawing historical allusions or extended metaphors, so (C) and (D) can also be eliminated. He does make some claims that could be considered "asides," but they are hardly for "didactic" (i.e., educational) purposes, and they are not the "most evident" stylistic feature, so eliminate (E) as well. The correct answer is (A) because the author uses a parallel, consistent syntactical structure throughout these paragraphs.

16. **D**   The author wants readers to see the connection between miniature people and landscapes in *Gulliver's Travels* and the common public entertainments of Swift's London. Thus, he emphasizes their "commonness," (D), over other features. This directly contradicts "obscurity" in (B), which can be eliminated. He does not emphasize merely the fact that they are small, so eliminate (A) as well. "Transcience," (E), which emphasizes their fleeting nature, is not discussed in the final paragraph; neither is "magnificence," (C), so both answer choices can be ruled out.

17. **B**   The series of quotes in the final paragraph substantiate the author's claim that *Gulliver's Travels* was at least somewhat based on the kinds of popular entertainments that people often saw in London. Therefore, (B) is the correct answer. The author does not really aim his argument at other scholars or at claims that "*Gulliver's Travels* was purely imaginative," so eliminate (A) and (C). While he certainly does include information from other sources, his primary purpose is not to "inform readers of the sources," so eliminate (E).

18. **E**   The first section of the essay introduces readers to the connection between *Gulliver's Travels* and popular entertainments, while the second section provides evidence to support that claim. Thus, (E) is correct. There really are no "series of questions," "positions of scholars," or "technical definition," so (A), (C), and (D) can be eliminated. It is not accurate at all that the second choice "challenges" claims made in the first, so (B) is wrong as well.

19. **C**   Footnote questions were added to the test in response to concerns raised by colleges and universities. In these days of easy access to information via the Internet, colleges are becoming increasingly concerned that students do not take seriously the intellectual property of authors and end up plagiarizing, knowingly or not. Footnotes give information about authorship and publication place and date, and can also provide hints as to the purpose of a piece of writing or its context. This particular footnote simply indicates that the quote about Lilliput does indeed come from *Gulliver's Travels*, part of a 14-volume set of works by Swift.

20. **D**   This quote from *Social Life in the Reign of Queen Anne* helps to set an elaborate scene, and the footnote helps to lend credibility to Todd's purpose in describing the imaginative miniature worlds of Swift's day.

21. **B**   By paying attention to the title, author, subject matter, and footnotes, you can use POE to eliminate (D) and (E). And while the subject matter of this essay might be of interest to an anthropologist, (A), the content and format is inconsistent with literary criticism, (C). The answer is (B).

22. **B**   The tone of this passage is scholarly and generally positive, which is somewhat more difficult to detect than more overtly negative tones. Therefore, (B) is correct. He does support his claims, but not frantically, so (A) is incorrect. He is not "dejected" (i.e., sad), so (C) is also incorrect. "Intransigent" basically means stubborn, so eliminate (E). And while this passage certainly is "erudite" (i.e., learned), he does not show any signs of cynicism, so (D) is incorrect.

23. **B**   POE is the best way to approach this question. Choices (A), (C), (D), and (E) are all partially wrong (and therefore completely wrong). Take a look at (B). The author is being ironic when she says in the first line, "My own sex, I hope, will excuse me, if I treat them like rational creatures…." The second part of (B), "exposition," is defined as "a setting forth of meaning or intent," and that is exactly what the author is doing in this first paragraph. Choice (B) is correct. Note that in this context, "apology" has nothing to do with being sorry; it most nearly means "defense of an idea."

24. **A**   The author addresses women directly and pretends to excuse herself for addressing them as strong, confident people, instead of the weak, overly sentimental creatures that society wants (and expects) them to be. The correct answer is (A).

25. **E**   Since men aren't mentioned anywhere in the first paragraph, your choice should boil down to (D) and (E). When the author says, "I wish to persuade women to endeavour to acquire strength, both of mind and body," she means intellectual and physical strength, (E). Had she wanted to stress emotional strength, she would have replaced *mind* with *heart*.

26. **E**   "Soft" and "weakness" are important words in both paragraphs; the author uses them in the second paragraph to tie this paragraph in with the first one. The correct answer is (E).

27. **A**   Narrow down your choices to (A) and (B). The best way to approach this type of question is to substitute each of the answer choices for the original word to see which one makes the most sense. Try (A): "supposed to be the sexual characteristics of the weaker *sex*." This seems great, but try (B) too, just in case: "supposed to be the sexual characteristics of the weaker *woman*." Not as good. Naturally, in this case, the weaker sex is woman, but you are asked to find the meaning for "vessel" only. Choice (A) is the best answer.

28. **C**   Using Process of Elimination, get rid of choices (B), (D), and (E). Now you have choices (A) and (C). The author states that "the first object of laudable ambition is to obtain a character as a human being, regardless of the distinction of sex." Thus, you should eliminate (A) because she is not suggesting that a comparison be made between a man and woman. This leaves choice (C) as the answer.

29. **A**   The author wishes to convince the reader by the force of her cogent arguments and the sincerity of her emotions, so the answer is (A). If "cogent" is not on your vocabulary list, add it now. It means "appealing to the intellect or powers of reasoning; convincing." You can eliminate the other choices because the author states unequivocally that she does not wish to polish her style, to employ the bombast and periodic sentences of a rhetorical style, to write elegantly, or to use flowery diction.

30. **C**   The author points out that the "flowery diction" expected of women relegated them to a world outside that of men. The difference in the social level of men and women was reflected in the way they used language. Only men could use the crude words that attempt to express the harsh realities of life. Women were not supposed to know those same harsh realities and, therefore, could not use the crude words that fit with those realities.

31. **E**   The sugary diction becomes associated with the taste of a cloyingly sweet delicacy. This is an extended metaphor, so Process of Elimination allows you to eliminate (A), (B), and (D); this is not a caricature of women, nor is it a critique of bombast (pompous speech or writing). If you do not know the meaning of "panegyric," then add it to your list of vocabulary. A panegyric is a statement of high praise. It should be clear that the author does not sing the praises of sugary writing.

32. **E**   In this passage, the author suggests that women have the capacity to be independent equals of men. Therefore, she is most likely to agree that if women were educated in the same manner as men, they would be more likely to be viewed as equal with men in the eyes of the world. The correct answer is (E).

33. **A**   Use Process of Elimination, especially if you don't know what "sardonic" means (harsh, bitter, or caustic). "Lyrical" is far too positive, so rule out (B). "Frivolous," (D), is a trap: the women are perceived as frivolous, but that is not the author's tone. The author is quite passionate and not at all reserved, so rule out (E). "Condescending," (C), is a trap as well; lines 55–59 seem to convey this mood, but it directly contradicts the message of line 2 ("rational creatures") as well as the main idea of the passage as a whole. The last line of the passage betrays the author's true purpose: to point out the illogic of assuming that women are helpless, useless creatures unfit for positions of responsibility.

34. **C**   The entire passage is about learning and, most importantly, the reason for learning. This is simply a big-picture question in disguise. In this passage, the writer claims that teaching methodologies are overrated because there are many ways to teach and learn; what is important is having a reason for learning. The correct answer is (C).

35. **A**   The phrase "So it is with learning," which follows the example of the ways to learn tribal lays, is a big clue that an analogy, (A), is being used here. The other answer choices are not plausible; Process of Elimination can lead you with certainty to the correct answer.

36. **C**   Don't be thrown off by the use of the term "infinitives" in this question. Infinitives are verb forms that function as substantives (a noun) while retaining some verb characteristics. Some examples of sentences with infinitives are "We want him *to win* the lottery," or "*To go* willingly will prove that you are innocent." So this question specifically refers to the line "There is no one who can say that this or that is the best way to know things, to feel things, to see things, to remember things, to apply things, to connect things and that no other will do as well." Based on the context, learning is a positive experience, so any answer choice that uses a negative adjective should be eliminated. Learning is (not supposed to be) "tedious," "impersonal," "trivial," or even "mechanical"; this leaves you with only (C). In fact, learning is an active and varied process.

37. **D**   If you have a good grasp of the passage, you should be able to narrow your choices to (C) and (D); motivation, in the author's words, is fleeting (or momentary). Although the author does not say outright that a motivation is concrete, he does set up a clear rhetorical contrast between motivation and reason. Given that he describes reason as abstract, it figures that motivation should be roughly the opposite—or at least not the same. The only textual clue that tells us motivation is concrete is the word "event."

38. **E**   Remember the string of infinitives in the first paragraph; in the third paragraph, you may have already noticed the parallel series of prepositional phrases (in which the preposition "for" is repeated). Choice (E), notable parallelism, is correct. Review the other choices. An aphorism, (A), is a pithy saying or proverb. Syllogistic reasoning, (C), proceeds along the lines of a syllogism: a major premise, a minor premise, and a conclusion. Here is an example of syllogistic reasoning: all Princeton Review books are useful; this is a Princeton Review book; therefore, this book is useful. *Ad hominem* arguments, (D), consist of attacks against a person's character. If you were to say, "This book must be awful because you wrote it," you would be adducing an *ad hominem* argument to prove your point.

39. **C**   Choices (A) and (B) may trap readers who fail to consider the context in which the word is used; "god" in this case has nothing to do with religion. The entire second half of the text is about the reason for education. One big clue that the author isn't using the word "god" literally, is the phrase "must have a god to serve, or, even better, several gods." If this were a literal use of "god," then the term would not have been pluralized later.

40. **C**   In this case, the authority is Nietzsche, and the author gives a clear rhetorical statement of his use of analogy, (C), in the sentence that follows the quote: "This applies as much to learning as to living."

41. **A**   This might be a good time to review two terms that are closely related: *oxymoron* and *paradox*. An oxymoron is an apparent contradiction of terms; a paradox is an apparent contradiction of ideas. The important word here is "apparent." In this case, the last sentence is built on an apparent contradiction of terms: schooling will be brought to an end if it has no end. Nonsense? No. You are supposed to understand that, in context, the second "end" is synonymous with reason (or goal or objective). Choice (A) is correct.

42. **E**   In this passage, the author insists that education must serve a higher purpose; otherwise it has no meaning for students. Therefore, the contrast is between motivation—which the author defines as temporary and superficial—and purpose—which gives meaning to everything a student can do in a classroom. Therefore, (E) is correct. He alludes to religion, but it is hardly the "principal contrast," so (D) can be eliminated. Choices (A), (B), and (C) are all appealing because they refer to education in one way or another, but are wrong because they do not represent the central distinction in the passage.

43. **B**   As seen in the previous question, the author argues that students need more than temporary motivation to succeed in education, so (B) is correct. The author does not really examine the "historical development of educational institutions," so (A) is incorrect. And while the circumstances are "challenges" and he does lament a "lack" of something in education, neither (C) nor (D) is correct in its full form, so eliminate those choices as well.

44. **E**   Overall, this is a reasoned (and reasonable) argument rather than a "dramatic" or "impassioned" work, so eliminate (D) and (B). There is neither evidence of a "narrative" in the sense of a story, nor of objectivity, so (C) and (A) can be ruled out as well. Choice (E) is correct.

45. **B**   Process of Elimination should allow you to eliminate (C) and (E). Choices (A) and (D) are similar in meaning, and both imply that the speaker is a politician—of which we have no proof. Choice (B) is your best bet. If you noticed the allusions to law in the body of the text and the judgment of the final statement, then you may have realized that the passage is the dissenting opinion of a judge in a federal case—and you would have been correct to assume that this was a case that went before the Supreme Court.

46. **B**   Perhaps the biggest clue that tells you an analogy, (B), is being employed is the phrase "upon like grounds." Almost everyone would agree that it would be unthinkable, for example, to segregate passengers by religion (Catholic and Protestant). If you agree that this (and the other examples) are analogous to the case before the court (segregation of passengers by race), then you are forced to agree with this judge.

47. **A**   The "it" in this instance refers to the "white race" mentioned much earlier in line 25; therefore, (A) is the correct answer. If you think about the verb "remains" that follows immediately after "it" in line 28, follow the story back to its source. "It" is remaining "true to its great heritage." Whose great heritage? Keep working backward through the passage until you find out he is speaking about the "white race" in line 25 and its future.

48. **A** The brief sentence "There is no caste here" has the effect of changing the syntactical style of the sentence to restate the point made in earlier sentences. Thus, (A) is correct. He is not primarily concerned with the caste system as such, so both (B) and (E) are incorrect. He does use "a simple syntactical structure," so (D) is appealing, but it is incorrect because his primary purpose in this sentence is not to refute "the claims of his opponents" *per se*.

49. **B** Were you tempted to choose (C)? Did you choose (C)? If so, you fell into a trap. Today, it would be normal to expect this judge to propose both civil and racial equality, but the judge bases his arguments solely on the issue of civil rights. In fact, the judge says that the white race is the dominant one "in prestige, in achievements, in education, in wealth, and in power. So, I doubt not, it will continue to be for all time, if it remains true to its great heritage, and holds fast to the principles of constitutional liberty." Based on the passage, the speaker appears to believe that racial equality will never be a reality, although civil equality exists.

50. **E** If you do not know the meaning of the word "pernicious," use Process of Elimination. Choices (A) and (C) can be eliminated; their meanings are the opposite of the speaker's tone and meaning. If you know that "propitious" is roughly equivalent to (C), "useful," you can eliminate that choice as well. As for (B), although "unjust," like "harmful," fits the context, the latter choice is the better synonym for the original term ("pernicious"). As long as you can narrow the choices down to two or three, you should take a guess even if you are not sure. The definition of pernicious is "causing great harm."

51. **A** In this passage, the phrases "may be stricken down by congressional action, or by the courts" and "duty to maintain the supreme law of the land" provide the answer: the Louisiana law is subject to censure by either the United States Congress or the United States Supreme Court, (A).

52. **D** The word "mischievous" is often associated with playful mischief, which is why the test writers included choices like (A) and (C). But in this context, the meaning of "mischievous" is closer to "harmful," so (D) is correct. Always be sure to go back to read the word in context so that you are not distracted by the most common meanings of the word or by the wrong answer choices.

53. **C** The final paragraph of this decision outlines why the author will dissent from the majority opinion of the court. This makes (C) the correct answer. The author does not describe objections to his argument or contrasts to earlier claims; (A), (D), and (E) can be eliminated. The author is not primarily interested in his opponents in this paragraph, so (B), while appealing in some respects, is also incorrect.

54. **D** Process of Elimination is the way to go on this one. Remember to look for one inappropriate word in each answer. Neither adjective in (A) is really appropriate, so eliminate (A). Try (B). Although one may argue that the style is "dry," it is not "objective"—the speaker is arguing only one side of an issue, so (B) is out. The passage could be thought of as "legalistic," but it is not at all "abstract," so get rid of (C). As for (E), the passage is "probing," but it is certainly not "subtle." The speaker comes right out and says what he believes, calling this decision as pernicious as the Supreme Court's judgment of the Dred Scott Case. Therefore, (D) is the answer.

Free-Response Questions

Question 1—Synthesis Essay

The following essay would most likely receive a score of around 7. Its use of language is skilled, it is reasonably well constructed, and its thesis strikes an original stance straddling both views of humanity. However, its introduction is quite repetitive and a bit too long, which is a common occurrence. The well-argued first body paragraph is probably the strongest part of the essay, but the second body paragraph could be developed more. The conclusion acknowledges the possibility of a global citizen mentality, but then provides a nuanced point that it is something that people achieve for themselves through personal growth.

It is possible that people will always be able to embrace their role as global citizens, but that doesn't mean it's the only role that they have. In fact, the primitive roles of mother, father, son, daughter, sister, brother, or neighbor come first in life, and much more naturally. The basic fact is that many people also identify with the people around them, people in their community, people who they look like, talk like, eat like, and live like. This is the group that we come from and it's the one many people feel most comfortable belonging to. After all, this is how humanity lived for millions of years, isolated in small tribes and villages. While it's true that some people won't ever be able to see themselves as members of humanity, it's also true that with some effort most of us can see the bigger picture.

One of the greatest things that unites the world is trade. Often trade brings us together in positive ways. For example, in Source E, Pirie points out that economic ties help countries "grow into the habit of resolving disputes by negotiation and agreement instead of by armed conflict." This is what happened after World War II, when the countries in Europe decided that if they became economically dependent upon one another, they wouldn't ever have another massive war. This is one of the reasons for the birth of the European Union. However, sometimes trade can unite the world in negative ways. Source F shows us that China's enormous industrial economy has created air pollution that blows across the Pacific Ocean and lands in California, Oregon, and Washington. Instead of starting war with one another, the two parties recognize this negative effect and try to find a solution that will satisfy both groups.

Some people have trouble seeing themselves as global citizens because other groups have shut them out, and so they turn inwards toward one another. The Kurds, discussed in Source A, don't have their own country; they are scattered among six other countries, and have been treated badly by many of those governments. Doesn't it make sense that they would only trust one another, and see themselves as Kurds first and foremost? We can't attribute the tribal mentality only to ignorance.

Arguments to the contrary, such as Source G (an illustration of all the countries that have contributed to the International Space Station) definitely carry some weight, but they miss the underlying truth. We are not born citizens of the world; instead, we are born local, and only through conscious acts of will we build ourselves up to that role. This change can be accomplished through travel, foreign exchange students and study abroad, books, documentaries, and social media. While some of the people who see themselves as only members of their tribe are under-informed, detached, and even prejudiced, others may not have had the opportunity to change themselves yet.

Question 2—Rhetorical Analysis Essay

The following sample essay is a strong one; the writer could expect to receive a score of 8 or even a 9. One important thing to note about the essay is the well-organized structure. A clear thesis is stated up front in the introduction, which is concise and straightforward. Each of the body paragraphs focuses on a different strategy, and the student provides evidence directly from the text to support his or her assertions. The last body paragraph ends a bit too abruptly, and the conclusion could be stronger, but overall this is a well-developed, focused essay that sticks to the thesis throughout.

Emmeline Pankhurst's "Freedom or Death" address, given in 1913, reflects her intention and need to defend the tactics of the British suffragette movement, which was criticized at the time for being radical and militant. Upfront she declares that she is not there to "advocate women's suffrage"; rather, she reiterates the fact that "women are human beings" and then goes on to show why the tactics deployed by women suffragists are necessary and, in fact, logical. She directs her argument specifically to male listeners, using appeals to reason, war-related analogies, and both historical and relatable, real-life examples to bolster her case and convey her message.

As Pankhurst's speech is directed to men, she seems to use rhetorical strategies that would appeal to their sensibilities. Throughout the speech, she uses rhetorical questioning and examples to highlight the logic behind the movement's tactics; her aim is to show that its means of protest are based on reason. She asks, "Suppose the men of Hartford had a grievance, and they laid that grievance before their legislature, and the legislature obstinately refused to listen to them…what would be the proper and the constitutional and the practical way of getting their grievance removed?" The diction here is deliberate and helps to build her reason-based argument; she uses words such as "proper," "constitutional," and "practical." She then asks the men to imagine what recourse they would take if they did not have voting rights (like women) and poses another question: "what would men do then?" The "perfectly obvious" conclusion is that they would either need to accept their fate passively or "rise up."

This is where another rhetorical strategy comes into play: Pankhurst cites American history to show that the suffrage movement's tactics are based on historical precedent. This is also a clever appeal to U.S. patriotism. She states, "Your forefathers decided that they must have representation for taxation, many, many years ago…and when their arguments were absolutely disregarded, when every other means had failed, they began by the tea party at Boston, and they went on until they had won the independence of the United States of America." Later in the speech, she turns this example on its head, pointing out that the Boston Tea Party participants (all of whom, undoubtedly, were male) had sacrificed tea and not whiskey, calling the decision to deprive women of their tea but not men of their whiskey "extraordinary," which is both an ironic and hyperbolic use of the word. The rhetorical effect of this is twofold. First, it shows that throughout history, women have suffered from the actions of men. At the same time, it upholds her argument that in times of war—which is what she equates the suffrage movement to—sacrifice is necessary.

Another interesting rhetorical choice is Pankhurst's decision to use real-life examples and analogies to underscore and legitimize her point of view. These examples are relatable but perhaps more so to women. For instance, she uses an example of a crying baby as compared to a patient baby; in this scenario, the baby that is impatient, "cries lustily, screams and kicks and makes everybody unpleasant until it is fed" is attended to first. She uses this analogy to show why it is important to "make more noise than anybody else" and be obtrusive; it is this tactic that gets noticed and achieves results. Later in the speech, she uses a cooking metaphor to reinforce the reality of civil wars and movements: "you cannot make omelettes without breaking eggs." These analogies connect activism with the mundane, which listeners can relate to and agree with. They also juxtapose the traditional female experience (child-rearing, household work) with the more male-centered analogies and metaphors that appear in the speech. For example, early in the speech she calls herself a "soldier who has temporarily left the field of battle" in order to give the speech and explain the movement's position. Pankhurst is thus representing two opposing experiences—that of the home and that of war—which are joined in the women's suffrage movement.

One of the most effective lines in the speech is the rhetorical question she poses, "is there any limit to what we can do except the limit we put upon ourselves?" This reference to "ourselves," which refers to women, seems to be a rallying cry directed to female listeners. Thus, the speech as a whole speaks directly both to men and women and uses specific strategies to target both audiences simultaneously. She at once appeals to reason and history to build an argument that is irrefutable, while calling upon women to continue the fight, instilling in them the knowledge that they are capable of real change.

Question 3—Argument Essay

The following sample essay is very strong. The one noticeable flaw is the discussion of Switzerland; this detour pertains to neutrality, but it is not clear how it relates to racism. It is difficult to gauge just how deleterious the flaw may be. Certainly, the essay would earn a score of at least 7 and may get an 8.

Often, it is believed that if one ignores an issue or a problem, it will merely disappear. Mothers tell their children to ignore bullies, and even the Bible instructs us to turn the other cheek. However, when certain issues are not dealt with, they can fester until they become something far more serious than they were originally; racism is one such issue. As the passage suggests, colorblindness and neutrality are not equalizers; they are merely blinders that allow people to continue as though nothing is out of balance. By adopting a "neutral stand" and by failing to recognize the innate differences between racial groups, one not only perpetuates racism, but also promotes the homogenization of cultures and races, in itself a form of racism.

Sooner or later, the issues one faces must be dealt with. Ignorance, in this case, is not bliss; the longer a problem is put aside, the harder it is to conquer when one finally decides to face it. In the United States, the quintessential example of such a problem is racism. The 1950s and 1960s were a demonstration of just what can happen when an entire nation pretends that nothing is wrong or unequal. Race riots all over the country were the culmination of a race's mounting frustrations. The passage states that "identifying problems and actively promoting solutions are necessary to effect useful change." In fact change, in the form of various civil rights legislatures, only took place when racism was recognized and dealt with by the federal government. Only strong action, like the integration of the Central High School in Little Rock, Arkansas, could ever hope to remedy the situation. By bringing the problem into the spotlight and making everyone consider it and its implications, the government steps toward change, progress, and equality.

The only successful neutral stance ever taken in history was by Switzerland, during all the wars that raged around the country's borders. However, a neutral stance requires more effort to maintain than a stance that is evidently one-sided, because neutrality involves denying the "social and historical context for every situation...[and]...ignoring personal contexts." When this occurs, it would seem that one is assenting that we are all the same equal people, yet that very assertion is flawed, since it eliminates the "differences that exist." If one does not take a side or a stance, one is, in effect, resigning oneself to the current state of affairs, the status quo. As the author of the passage points out, ignoring inequalities and differences allows "the inequalities to continue to exist, given that [one] wouldn't do anything to help change them." Until the public began noticing and sympathizing with the victims of racism, it took no collective action to change the status quo. Finally recognizing the inequality which was the status quo, the public could no longer remain neutral—it split into those who wanted to maintain the status quo and those who wanted to change it and improve the situation.

In essence, neutrality is supposed to be an equalizer because it declares that there are no differences between human beings. However, that denial takes away that which makes us inherently human. Without our cultures and races, we would have nothing to separate one person from another. Thus neutrality states that it is better for a group of people to lack differences than to embrace those differences. Racism is looking down on and rejecting the differences between two people. In much the same way, neutrality turns a blind eye to differences, lending validity to ignorance. Without action and discussion, societies become stale. It is only with a firm stance that one can hope to incite progress and reform; there must be recognition and a definite lack of neutrality if racism is to be prevented. "Being neutral is consenting to the status quo," a status quo which is unequal, unfair, and socially unbalanced.

HOW TO SCORE PRACTICE TEST 1

Section I: Multiple-Choice

_____ × 1.2500 = _____
Number of Correct
(out of 54)

Weighted
Section I Score
(Do not round)

Section II: Free Response

(See if you can find a teacher or classmate to score your essays using
the guidelines in Chapter 4.)

Question 1 _____ × 3.0556 = _____
(out of 9)   (Do not round)

Question 2 _____ × 3.0556 = _____
(out of 9)   (Do not round)

Question 3 _____ × 3.0556 = _____
(out of 9)   (Do not round)

AP Score Conversion Chart English Language and Composition	
Composite Score Range	AP Score
112–150	5
98–111	4
80–97	3
55–79	2
0–54	1

Sum = _____
Weighted Section II
Score (Do not round)

Composite Score

_____ + _____ = _____
Weighted
Section I Score

Weighted
Section II Score

Composite Score
(Round to nearest
whole number)

Part III
About the AP English Language and Composition Exam

- The Structure of the AP English Language and Composition Exam
- How the AP English Language and Composition Exam Is Scored
- Overview of Content Topics
- How AP Exams Are Used
- Other Resources
- Designing Your Study Plan

THE STRUCTURE OF THE AP ENGLISH LANGUAGE AND COMPOSITION EXAM

Below is a helpful outline that describes the basic format for the exam. The total time allotted for the completion of this exam is 3 hours and 15 minutes, or 195 minutes.

Section I: Multiple Choice (1 hour)—counts for 45 percent of your grade

Total number of questions: 52–55

Section II: Free Response (2 hours, 15 minutes; includes a 15-minute reading period)— counts for 55 percent of your grade

Composed of three essays, which the College Board describes as follows:
1. **Synthesis essay:** You will read several sources on a topic and create an argument that integrates information from at least three of the sources to support your thesis.
2. **Rhetorical analysis essay:** You will analyze a nonfiction text and discuss how the author's language choices contribute to the purpose and intended meaning.
3. **Argument essay:** You will create an evidence-based argument in response to a given topic.

HOW THE AP ENGLISH LANGUAGE AND COMPOSITION EXAM IS SCORED

Your Multiple-Choice Score

In the multiple-choice section of the test, you are awarded 1 point for each question that you answer correctly, and you receive no points for each question that you leave blank or answer incorrectly. So, even if you are completely unsure, guess. In Part IV, Chapter 1, we'll show you how to narrow down your choices and make educated guesses.

Your Free-Response Score

Each AP essay is scored on a scale from 0 to 9, with 9 being the best score. Essay readers (who are high school or university English instructors) will grade your three essays, and the scores for your three essays will be added together. The resulting total (which ranges from 0 to 27) constitutes your free-response score.

We will go into the details of essay scoring in Part IV, Chapter 4, but, in general, an essay that receives a 9 answers all facets of the question completely, making good use of specific examples to support its points, and is "well-written," which is a catch-all phrase that means its sentences are complete, properly punctuated, clear in meaning, and varied (that is, they exhibit a variety of structure and use a large academic vocabulary). Lower-scoring essays are considered to be deficient in these qualities to a greater or lesser degree, and students who receive a "0" have basically written gibberish. If you write an essay that is not on the topic, you will receive a blank ("—"). This is equivalent to a zero.

The essay readers do not award points according to a standardized, predetermined checklist. The essays are scored individually by individual readers, each of whom scores essays for only one prompt. Thus, you will have three different readers, and each reader will be able to see only the single essay that he or she reads. The readers do not know how you did on the other essays or what score you received on the multiple-choice section.

Your Final Score

Your final score of 1 to 5 is a combination of your scores from the two sections. Remember that the multiple-choice section counts for 45 percent of the total and the essay section counts for 55 percent. This makes them almost equal, and you must concentrate on doing your best on both parts. If you can get a score of 36 (number correct) on a multiple-choice section with 54 questions, you have exactly a 99 percent chance of getting at least a score of 3 on the exam.

You will have the opportunity to calculate your final score for each Practice Test in this book. Both Answers and Explanations chapters include a worksheet to guide you through the scoring formula step by step. (Remember, this worksheet is meant to serve as a guideline only!)

What Your Final Score Means

After taking the test in early May, you will receive your scores sometime around the first week of July, which is probably when you'll have just started to forget about the entire harrowing experience. Your score will be, simply enough, a single number that will either be a 1, 2, 3, 4, or 5. Here is what those numbers mean.

Score meaning	Percentage of all test takers receiving this score*	Roughly equivalent first-year college course grade	Will a student with this score receive credit?
5—Extremely qualified	9.1%	A	Usually
4—Well qualified	18.4%	A–, B+, B	Usually
3—Qualified	27.8%	B–, C+, C	Maybe
2—Possibly qualified	30.7%	N/A	Very Rarely
1—Not qualified	14%	N/A	No

*Percentages are based on the May 2017 administration of the exam.

OVERVIEW OF CONTENT TOPICS

The AP English Language and Composition Exam tests your abilities to understand how authors use rhetoric and language to convey their purpose. Students are also expected to apply these techniques to their own writing and research projects. Some of the major skills tested include the ability to:

- identify an author's purpose and intended audience

- recognize rhetorical devices and strategies in an author's work

- demonstrate understanding of citations in research papers

- apply these skills and techniques to their own writing

- create and organize an argument defended with evidence and reasoning

- plan, write, and revise cogent, well-written essays

HOW AP EXAMS ARE USED

Colleges make their own decisions about the minimum AP score required to earn credit (points that count toward your college degree), the number of credit hours awarded, and whether advanced placement (the opportunity to skip introductory courses and enter higher-level courses) is offered.

Policies differ widely. Some colleges require a score of 3, while others require a 4, for instance. Some offer both credit and placement; some offer only credit, and some only placement.

The AP exam administrators have created a helpful tool that lets you check the AP credit policy for most colleges. Go to apstudent.collegeboard.org/creditandplacement/search-credit-policies and enter the names of the colleges that interest you. The tool will give you the minimum score required for credit and/or placement. It will also give you a link to the college's website so you can check the most up-to-date policy information.

Want to know which colleges are best for you? Check out The Princeton Review's College Advisor app to build your ideal college list and find your perfect college fit! Available for free in the iOS App Store and Google Play Store.

OTHER RESOURCES

There are many resources available to help you improve your score on the AP English Language and Composition Exam, not the least of which are your teachers. If you are taking an AP class, you may be able to get extra help from your teacher, such as obtaining feedback on your essays. If you are not in an AP course, reach out to an English teacher and ask if he or she will review your essays or otherwise help you review.

Another wonderful resource is **AP Students,** the official student site for the AP exams. The scope of the information at this site is quite broad and includes:

- a Course Description, which provides details on what is covered and sample questions

- the 2001 and 2007 AP English Language and Composition Released Exams, available for purchase at the College Board Store

- essay prompts from previous years

- frequently Asked Questions (FAQs)

- practice material for grammar, including a quiz and grammar guide

- tips for succeeding on the essays

The AP Students home page address is: apstudent.collegeboard.org/home

The AP English Language and Composition Course home page address is: apcentral.collegeboard.org/courses/ap-english-language-and-composition/course

Finally, **The Princeton Review** offers tutoring and small group instruction for the AP English Language and Composition Exam. Our expert instructors can help you refine your strategic approach and add to your content knowledge. For more information, call 1-800-2REVIEW or visit princetonreview.com/academic-tutoring/subjects/ap-english-language for AP English Language Homework Help.

AP Student Tools
Our online portal for the AP exams, AP Student Tools, contains a bunch of helpful resources, including a study guide, printable bubble sheets, admissions advice, and more. Follow the instructions on the Get More (Free) Content page at the front of this book to access this great content!

Break up your review into manageable portions. Download our helpful study guide for this book once you register online.

DESIGNING YOUR STUDY PLAN

In Part I, you identified some areas of potential improvement. Now let's delve further into your performance on Practice Test 1, with the goal of developing a study plan appropriate to your needs and time commitment.

Read the answers and explanations associated with the multiple-choice questions (starting on page 35). After you have done so, respond to the following questions:

- Review the Overview of Content Topics on page 50 and, next to each skill listed, indicate your rank as follows: "1" means "I need a lot of work on this," "2" means "I need some review of this," and "3" means "I have sufficiently mastered this."

- How many days/weeks/months away is your 2019 exam day?

- What time of day is your best, most focused study time?

- How much time per day/week/month will you devote to preparing for your exam?

- When will you do this preparation? (Be as specific as possible: Mondays and Wednesdays from 3:00 to 4:00 P.M., for example.)

- Based on the answers above, will you focus on strategy (Part IV) or the terms and modes review (Part V) or both?

- What are your overall goals in using this book?

Based on your answers to these questions, you should now have a better understanding of how to study for the exam. Use your answers to tailor the online study guide available for download when you register your book online.

Part IV
Test-Taking Strategies for the AP English Language and Composition Exam

PREVIEW

Review your responses to the questions on page 2 of Part I and then answer the following questions:

- How many multiple-choice questions did you miss even though you knew the answer?

- On how many multiple-choice questions did you guess blindly?

- How many multiple-choice questions did you miss after eliminating some answers and guessing based on the remaining answers?

- Did you create an outline before you wrote each essay?

- Did you find any of the essays easier or harder than the others—and, if so, why?

Those answers will give you an idea of what you're doing now and where you could improve your performance on the multiple-choice section and the three essays.

- Did you miss too many multiple-choice questions when you knew (or think you should have known) the answer? Perhaps you're not working carefully enough, or you're letting test anxiety get the better of you.

- Did you guess blindly at more than a few questions? Maybe you didn't make your guesses in the most successful way.

- Did you use POE (Process of Elimination) to get rid of the obviously wrong answers, and still miss the correct response when you took a guess from the remaining answers? The "Letter of the Day" approach probably would have helped there, too. You'll learn about this approach shortly.

- Did you simply start writing your essay without planning what you were going to say and organizing your points? A few minutes spent on an outline will save you from getting half an hour into your essay time and realizing you're seriously off track.

- If you found one essay more difficult than the others (typically the rhetorical analysis essay gives students the most grief), you know where to focus your efforts. The techniques and practice you'll find in the essay chapters will help you gain confidence in tackling all three of the essays on the exam.

HOW TO USE THE CHAPTERS IN THIS PART

Before you read the following strategy chapters, think about the previous strategies you learned and used for Practice Test 1. As you read on you'll start to recognize ways you can change your current approach in order to be more successful on each section of the exam. At the end of Part IV, you'll have the opportunity to reflect on the changes you plan to make.

Chapter 1
How to Approach Multiple-Choice Questions

WHAT TO EXPECT IN THE MULTIPLE-CHOICE SECTION

The multiple-choice section counts for 45 percent of your total score, but you're given only 31 percent (1 hour) of the total exam time to earn that large chunk of points. So how you spend that hour is extremely important.

The exam presents you with five passages, all nonfiction. Some are from the 20th and 21st centuries, and some are pre-20th century. Our practice tests include passages from earlier works just like the real exam does, so that type will be familiar by the time you get to the test.

"Nonfiction" is a very broad term, so you could find passages taken from all sorts of works— essays, biographies, diary entries, speeches, letters, literary criticism, science and nature writing, and writings about politics or history. The passages will also run the gamut as far as types of diction (word choice), syntax (how words are combined into phrases and sentences), imagery, tone, style, point of view, and purpose. You have an hour to read them and answer 55 questions, divided roughly equally among the five passages. Your responses are then scored by computer.

The questions emphasize not just *what* the author is saying, but especially *how* the author says it. The idea is to get you to focus on rhetorical devices, figures of speech and intended purposes, under rigid time constraints and with material you haven't seen before. You'll need to identify rhetorical devices and structures in a passage, and understand why and how the author used them. (Review Chapters 8–11 to learn more about rhetorical strategies. You'll find this helpful for the rhetorical analysis essay, too.) The multiple-choice section is a challenging opportunity to demonstrate your ability to analyze how writers use language to achieve their purposes.

In at least one of the passages in the multiple-choice section, you'll also find several questions about citations, which are usually presented as footnotes to the passage. Citations often give credit to sources from which the passage author drew ideas or information. The citation could state a source's date and place of publication, which might be important in evaluating that source. (For example, a very old source might be questionable if there have been more recent discoveries about a topic.) Citations can also supplement information in the passage without cluttering up the main text with details that might distract readers.

So where do you start preparing to get that much done in such a short time? In this chapter you'll find techniques for reading the passages and answering multiple- choice questions under the conditions that will confront you in the exam.

Active Reading

The passages on the exam are often heavy reading, particularly the older nonfiction, with the long sentences and sometimes obscure words that were common at the time. You need to read quickly but with understanding. If you just skim through the passage, you will have wasted much of your precious two or three minutes of reading time and will likely have to keep rereading parts just to gain a sense of what the author is talking about.

The solution? Active reading. That means you take control of the passage instead of simply letting it pour sentences and paragraphs into your head. Engage with it.

As you read each paragraph, ask yourself these questions:

- What is the author's main point in this paragraph?

- How does it connect to the paragraph that came before it?

- Where is it likely to lead in the next paragraph?

At the end of the passage, ask yourself the following questions:

- What is the author's "big picture" purpose and main point in this passage as a whole?

- Did the author convince me? Interest me? Lead me to disagree strongly? How did the author achieve that effect on me as a reader?

- What impact would this passage likely have had on readers who lived when it was written? What techniques did the author use to achieve that effect?

You can practice this type of active reading with any written material—textbooks, printed ads, or product descriptions, for example. Once you get into the habit, you'll find that your reading comprehension increases considerably, along with your critical thinking skills. With enough practice, active reading will be second nature to you by the time you encounter the AP English Language and Composition Exam passages, where it's a necessity if you're to wade through most, if not all, of the questions and answer them successfully.

Active Reading
Look for the main point of the passage, the author's purpose, and the rhetorical strategies used to achieve that purpose.

Words in Context

Chances are you'll encounter some unfamiliar words on the exam, particularly in the nonfiction passages. Another active reading technique can take you over that hurdle, too: guessing the meaning of a word from its context. For example, let's say the passage is describing a politician who is trying to sell an unpopular new law to the voters in his constituency.

Words in Context
Guess the meaning of an unfamiliar word from its context.

> The speaker's passion and ebullience began to cut through the dour mood of the audience that confronted him.

If you have no idea what "ebullience" and "dour" mean, you can still figure them out from the context. The speaker is passionate about this law he's trying to promote, so—paired with "passion"—"ebullience" must have something to do with enthusiasm and excitement. The voters, on the other hand, don't like it at all, so "dour" must signify something opposite—gloomy, unreceptive. The word even sounds dark and unfriendly.

Guessing a word's meaning from its context is something you can practice on material you encounter in your daily life. Then you can check a dictionary or thesaurus to see how your skill is improving.

Attack the Questions and Go Back to the Passage

Each question is setting a specific task for you. Make sure you understand exactly what it's telling you to do. Read the question stem carefully, word for word.

Don't Play Mind Games

Your memory will fool you. Always go back to the passage.

When a question refers to specific lines in the passage, always go back to the passage and reread them. You should also read a few lines before and after the specified lines; context is often critical in determining the correct answer.

Relying on your memory—particularly in the dense, nonfiction works you'll encounter on the exam—can easily lead you astray. Sometimes a sneaky answer choice will start out partly correct, but then make a U-turn into something that is not supported by the passage. But if you're relying on your memory and get a glimmer of recognition from the first part, you might pick the wrong answer and miss out on scoring a point. Remember, half wrong is all wrong.

POE—Process of Elimination

After you understand the question task and have gone back to the passage to review the lines it specifies, look at the answer choices. Your active reading, careful analysis of the question task, and rereading of specific lines will most likely show you at least a couple of answer choices that are clearly wrong. Now instead of five possible answers, you have only three or perhaps two, and your chances of choosing—or even guessing at—the correct answer just went up substantially.

Main Steps of POE

First, eliminate the answers you know are wrong.

Then look for the right answer within the remaining choices.

So start there—by quickly getting rid of choices that are obviously wrong—instead of starting by puzzling through five possible answers looking for the one right choice. That's the Process of Elimination approach, and it will increase your success rate on multiple-choice questions significantly.

Guessing and the Letter of the Day

So you've tossed out two clearly wrong answers using POE, and narrowed five possible choices down to three. Suppose you still can't tell *which of* those three is the correct answer, though.

What do you do? Two things: guess and use the Letter of the Day.

Guessing

You get no points for a question that isn't answered at all. The good news with this exam, though, is that you don't lose any points for incorrect answers. So answer every single question, even if your answer is a guess. By using POE, you've raised your chances of guessing correctly within a smaller number of possible answers.

There's another technique you can add that will increase your guessing success rate even more.

Letter of the Day

If you make a random guess for each question you can't answer—(A) for one and (D) for another and maybe (E) for this one—you've just made an excellent start at getting every one wrong. The solution? Pick one letter—any letter—and use it for every single guess. That's the Letter of the Day approach.

Let's say there are 10 questions you can't answer. If you pick, for example, (B) as your Letter of the Day and answer (B) on every one of those 10 questions, what are the chances that (B) really is the correct answer to at least one of them, possibly more? Pretty good. On the other hand, if you jump around with a different random letter for each guess, you stand a good chance of missing the correct answer on every one.

Proven Techniques
Use POE, Letter of the Day, and the Two-Pass System to help boost your score.

The Two-Pass System

With around 55 questions and 5 passages, you have roughly 1 minute to answer each question, about 12 minutes for each passage and accompanying set of questions. The Two-Pass System will help you use that time most efficiently. Here are the steps to take:

On your first pass through the questions,

- Answer all the easy questions first. If you can answer a question as you come to it, do so.

- Each time you come to a hard question that you can't answer, fill in a "guess" answer using your Letter of the Day and circle the question.

> ### The Two-Pass System
> Pass 1: Answer the easy questions and guess at the hard ones, using the Letter of the Day.
>
> Pass 2: Tackle as many of the hard ones as you can during the time left for that passage.

On your second pass through,

- Look at your watch to see how much time you have left for this passage. Go back to the hard questions you circled and tackle as many as you can before the chunk of time available for that passage runs out.

This system works well since all the questions are worth the same number of points, regardless of whether you think they're easy or hard, and since the order in which you answer the questions doesn't matter.

Now let's examine a sample passage.

SAMPLE PASSAGE—HERE'S HOW IT'S DONE

The following passage is excerpted from *A Technical Guide for Monitoring Wildlife Habitat* by the United States Department of Agriculture Forest Service.

The publication that includes this excerpt is intended as a guide for professionals involved in forest planning and wildlife habitat monitoring. It was published in 2013 by the USDA Forest Service, which aims to balance the use of public resources with the protection of those resources. The authors are professionals in such fields as ecology, biology, and forestry.

Management Considerations

Management objectives will differ substantially among species and, thus, influence habitat monitoring objectives. Emphasis species for which habitat may be monitored
Line may come from a wide spectrum of conservation cat-
5 egories from taxa listed under the Federal Endangered Species Act to ubiquitous species that may be hunted or trapped.

The process of identifying monitoring priorities begins with a review of pertinent laws, regulations, policies,
10 regional and forest management objectives, and prior-ities set through partnerships and agreements to deter-mine those emphasis species for which monitoring of populations is required. Recovery plans for threatened or endangered species often require that cooperating
15 agencies monitor population parameters for the species.[1] Others commit the Forest Service to monitor habitat.[2] Memoranda of understanding with State wildlife agen-cies obligate the Forest Service to assist with monitoring populations of important game species.[3]
20 Regional and forest management objectives also influence whether habitat is monitored for an emphasis species. If a land and resource management plan specifies management activities in ecological systems that also provide habitat for an emphasis species, it may be advis-
25 able to monitor habitat for that species.[4] Conversely, an emphasis species associated with habitat that is not likely to be influenced by planned management actions may be a poor candidate for habitat monitoring.[5]

Biological Considerations

Habitat monitoring should focus primarily on species
30 that are most likely to respond to changes in habitat condition because of management actions, disturbances, or climate change. In particular, management actions may impact systems in ways that are detrimental or positive but remain uncertain and require monitoring. Thus,
35 selecting emphasis species should include not only those that are associated with forest plan objectives or desired conditions, but also those that have the potential to be affected by management actions that modify habitat.

In addition, developing a successful habitat monitor-
40 ing program requires making a clear distinction between habitat and population monitoring.[6] In some cases, the monitoring objective for a species at risk will specify the

detection of relatively small changes in population size
(especially decreases) or occupancy. Depending on the
45 management concern, monitoring objective, detectability,
demography, and ecological relationships of a species, it
may be prudent to monitor only populations, rather than
to also track habitat. Under some limited circumstances,
behavioral and spatial relationships may exist that allow
50 populations to be closely linked to specific habitat attributes.[7] If strong evidence indicates that habitat features
are directly associated with population size of an emphasis species, then habitat monitoring, with the objective of
indirectly monitoring populations may be an acceptable
55 approach under a limited range of management circumstances.[8] Species that are difficult to detect and, therefore, difficult to monitor for population abundance are
good candidates for habitat monitoring if strong habitat
relationships have been documented and if informa-
60 tion on annual population fluctuations are not needed.
Under these circumstances, compare habitat monitoring
results periodically with population data to ensure that
the assumed relationship between habitat and population
remains.[9] The indirect nature of the monitoring program
65 relative to the link between habitat and populations must
always be considered when the resulting monitoring data
are used.

1 e.g., red-cockaded woodpecker [Picoides borealis] USDI USFWS. 2003. Recovery plan for the red-
cockaded woodpecker (Picoides borealis). 2nd rev. Atlanta, GA: U.S. Department of the Interior, U.S.
Fish and Wildlife Service, Southeast Region. 296 p.

2 e.g., Mexican spotted owl [Strix occidentalis lucida] USDI U.S. Fish and Wildlife Service (USFWS).
1995. Recovery plan for the Mexican spotted owl (Strix occidentalis lucida). Albuquerque, NM: U.S.
Department of the Interior, U.S. Fish and Wildlife Service, Southwest Region. 172 p.

3 e.g., Sitka black-tailed deer [Odocoileus hemionus sitkensis] in the Alaska Region

4 e.g., woodland caribou. [Rangifer tarandus caribou]. USDA Forest Service. 1987. Forest plan Idaho
Panhandle National Forests. Missoula, MT: U.S. Department of Agriculture, Forest Service, Northern
Region. Irregular pagination.

5 e.g., gray-crowned rosy finch [Leucosticte tephrocotis] in alpine habitats relative to timber management
activities

6 i.e., habitat monitoring should not be confused with population monitoring (See chapter 1).

7 e.g., amount of recently burned conifer forest is directly related to populations of black-backed
woodpeckers [Picoides arcticus]. Hutto, R.L. 1995. Composition of bird communities following stand-
replacement fires in northern Rocky Mountain (U.S.A.) conifer forests. Conservation Biology.
9: 1041–1058.

8 Haufler, J.B.; Mehl, C.A.; Roloff, G.J. 1999. Conserving biological diversity using a coarse-filter
approach with a species assessment. In: Baydack, R.K.; Campa, H., III; Haufler, J.B., eds. Practical
approaches to the conservation of biological diversity. Washington DC: Island Press: 107–125. Molina,
R.; Marcot, B.G.; Lesher, R. 2006. Protecting rare, old-growth, forest-associated species under the survey
and manage program guidelines of the Northwest Forest Plan. Conservation Biology. 20: 306–318.

9 See chapter 1.

Analyzing the Passage

In active reading mode, you should be looking for and writing down the main point of each paragraph in the margins before you move on to the next. From those building blocks, you can identify the main point of the excerpt and the author's purpose.

The first section focuses on forest or other environment management programs. The first paragraph stresses flexibility: objectives and species can encompass a broad range. The authors are providing guidance that can be applied to just about any situation readers face. The second paragraph outlines a framework of requirements and partnerships for undertaking monitoring programs—again, within a broad range of situations. The third paragraph positions habitat monitoring within larger management programs, and gives examples of when it may or may not be appropriate to monitor habitats.

The excerpt then looks at selecting species for habitat monitoring. The fourth paragraph specifies that species likely to be affected by a change in habitat should be selected. The long fifth paragraph then makes a point the authors want to emphasize: habitat monitoring should be distinguished from population monitoring. The paragraph gives examples of when both types of information could be considered, or even when population monitoring could be carried out on its own. However, the two types of monitoring are always considered as distinct activities.

The introductory comments provide context that helps identify the authors' purpose and the rhetorical strategies they use. The excerpt is part of a guide written by nature management professionals for professionals. In order to influence readers to follow their recommendations and practices, the authors need to gain trust and build credibility. Rhetorical techniques they use include formal language, drawing on authorities, and providing examples. The authors do have a clear bias for distinguishing habitat monitoring from population monitoring; however, their tone is neutral and unemotional. They allow for exceptions, and they use qualified language such as "may be prudent" and "may be an acceptable approach." They avoid complex industry jargon, making their information accessible to readers from a broad spectrum of disciplines and with varying degrees of expertise. As a result of these techniques, the authors sound like trustworthy, experienced scientists who are making sound recommendations but not alienating readers by being authoritarian.

Let's look at a typical "big-picture" question.

1. The authors' main purpose in this excerpt is to

   (A) encourage professionals to adopt a monitoring approach that is similar to the Forestry Service's approach

   (B) influence habitat monitoring professionals to monitor populations, too

   (C) concentrate wildlife monitoring efforts on bird populations

   (D) educate readers about how to monitor wildlife habitats

   (E) direct resources toward protecting endangered species

Through active reading, you should have identified not only the main point of each paragraph, but also the authors' overall purpose. The correct answer is (A). The excerpt outlines the Forestry Service's approach and, through the frequent use of "should," encourages readers to follow a similar approach. The guide specifies that habitat and population monitoring should be distinct activities, and that they should be combined in only limited circumstances, so (B) is clearly wrong and could have been eliminated right away using POE. Although the footnote comments give several examples of birds, they also mention deer and caribou, (C). The intended audience is made up of professionals in the field, so they would not need to be educated about how to monitor wildlife habitats, (D). The authors specify that habitat can be monitored for any species, from the endangered and at risk to the thriving, so they intend to cover a broad spectrum of situations, making (E) incorrect.

Here's another "big picture" question, focused on only one paragraph this time.

2. Paragraph 4 implies that
    (A) resources available for habitat monitoring are limited
    (B) forest management programs focus only on the physical environment
    (C) the impact of forest management programs cannot be predicted
    (D) forest management programs include climate change
    (E) habitat monitoring should not be confined to species that are part of forest management programs

The answer is (E). The authors recommend also monitoring species that aren't part of the forest plan but which could be affected by any resulting changes to their habitat. This recommendation makes (A) incorrect; resources do not appear to be limited when the scope of the monitoring could be expanded beyond the original plan. The paragraph discusses both the physical environment and the species that inhabit it, so (B) is incorrect. In addition to being wrong, though, (B) is also too extreme ("focus only on"). On the AP exam, it's unusual for an "all or nothing" response such as this to be correct. Extreme choices can usually be eliminated right away using POE. While the authors acknowledge that the impact of forest management actions may be uncertain, they don't claim that it's not possible to predict the impact in every case, so eliminate (C). Forest management programs are planned and run by humans; climate change is not, so (D) is incorrect.

Here's another question in which you're asked to make an inference from something stated in the passage.

3. The last sentence of paragraph 2 suggests that

    (A) readers must consult the Forest Service if they want to monitor habitats for endangered species

    (B) the Forest Service requires State wildlife agencies to include it in monitoring game species populations

    (C) the Forest Service must be involved in population monitoring programs for certain game species

    (D) permission must be obtained from the Forest Service before game populations are monitored

    (E) the Forest Service demands control of game species population monitoring programs

A set of relatively close answers such as this one demonstrates the importance of going back to the passage instead of relying on your memory. You need to review exactly what the sentence says to avoid being tripped up by a choice that sounds close but has something wrong with it. Reread only as much as you need to, though. If you can't answer a question without spending too much time rereading, then guess at the answer (using your Letter of the Day) and, if you have time, return to it on your second pass through the questions for that passage.

The correct answer is (C). As you found when you identified the main point of paragraph 2, the authors are cautioning that a framework of requirements governs monitoring programs. Readers can't necessarily just set off on their own. In the last sentence of paragraph 2, the authors state—in a gentle, non-threatening way —that the Forest Service is "obligated" to "assist" with population monitoring programs for important game species. Choice (A) can be eliminated immediately because the sentence mentions game species, not endangered species. The authors don't specify which organization initiated the agreements with State wildlife agencies, so we can't say for sure whether (B) is true. Choice (D) would suggest getting permission and then going off and conducting the monitoring program without any further involvement by the Forest Services, which is incorrect. Choice (E) is too extreme ("demands control") and can be eliminated on that basis.

Here are a couple of questions dealing with rhetorical strategies—*how* the authors say what they say in order to achieve their purpose with a specific audience in a particular context.

4. In the rhetorical strategies they use, the authors are trying to convince readers that they are

    (A) expert authorities in the field

    (B) a trustworthy source

    (C) a benign enforcement mechanism

    (D) independent thinkers

    (E) set in their ways as a result of extensive experience

The correct answer is (B). Through their formal language, objective tone, supporting citations, and flexibility in acknowledging exceptions, the authors position themselves as a source whose recommendations can be trusted by professionals in the field. While the authors do cite some other U.S. environmental agencies in the footnotes, they also give references to nongovernment research results. They position themselves as experienced guides, not as expert authorities, (A). The authors do not suggest that they can or will enforce compliance with the monitoring practices they describe, so (C) is incorrect. Even when they outline "laws, regulations, policies," they don't specify penalties for noncompliance. There is no suggestion that the authors are advocating an approach that differs markedly from established monitoring practices, (D). At several points, the authors demonstrate flexibility by acknowledging that there may be exceptions to their recommendations, demonstrating an openness that makes (E) wrong.

5. One rhetorical strategy the authors use in order to achieve their purpose with their professional audience is

(A) examples of the negative results of combining population and habitat monitoring

(B) appeals to authority

(C) specialized technical language

(D) understatement

(E) appeals to logical reasoning

Choice (B) is the correct answer. In several of the footnotes, the authors draw on published works and authorities in the field to support their points. The citations in the footnotes become part of the authors' rhetorical strategy. The authors actually acknowledge that the two types of monitoring can be combined in certain circumstances. They do not give any examples of negative results from combining them in the wrong circumstances, (A). The authors do give the correct scientific classification for certain species, and they use the term "emphasis species" to signify a monitoring target. However, their use of technical language is not extensive. The authors are aiming at a diverse range of industry participants, so in general they use formal language to signify their professionalism while not excluding readers by using highly technical language from one specific field, so (C) is incorrect. The authors' tone is objective and neutral. They do not understate, (D), or overstate the impact of not following their general practice of distinguishing habitat monitoring from population monitoring. The authors don't rely on logical arguments, (E), such as "X and Y are the case; therefore, you should do Z or else *this* will happen because of *this*."

This next question shows the type of detail some questions can cover.

6. The term "taxa" in paragraph 1 refers to

(A) characteristics of a group of organisms that distinguish them from other groups

(B) criteria used to determine whether a species is endangered

(C) a grouping of certain species of organism

(D) the unusually frail members of a larger group of animals who likely would not survive without habitat support

(E) any group of widespread and thriving organisms

This question demonstrates the importance of context in guessing the meaning of an unfamiliar word, and the need to go back to the passage to find the answer. Remember to read a line or two above and below the word specified, too, so you won't miss any important information from the context.

Here, the correct answer is (C). The paragraph states that habitat monitoring is appropriate for a full range of organisms, from those on the endangered species list to those that are so numerous and widespread ("ubiquitous") that they can be hunted. It sets up a contrast between species on both extreme ends of the range. Using the technical term "taxa" allows the authors to avoid repeating the word "species" three times in the same sentence. However, "taxa" could accurately be replaced by "species" in this sentence. Choice (A) is incorrect because "taxa" (the plural of "taxon," which would indicate a single species) refers to the groups themselves, not to the characteristics of those groups. Both (B) and (E) are incorrect as meanings for "taxa" because species could be either endangered or thriving. Choice (D) is incorrect because "taxa" refers to entire groups, not to individual members of those groups.

Here are some typical questions about citations, which are shown as footnotes. That means you'll need to read the footnote as well as go back to the corresponding place in the passage (indicated by the superscript number of the footnote). Read a couple of lines above and below the footnote number so you understand the context in which the authors cite a particular source or make a supplementary comment.

7. The primary function of footnote 9 is most likely to

   (A) give readers a method for carrying out a procedure
   (B) explain the reason for the authors' recommendation
   (C) provide an additional source for readers who are interested in more information
   (D) convince readers that they need more information before they can follow the authors' recommendations successfully
   (E) provide an authority to support the authors' point

Choice (A) is correct. The excerpt doesn't say what is in Chapter 1, so you'll need to guess at the most likely primary reason for referring readers to it. Since the footnote occurs at the end of a sentence that describes a procedure (comparing habitat monitoring results with population data to confirm an assumed relationship between the two), (A) is the best choice. The footnote is simply a side comment, not an integral part of the text, where the authors would likely have explained their reasoning, (B), or made a convincing case, (D), if they felt the need to do so. Choice (C) is too vague when the footnote follows the description of a specific procedure. Since the footnote sends readers to another spot in the same publication, it is not providing a supporting authority, (E).

8. The most unique aspect of footnote 8 in paragraph 5 is its

   (A) support for the separation of habitat and
       population monitoring
   (B) seven-year time span of support for the program
       objective of monitoring populations
   (C) geographical diversity of the resources cited
   (D) additional support for the authors'
       acknowledgement of a situation that would favor
       incorporating some population monitoring into a
       habitat monitoring program
   (E) acknowledgement of an opposing position

The answer is (D). Footnote 8 is the only one that cites two sources of support for the same point (indirect population monitoring as an objective of habitat monitoring). The sources are cited as support for a condition in which habitat and population monitoring could be combined, not separated. Going back to the passage should have allowed you to eliminate (A) immediately using POE. While there is a seven-year time span between the two references, the two sources are not cited as support for only monitoring populations. Choice (B) is half wrong; therefore, it's all wrong. Although the second study in the footnote specifies the northwest, the first study doesn't indicate which geographical area it covers; eliminate (C). The sources are cited in support of, not in opposition to, the authors' position; eliminate (E). Again, going back to the passage should have eliminated this choice right away.

9. The main effect of footnote 7 is to

   (A) support the authors' point
   (B) convince readers who might be skeptical about the
       authors' point
   (C) illustrate and support the authors' point
   (D) explain the authors' point
   (E) support and qualify the authors' point

Choice (C) is correct. The example of the impact of forest fires on woodpecker populations illustrates the authors' point, and the citation from published research supports it. While this footnote supports the authors' point with a reference to published research, that's not the only thing it does, eliminating (A). It's possible that an example and citation might convince skeptical readers, but the question asks for the *main* effect. The footnote is not worded as if its main objective were to convince skeptical readers, so you can get rid of (B). The footnote gives an example; it doesn't explain what the authors mean, so (D) can be eliminated. This footnote does support the authors' point. However, they already qualified their point in the main text ("Under some limited circumstances..."), not in the footnote. Remember, half wrong is all wrong. Eliminate (E).

Incidentally, if you had guessed at every one of these answers and had chosen (C) as your Letter of the Day, you would have gotten three correct answers on this passage. No, of course you can't know in advance which letter is best, but this example shows the results that are possible with the Letter of the Day technique.

You'll have the opportunity to practice what you've learned in the drills in Chapter 3. First, let's look a bit more closely at some approaches to two essential aspects of doing well on the multiple-choice questions: timing and pacing.

Summary

- Use active reading to identify the main point of each paragraph (or chunk) of the passage; then see how they connect to form the main point of the passage as a whole.

- Concentrate on the author's purpose, tone, and point of view.

- Look for the rhetorical strategies the author uses to achieve that purpose.

- Always go back to the passage when multiple-choice questions refer you to specific lines. Relying on your memory can easily lead you to select a close—but incorrect—answer.

- Read a couple of lines above and below the lines specified in the question. The context of the lines is almost always critical in determining the correct answer.

- Pace yourself. Divide the multiple-choice section into 12-minute chunks for each passage.

- Use the Two-Pass System. On your first pass, answer the questions you can and guess at the rest, using your Letter of the Day. Circle the questions you guessed at, and go back to them later if time remains in your 12-minute chunk.

- Use POE to eliminate wrong answers instead of looking for the right answer among five alternatives.

Chapter 2
Using Time
Effectively to
Maximize Points

STUDYING ISN'T EVERYTHING

Very few students stop to think about how to improve their test-taking skills. Most assume that if they study hard, they will get a high score, and if they do not study, they will do poorly.

Have you ever studied really hard for an exam and then blown it on test day? Have you ever aced an exam for which you thought you probably hadn't studied enough? Most students have had one, if not both, of these experiences. The lesson should be clear: factors other than how much you've studied influence your final test score, particularly on a test such as the AP English Language and Composition Exam, where timing and pacing are important aspects of thorough preparation.

This chapter will provide you with some insights that will help you perform better on the multiple-choice section of the AP English Language and Composition Exam, and on other exams as well.

Pacing and Timing

A big part of scoring well on an exam is sharpening your awareness of time. Another is working at a consistent pace.

Don't Waste Your Time
If you can't answer a question, make an educated guess and move on to the next question. Although you don't lose any points for wrong answers in the multiple choice section, you don't want to waste time on a question you're unsure of because you will take away time from questions you're more likely to get correct.

The worst mistake made by inexperienced test takers is that when they come to a question that stumps them, rather than just skipping it, they panic and stall. Time stands still when you're working on a question you can't answer, and it is not unusual for students to waste five minutes on a single multiple-choice question (especially a question involving a long selection from the passage or the word EXCEPT) instead of cutting their losses and moving on to questions they *can* answer.

Every question is worth the same one point, whether it's a hard question or an easy one. The computer that scores your responses doesn't know whether you agonized for three minutes over a hard question or breezed through an easy one in a few seconds; it only knows whether your answer is right or wrong.

It is important to be aware of how much time you have spent on a given question or section. There are several ways to improve your pacing and timing for the test.

- **Know your average pace.** While you prepare for your test, gauge how long you take on a passage with 11 or so questions. Knowing how long you spend on average per passage (and per question) will help you identify how many passages you can read (and questions you can answer) effectively in 60 minutes, and how best to pace yourself for the test.

- **Have a watch or clock nearby.** You are permitted to have a watch or clock nearby to help you keep track of time. However, constantly checking the clock is in itself a waste of time and can be distracting and stressful. Devise a plan. Try checking the clock after every passage or two to see whether you are keeping the correct pace or need to speed up. This will ensure that you're managing your time but won't permit you to fall into the trap of dwelling on it.

- **Know when to move on.** Because all of the multiple-choice questions are scored equally, and you are not penalized for wrong answers, investing long stretches of time on a single question is inefficient and can potentially deprive you of the chance to answer easier questions later on. If you can eliminate answer choices with POE, do so, but on your first pass through the questions, just guess from among the remaining choices (using your Letter of the Day) and move on if you can't find the correct answer. Remember, tests are like marathons: you do best when you work through them at a steady pace.

- **Be selective.** You don't have to do the multiple-choice questions in order. If you are stumped by a question, guess, skip it, and choose a different one. You might not have to answer every question correctly to achieve the score you need for your first choice of college. Select the questions you can answer and work on them first. This will boost your confidence, make you more efficient, and give you the greatest chance of getting the most questions correct.

- **Use Process of Elimination on every question.** Every answer choice that can be eliminated increases the odds that you will answer the question correctly.

Remember, when all the questions on a test are of equal value, and you don't lose any points for incorrect answers, no one question is that important. Your overall goal for pacing is to get the most questions correct.

Getting the Score You Need

Depending on the score you need, it may be in your best interest *not* to try to work through every multiple-choice question. Check with the schools to which you are applying. If you're aiming for credit hours and need to score a 5, it's best to find out as early in your preparation as possible. On the other hand, if you're simply aiming for placement and you find out your first choice of college sets the cut-off point at a score of 3, some of the pressure is off and you can prepare without feeling crushed by anxiety.

Reducing Test Anxiety

No matter what score you need, everybody experiences anxiety before and during an exam. To a certain extent, test anxiety *can* be helpful. Some people find that they perform more quickly and efficiently under stress. If you have ever pulled an all-nighter to write a paper and ended up doing good work, you know the feeling.

However, too much stress is definitely a bad thing. If you find that your stress level prevents you from doing your best work during exams, here are a few actions you can take to stop excessive stress in its tracks.

Lit Lover?
Are you taking AP English Literature and Composition as well? Check out our *Cracking the AP English Literature and Composition Exam!*

- **Take a reality check.** Evaluate your situation before the test begins. If you have understood and practiced all of the techniques we give for success on the exam, remind yourself that you are well prepared. Remember that many others taking the test are not as well prepared as you are, and you're being graded against them, so you have an advantage.

- **Don't fixate on how much you don't know.** Your job is to score as high as you can by maximizing the benefits of what you do know. Think of a test as a game. How can you get the most points in the time allotted?

- **Try to relax.** Slow, deep breathing works for almost everyone. Close your eyes, take a few slow, deep breaths, and concentrate on nothing but your inhalation and exhalation for a few seconds. This is a basic form of meditation, and it should help clear your mind of stress and, as a result, concentrate better on the test. If you have ever taken yoga classes, you probably know some other good relaxation techniques you could use in the test setting.

- **Visualize.** Imagine your favorite park, beach, hiking trail, or room, and visualize yourself sitting there taking the exam—all alone, calm and relaxed, and enjoying your surroundings. You're still taking the test, but in a pleasant place instead of in a stress-filled atmosphere. Most likely you'll need to practice this technique in advance in order to be able to slip into another place mentally while you're taking the test. Try it while you're having breakfast, or riding the bus, or walking down a noisy, chaotic street.

- **Eliminate as many surprises as you can.** Make sure you know the testing location, how long it will take you to get there, and where to park if you're driving. Take a "dry run" trip to the test center before the day of the exam. Know when the exam room will open, when the actual exam starts, what type of questions you will be asked, and how long each section of the test will take. You don't want to be worrying about any of these things on the test day.

- **Plan to reward yourself.** After all, you deserve a reward for all of your hard work. Make a plan for doing something enjoyable right after the test is over. While you're preparing, keep thinking of the reward you've promised yourself.

The best way to avoid stress is to become familiar with the test material and practice doing exam questions under actual time constraints. (By reading this book, you are taking a major step toward a stress-free AP English Language and Composition Exam.)

In the next chapter, you'll have an opportunity to practice the strategies you've learned.

Remember...
Your purchase of this book comes with access to AP Student Tools, a resource hub filled with bonus material like study guides and college advice. Follow the instructions on the Get More (Free) Content page to start using your AP Student Tools.

Chapter 3
Pacing Drills

DRILL 1

Questions 1–8. Read the following passage carefully before you choose your answers.

This passage is excerpted from the British Prime Minister's 1846 speech about the repeal of the Corn Laws.

Sir, believe me, to conduct the Government of this country is a most arduous duty; I may say it without irreverence, that these ancient institutions, like our physical
Line frames, are "fearfully and wonderfully made." It is no easy
5 task to ensure the united action of an ancient monarchy, a proud aristocracy, and a reformed constituency. I have done everything I could do, and have thought it consistent with true Conservative policy to reconcile these three branches of the State. I have thought it consistent with true
10 Conservative policy to promote so much of happiness and contentment among the people that the voice of disaffection should be no longer heard, and that thoughts of the dissolution of our institutions should be forgotten in the midst of physical enjoyment. These were my attempts,
15 and I thought them not inconsistent with true and enlarged Conservative policy. These were my objects in accepting office—it is a burden too great for my physical, and far beyond my intellectual structure; and to be relieved from it with perfect honour would be the greatest favour that
20 could be conferred on me. But as a feeling of honour and strong sense of duty require me to undertake those responsible functions, I declare, Sir, that I am ready to incur these risks, to bear these burdens, and to front all these honourable dangers. But, Sir, I will not take the step with
25 mutilated power and shackled authority. I will not stand at the helm during, such tempestuous nights as I have seen, if the vessel be not allowed fairly to pursue the course which I think she ought to take. I will not, Sir, undertake to direct the course of the vessel by the observations which have
30 been taken in 1842. I will reserve to myself the marking out of that course; and I must, for the public interest, claim for myself the unfettered power of judging of those measures which I conceive will be better for the country to propose.
35 Sir, I do not wish to be the Minister of England; but while I have the high honour of holding that Office, I am determined to hold it by no servile tenure. I will only hold that office upon the condition of being unshackled by any other obligations than those of consulting the public inter
40 ests, and of providing for the public safety.

1. The opening sentence of the passage contains

   (A) an expression of fear
   (B) an appeal to authority
   (C) a humorous simile
   (D) an irreverent attack
   (E) equivocation

2. The speaker is addressing

   (A) a friend
   (B) a group of his peers
   (C) a king
   (D) a crowd of voters
   (E) his political adversaries

3. The most significant transition takes place in

   (A) line 9 ("I have thought it consistent…")
   (B) line 16 ("These were my objects…")
   (C) line 20 ("But as a feeling of honour…")
   (D) line 24 ("But, Sir, I will not…")
   (E) line 28 ("I will not, Sir, undertake…")

4. All of the following are part of the same extended metaphor EXCEPT

   (A) "helm" (line 26)
   (B) "vessel" (line 27)
   (C) "fairly" (line 27)
   (D) "course" (line 29)
   (E) "unshackled" (line 38)

5. Which term in the first paragraph serves to prepare the dominant point of the final paragraph?

   (A) "disaffection" (lines 11–12)
   (B) "enjoyment" (line 14)
   (C) "dangers" (line 24)
   (D) "tempestuous" (line 26)
   (E) "unfettered" (line 32)

6. Based on the passage, the speaker's motivation to serve as prime minister is dictated mostly by

   (A) greed
   (B) political ambition
   (C) sense of honor
   (D) political power
   (E) youthful exuberance

7. The tone of the entire passage

   (A) remains consistently cynical
   (B) shifts according to the speaker's mood
   (C) shifts from light to serious
   (D) becomes more frivolous in the final paragraph
   (E) remains consistently lighthearted

8. Which of the following best describes the rhetorical function of lines 17–20 ("it is a burden too great… the greatest favor that could be conferred upon me")?

   (A) It makes an appeal to emotion.
   (B) It states the overall thesis of the passage.
   (C) It expresses a causal relationship between events in the past and events in the present.
   (D) It provides a specific example for the preceding argument.
   (E) It reinforces the author's claim of responsibility in the following sentence.

DRILL 2

Questions 9–16. Read the following passage carefully before you choose your answers.

This passage is excerpted from an influential work published in 1839.

This archipelago consists of ten principal islands, of which five exceed the others in size. They are situated under the Equator, and between five and six hundred miles
Line westward of the coast of America. They are all formed
5 of volcanic rocks; a few fragments of granite curiously glazed and altered by the heat, can hardly be considered as an exception. Some of the craters, surmounting the larger islands, are of immense size, and they rise to a height of between three and four thousand feet. Their flanks are
10 studded by innumerable smaller orifices. I scarcely hesitate to affirm, that there must be in the whole archipelago at least two thousand craters. These consist either of lava or scoriae, or of finely-stratified, sandstone-like tuff. Most of the latter are beautifully symmetrical; they owe their
15 origin to eruptions of volcanic mud without any lava: it is a remarkable circumstance that every one of the twenty-eight tuff-craters which were examined had their southern sides either much lower than the other sides, or quite broken down and removed. As all these craters apparently have
20 been formed when standing in the sea, and as the waves from the trade wind and the swell from the open Pacific here unite their forces on the southern coasts of all the islands, this singular uniformity in the broken state of the craters, composed of the soft and yielding tuff, is easily
25 explained.

The *Beagle* sailed round Chatham Island, and anchored in several bays. One night I slept on shore on a part of the island, where black truncated cones were extraordinarily numerous: from one small eminence I counted sixty of
30 them, all surmounted by craters more or less perfect. The greater number consisted merely of a ring of red scoriae or slags, cemented together: and their height above the plain of lava was not more than from fifty to a hundred feet; none had been very lately active. The entire surface of this
35 part of the island seems to have been permeated, like a sieve, by the subterranean vapours: here and there the lava, whilst soft, has been blown into great bubbles; and in other parts, the tops of caverns similarly formed have fallen in, leaving circular pits with steep sides. From the regular
40 form of the many craters, they gave to the country an artificial appearance, which vividly reminded me of those parts of Staffordshire, where the great iron-foundries are most numerous. The day was glowing hot, and the scrambling over the rough surface and through the intricate thickets,

45 was very fatiguing; but I was well repaid by the strange Cyclopean scene. As I was walking along I met two large tortoises, each of which must have weighed at least two hundred pounds: one was eating a piece of cactus, and as I approached, it stared at me and slowly walked away; the
50 other gave a deep hiss, and drew in its head. These huge reptiles, surrounded by the black lava, the leafless shrubs, and large cacti, seemed to my fancy like some antediluvian animals. The few dull-coloured birds cared no more for me than they did for the great tortoises.

9. This passage is most notable for its

   (A) meticulous classification
   (B) unusual point of view
   (C) precise description
   (D) resourceful analogies
   (E) lyrical prose

10. The speaker in the passage can best be described as

   (A) a scientist making entries in a nature journal
   (B) a professional sailor touring a remote island
   (C) a fiction writer on holiday
   (D) a surveyor measuring land for future development
   (E) a volcanologist studying the site of a recent eruption

11. In context, one can infer that "tuff" (line 13) is

   (A) an alternate spelling for "tough"
   (B) a kind of sand
   (C) made up principally of grass
   (D) volcanic rock
   (E) dense and resistant

12. In this passage, the speaker is most notably impressed by

   (A) the flora on the islands
   (B) the force of the Pacific Ocean
   (C) the fragments of granite
   (D) the symmetrical craters on the islands
   (E) the topography of the smaller islands

13. Which of the following phrases represents a literary allusion?

   (A) "parts of Staffordshire" (lines 41–42)
   (B) "the strange Cyclopean scene" (lines 45–46)
   (C) "situated under the Equator (lines 2–3)
   (D) "the coast of America" (line 4)
   (E) "the swell from the open Pacific" (line 21)

14. Which of the following landscape features are described throughout the entire passage?

   (A) Craters and lava
   (B) Craters and tortoises
   (C) Tortoises and birds
   (D) Islands and bays
   (E) Tuff and volcanic mud

15. In line 52, "antediluvian" most nearly means

   (A) artificial
   (B) lifeless
   (C) prehistoric
   (D) volcanic
   (E) enormous

16. Which of the following are virtually synonymous as presented in the author's description?

   (A) "ten principal islands" (line 1) and "two thousand craters" (line 12)
   (B) "tuff" (line 13) and "volcanic mud" (line 15)
   (C) "iron-foundries" (line 42) and "intricate thickets" (line 44)
   (D) "craters" (line 40) and "caverns" (line 38)
   (E) "tortoises" (line 47) and "birds" (line 53)

DRILL 3

Questions 17–25. Read the following passage carefully before you choose your answers.

This passage is excerpted from an essay by a nineteenth-century British writer.

Art begins with abstract decoration, with purely imaginative and pleasurable work dealing with what is unreal and non-existent. This is the first stage. Then Life
Line becomes fascinated with this new wonder, and asks to
5 be admitted into the charmed circle. Art takes Life as part of her rough material, re-creates it, and refashions it in fresh forms, is absolutely indifferent to fact, invents, imagines, dreams, and keeps between herself and reality the impenetrable barrier of beautiful style, of decorative
10 or ideal treatment. The third stage is when Life gets the upper hand, and drives Art out into the wilderness. That is the true decadence, and it is from this that we are now suffering.

Take the case of the English drama. At first in the hands
15 of the monks Dramatic Art was abstract, decorative and mythological. Then she enlisted Life in her service, and using some of life's external forms, she created an entirely new race of beings, whose sorrows were more terrible than any sorrow man has ever felt, whose joys were keener
20 than lover's joys, who had the rage of the Titans and the calm of the gods, who had monstrous and marvelous sins, monstrous and marvelous virtues. To them she gave a language different from that of actual use, a language full of resonant music and sweet rhythm, made stately
25 by solemn cadence, or made delicate by fanciful rhyme, jeweled with wonderful words, and enriched with lofty diction. She clothed her children in strange raiment and gave them masks, and at her bidding the antique world rose from its marble tomb. A new Caesar stalked through
30 the streets of risen Rome, and with purple sail and flute-led oars another Cleopatra passed up the river to Antioch. Old myth and legend and dream took shape and substance. History was entirely rewritten, and there was hardly one of the dramatists who did not recognize that the object of Art
35 is not simple truth but complex beauty. In this they were perfectly right. Art itself is really a form of exaggeration; and selection, which is the very spirit of art, is nothing more than an intensified mode of over-emphasis.

But Life soon shattered the perfection of the form. Even
40 in Shakespeare we can see the beginning of the end. It shows itself by the gradual breaking-up of the blank-verse in the later plays, by the predominance given to prose, and by the overimportance assigned to characterization. The passages in Shakespeare—and they are many—where
45 the language is uncouth, vulgar, exaggerated, fantastic, obscene even, are entirely due to Life calling for an echo of her own voice, and rejecting the intervention of beautiful style, through which alone should life be suffered to find expression. Shakespeare is not by any means a
50 flawless artist. He is too fond of going directly to Life, and borrowing Life's natural utterance. He forgets that when Art surrenders her imaginative medium she surrenders everything.

17. The author of this passage is most likely

(A) a poet
(B) a novelist
(C) an art critic
(D) a journalist
(E) an actor

18. The author relies principally on which of the following to substantiate his thesis?

(A) A faulty analogy
(B) Process analysis
(C) Deductive reasoning
(D) An accumulation of facts
(E) Illustration by example

19. "…when Art surrenders her imaginative medium she surrenders everything" (lines 51–53) is in the form of

(A) a maxim
(B) a chiasmus
(C) an antithesis
(D) an understatement
(E) an analogy

20. Above all else, the author reveres

(A) beauty
(B) life
(C) Shakespeare
(D) Caesar
(E) English drama

21. In the context of the entire passage, "Life gets the upper hand" (lines 10–11) is best interpreted as having which of the following meanings?

(A) Art is favored over Life in English drama.
(B) Life rewrites history.
(C) Life drives Art out of English drama.
(D) Life is uncouth, vulgar, and unsophisticated.
(E) Life dominates Art in English drama.

22. The quality discussed in lines 23–27 is most directly the antithesis of which of the following?

(A) "marble tomb" (line 29)
(B) "The passages in Shakespeare" (line 44)
(C) "to find expression" (line 49)
(D) "her imaginative medium" (line 52)
(E) "a flawless artist" (lines 49–50)

23. The author's observation in the first three sentences (lines 1–5) is best described as an example of which of the following?

(A) Personification
(B) Linguistic paradox
(C) First-person narrative
(D) Dramatic irony
(E) Authorial intrusion

24. In line 27, "She" refers to which of the following?

I. "Dramatic Art" (line 15)
II. "English drama" (line 14)
III. "Life" (line 16)

(A) I only
(B) II only
(C) I and III only
(D) II and III only
(E) I, II, and III

25. The author's tone in the passage as a whole is best described as

(A) harsh and strident
(B) informal and analytical
(C) rueful and expository
(D) superficial and capricious
(E) enthusiastic and optimistic

DRILL 1 EXPLANATIONS

1. **C** The simile in this first sentence compares the great and ancient parliamentary institutions with the august, but somewhat ancient, bodies of the members of Parliament. The speaker is warming up his audience with a bit of humor before launching into what amounts to a very serious ultimatum: that the speaker will continue to serve as prime minister, but only if they concede to him much greater authority than before (1842). The answer is (C).

2. **B** The speaker is addressing a group of his peers, (B), who are the other members of Parliament. The tricky part here is, of course, the repetition of "Sir," a political convention in Great Britain—it is as if the prime minister were addressing each member of Parliament as an individual. We know that he is the British prime minister because of the final sentences, and these sentences also reveal definitively that he is speaking to peers: "Sir, I do not wish to be the Minister of England; but while I have the high honour of holding that Office, I am determined to hold it by no servile tenure. I will only hold that office upon the condition of being unshackled by any other obligations than those of consulting the public interests, and of providing for the public safety."

3. **D** Everything before this line is an introduction to the prime minister's real message; until this point, he has joked, given a general review of his former motivations and actions as the leader of the Conservative party, and explained his reasons for accepting to serve again as prime minister ("feeling of honour") in spite of his failing health and aged mind ("a burden too great for my physical, and far beyond my intellectual structure"). The transition comes with "But, Sir, I will not take the step with mutilated power and shackled authority." He will do the country and his peers a favor, but only if he is granted much more authority to rule. Choice (D) is the answer.

4. **E** Eliminate (A), (B), and (D) so you're left with (C) and (E), which do not fit neatly into the nautical terminology. Choice (C) is the one to eliminate. All the other terms fit neatly into the nautical terminology. However, one could stretch a point and claim that "fairly" is related to fair weather, whereas "unshackled" is clearly unrelated to this metaphor. The answer is (E).

5. **E** The first step is to determine the "dominant point" of the final paragraph. Thankfully, the second paragraph is short—it is the rhetorical summation of his ultimatum. The key phrases are "servile tenure" and "unshackled by any other obligations." Of course, "unfettered" and "unshackled" are synonyms, so the best answer is (E), "unfettered."

6. **C** The prime minister states unequivocally that honor is his motivation, in the following passage in particular: "and to be relieved from it [the position] with perfect honour would be the greatest favour that could be conferred on me. But as a feeling of honour and strong sense of duty require me to undertake those responsible functions, I declare, Sir, that I am ready to incur these risks, to bear these burdens, and to front all these honourable dangers." The word "honor" comes up numerous times in this excerpt. Choice (C) is correct.

7. **C** You should be able to narrow your options to (B) and (C). But be careful! Do you think that the speaker, the most powerful man in Great Britain, allowed his mood to shift or to affect his tone? The speech was carefully constructed, and the tone was coolly calculated when the author wrote it. The prime minister begins with a light tone because he is looking to set up his audience, not because he starts his speech in a good mood. In fact, his real mood never shifts: he manipulates tone for maximum effect.

8. **E** In lines 17–20, the prime minister describes his time in office as a "burden" and how he wishes to be "relieved of it." But in the following sentence, lines 21–24, he states that "a strong sense of duty" requires him to "incur these risks, bear these burdens, and to front all these honourable dangers." So he is burdened but feels a sense of responsibility. This aligns with (E). Although readers may feel sympathy with the the prime minister, an appeal to emotion is not the primary goal, so eliminate (A). The overall thesis of the passage has more to do with duty than burden, so (B) can be eliminated as well. The author's sense of burden did not cause anything to happen, which eliminates (C), and there is no specific example, so rule out (D).

DRILL 2 EXPLANATIONS

9. **C** This is a scientifically precise description of the Galapagos Islands. Choice (A) is incorrect because nothing is being classified in this passage. Choice (B) is also wrong—no point of view is presented here, just facts. The passage is not dominated by analogies, so (D) is incorrect. Finally, you know that (E) is also incorrect because "lyrical" pertains to personal sentiment, and there are practically no personal feelings expressed at all; the closest we get to personal sentiment is the statement that some of the craters are "beautifully symmetrical."

10. **A** You can use POE to answer this question. Choice (C) is the easiest to eliminate; the passage is factual, not fictional. The passage is about the islands themselves, not about volcanoes as (E) suggests, and, according to the second paragraph, "none had very lately been active." Choices (B) and (D) are somewhat plausible; however, there is no evidence that the author is a "professional" sailor, nor that he has done any formal "surveying." The passage contains a detailed description of nature, so (A) is the best match.

11. **D** In this case, the answer is made clear from the passage; the craters have a border of soft stone (tuff) that has worn away on the southern side. The specific line from the passage that allows you to answer this question is this: "These consist either of lava or scoriae, or of finely stratified, sandstone-like tuff." Sandstone is a type of rock. Tuff is actually a rock composed of compacted volcanic ash varying in size from fine sand to coarse gravel. Choice (D) is correct.

12. **D** The author doesn't address (A) or (E), so you can eliminate those and look more closely at the middle three choices. Although the author mentions the Pacific Ocean and the fragments of granite, he incorporates these elements in his overarching discussion of the symmetrical craters.

13. **B** A literary allusion is a reference, usually to a character from art, literature, or mythology, which requires the reader to have some outside knowledge of the topic. Staffordshire, (A), is a place, but not a feature of literature or mythology. The Cyclops, (B), is a character from Greek mythology, so this is the best match. Choices (C), (D), and (E) are geographical references, not literary or mythological.

14. **A** Check BOTH paragraphs. Tortoises are mentioned only toward the end of the passage and are not landscape features, so eliminate (B) and (C). Tuff is mentioned only in the first paragraph, so eliminate (E). Bays are mentioned only at the beginning of paragraph 2, so eliminate (D). Craters and lava are mentioned throughout the passage, making (A) the best answer.

15. **C**   If you know the definition of "antediluvian," then you have a distinct advantage here; if not, you can get clues from the context of the passage. Since the word is describing animals, they would not be "artificial" or "volcanic," so eliminate (A) and (D). The tortoises are not "lifeless," (B), since one of them hisses at the author. "Enormous," (E), is tempting, since the tortoises are described as "huge," but that would ignore the middle phrase in that sentence and create a redundancy. "Black lava," "leafless shrubs," and "large cacti" are not features of many modern landscapes, and the tortoises are larger than normal, so "old" or "primordial" is the meaning we're looking for here. Choice (C) is the closest choice.

16. **D**   Synonymous phrases would represent virtually the same idea. The islands have craters, but they are not, in themselves, actual craters, so eliminate (A). Tuff and volcanic mud, (B), may be associated together in the first paragraph, but you don't know for sure whether they are the same substance. Iron-foundries are more closely aligned to craters, not thickets, (C). And the tortoises and birds are in opposition, according to the author, because they react to him in different ways. That leaves you with (D): both craters and caverns are holes in the landscape.

DRILL 3 EXPLANATIONS

17. **A**   In reality, the author is both a poet and a novelist, but you are asked to make a judgment based on the passage. To answer this question correctly, you need to use POE and your best judgment to eliminate all of the least likely answer choices. The passage is an attack against the intrusion of prosaic life into the realm of art. The panegyric (high praise) of classical language is a key to understanding the author's point of view: "a language different from that of actual use, a language full of resonant music and sweet rhythm, made stately by solemn cadence, or made delicate by fanciful rhyme, jeweled with wonderful words, and enriched with lofty diction." In a word, this is poetry. Choice (A) is correct.

     The writing is far too lyrical for the author of the passage to be a journalist, (D), or an actor, (E); the latter choice is thrown in for readers who assume that a passage dealing with English drama should be somehow related to a theatrical term. The same may be said for (C). The author capitalizes "art" because he is not discussing painting specifically, but the general realm of artistic creation that encompasses all the arts.

18. **E**   The example is stated rhetorically—"Take the case of the English drama"—and lasts for most of the passage. "Illustration by example," (E), is definitely the defining rhetorical device of this passage.

19. **A**   A maxim is a truism or pithy saying, a gnomic statement similar to a proverb, so (A) is the best answer. POE can help you narrow down your choices. Clearly, the statement does not compare Art to something else, so you can eliminate (E). If anything, the statement is overstatement (hyperbole), and for that reason (D) can be discarded. For the statement to be an antithesis, the author would have needed to put two things or concepts in opposition, but we have only one element (Art); thus, you can eliminate (C). At this point, your chances are fifty-fifty, so you could guess and move on. But look at (B). A "chiasmus" is a syntactic figure wherein the elements in one clause are reversed in another. The most famous example is President Kennedy's statement: "Ask not what your country can do for you, but what you can do for your country."

20. **A**   The author does not revere life above everything else—for example, he clearly states that he doesn't like life as an intrusion on Art, at the very least or as it appears in certain parts of William Shakespeare's work. He includes these examples of Caesar and English drama for rhetorical reasons, and while he admires English drama, he does not appear to revere it. (By the way, to "revere" something is "to regard it with awe, deference, and devotion.") Beauty is held up as an ideal, and this is clear when the author says, "the object of Art is not simple truth but complex beauty." The answer is (A).

21. **E**   The idiom "getting the upper hand" means having an advantage over something or someone. If "Life gets the upper hand," then (A) is wrong. Choice (D) is a trap, since it sounds like a direct quote from line 45 and does not connote having an advantage. Choice (B) is likewise irrelevant to "getting the upper hand." Choices (C) and (E) have very close meanings, but (C) is too extreme, since we can't say for sure that Art is absent from all English drama. Choice (E) is the best choice.

22. **B**   The quality in lines 23–27 is "a language full of resonant music and sweet rhythm." This is the antithesis (direct opposite) of the author's description on Shakespeare's writing in line 44. Choice (B) is the best answer.

23. **A**   Throughout the first paragraph, the author refers to Life and Art as though they were people: "Life becomes fascinated" (lines 3–4), "Art takes life as part of her rough material" (lines 5–6). This is known as personification, (A). Although Life and Art are in opposition to each other, there is no inherent confusion or contradiction, (B). The passage is not written in first-person narration ("I," "me," etc.), so eliminate (C). And there is no sense that circumstances are the opposite of how one might anticipate, so eliminate (D). Authorial intrusion is an interruption in the narrative, so rule out (E).

24. **A**   Check the beginning of the paragraph. In line 15, "Dramatic Art" is mentioned. In line 16, "she enlisted Life." So the "she" used throughout this paragraph is "Dramatic Art," not "Life," and certainly not "English drama" as a whole.

25. **C**   First, eliminate the extreme answers: (A) and (E). "Informal," (B), is not a good match, since the passage is written in a rather lofty style. Choice (D) would make the author seem petty or unpredictable. Overall, the author laments the "takeover" of Art by Life. This is especially obvious in the last line of the passage. Thus, he is "rueful," (C). "Expository" simply means that the author is "exposing" the supposed problem with English drama.

Chapter 4
How to Approach
the Essays:
Basic Principles

ESSAY SECTION TASKS

Yes, that's right—tasks. You'll need to write three different essays: synthesis, rhetorical analysis, and argument.

In the **synthesis essay**, you'll be given a scenario and tasked with writing a response using at least three of six or seven short accompanying sources for support. You'll need to cite the sources you use (in a simple format such as "Source A"), and incorporate them into your own position (instead of simply quoting them). At least one of the sources will be a visual (such as a picture, drawing, or graph) rather than text.

The **rhetorical analysis essay** asks you to analyze the techniques (such as choice of language or organization of points) an author uses, and discuss how those techniques contribute to the author's purpose. The passage you'll be asked to analyze is typically about a page long.

The **argument essay** presents a claim or assertion in the prompt and then asks you to argue a position based on your own knowledge, experience, or reading. You can choose to agree with the claim, disagree with it, or give it qualified support (for example, arguing that the claim is true only in certain circumstances).

In Chapters 5–7, you'll learn more about the approach and expectations for each type of essay.

For all three essays, you will be writing cold on a prompt or passage you read just two minutes ago for the first time. You have to come up with good ideas and get them written down efficiently—on the very first try.

Writing a clear, effective, well-organized essay under rigid time constraints is a learned skill; writing three consecutive essays under such conditions requires special techniques and lots of practice. Fortunately, this book provides you with both of those.

Time Crunch

You'll have 2 hours to write all three essays, which allows about 40 minutes for each. Before you even start working on the essays, though, you'll have 15 minutes to read all three prompts and the source documents for the synthesis essay. While we suggest you use all 15 minutes, if you finish reading the prompts and the documents early, you may start writing your response.

This 15-minute period is crucial for building a solid foundation in understanding the prompts and the source documents. You'll need to put your active reading skills in high gear to get the best possible head start from the reading time available.

Three Rules for Successful Essay Preparation

1. Do plenty of TIMED practice on all three essay types.

2. Hand-write your practice essays; don't use a computer.

3. Ask for feedback on your essays from a trusted source (such as an English teacher or Princeton Review tutor).

Why *Three* Essays?

The AP English Language and Composition Exam is designed to predict your ability to perform college-level work on such assignments as research papers and on-demand essay questions on tests. The AP exam's three types of essays essentially give you an opportunity to demonstrate some of the important skills required for those types of college assignments:

- using research sources to support your own position

- examining sources critically in order to assess credible or faulty support

- arguing your own position persuasively

The three essays simply separate—and highlight—these skills. In college work, you'll often be combining them.

HOW ARE THE ESSAYS SCORED?

The essays are scored separately on a scale of 0–9; then the three scores are combined. Each essay has equal weight in that combined score, which is then combined with the result of the multiple-choice section to yield a final AP score of 1–5.

Together, the essays count for 55 percent of your final score. However, they take up 69 percent of the exam time, so it's easy to lose perspective and feel as if the essay section is more crucial to your success than it actually is. Doing well on the multiple-choice section is almost as important, even though it's only an hour long.

The grading is holistic, meaning that the reader will assess the overall quality of the essay rather than using a point-by-point checklist to arrive at a score. There are only a couple of exceptions, such as using fewer than three sources in the synthesis essay or consistently expressing ideas in such a confused way that the reader has great difficulty following the argument. Such lapses automatically knock an essay down to a lower point on the scoring scale.

Essays are graded holistically, based on the overall impression created by

- your grasp of the prompt

- your ability to present concrete evidence and link it to your thesis

- your skillful use of language to develop your argument

Who Does the Scoring?

The readers are college English professors and AP course teachers who come together in June for an intense week of scoring. Thousands of readers go through thousands of essays in a few short days. A different person will read each of your essays.

Before the scoring starts, though, readers are trained in assessing that particular year's group of essays. Educational Testing Service (ETS), the nonprofit organization that develops the exam, combs through the current crop of essays looking for work that represents a top-level 9 synthesis essay, a mediocre 4 rhetorical analysis essay, and so on, from that year's group. These sample essays are used to train the readers so the scoring will be as standardized as possible, given that the readers are still human beings who make subjective decisions.

So what? Well, the readers are your audience—the people you're addressing in your essays—and this scoring process tells you a few important things about them.

- First, they're buried in student essays, most of them mundane and mind-numbingly similar, and are just hoping for that one brilliant piece of writing that breaks the monotony and is a pleasure to read.

- Second, the readers have been trained to score your essays in relation to the work of the other students who took the exam that year. They're not judging your work in relation to some ideal standard of what a "perfect" essay should be.

- Third, these are teachers who guide students through English composition for a living. They know that polished essays require time, draft after draft, revision after revision. They don't expect an essay written in 40 minutes to be polished or perfect—they couldn't produce a flawless essay themselves in 40 minutes.

The essay section is the only place in this exam where your personality—at least to a limited degree—will shine through to test graders. Use it as an opportunity to show off what an exceptional thinker and writer you are.

What Are the Characteristics of Each Score Level?

The 0–9 scale breaks down into four categories: effective, adequate, inadequate, and little success.

Effective essays score between 7 and 9. These are the essays with thorough and convincing discussions, perceptive analyses, well-developed positions, smooth organization, and sophisticated control of expression. They demonstrate that the writer has understood and thought about the prompt and created an original response.

Adequate essays score 5 or 6. They address the prompt with appropriate explanations and evidence, do an adequate job of organizing and developing points, and express the writer's ideas clearly.

Inadequate work receives a score of 3 or 4. In these essays, the writer may have misunderstood the prompt or (in the case of the synthesis essay) the sources. Evidence and explanations are limited or simplistic, or even flat-out inappropriate. The organization does not flow smoothly, and the writer has less control of English language conventions in expressing ideas.

Essays that demonstrate **little success** receive a score of 0, 1, or 2. Here the writer has oversimplified or completely misunderstood the prompt, and presented evidence that is inappropriate or just plain unrelated. These essays show a consistent weakness in expressing ideas in a clear, organized, and grammatically correct way.

Essays fall within one of those four categories based on the general characteristics of that category. The specific score within the two higher bands reflects more or less skill and depth in demonstrating those characteristics. Within the two lower bands, the number score reflects varying degrees of problems.

For all three essays, the 2016 mean score—the mid-point in the range, where half of the essays scored higher and half lower—around 4.5, which could be considered "high inadequate" (if you can imagine such a concept).

In Chapters 5–7, you'll learn some more details about how these score levels apply to each type of essay.

WHAT ARE THE KEYS TO REACHING THE "EFFECTIVE" BAND?

Your goal is to rise above the vast middle bulge of essays that score 4 or 5. You're aiming for the "effective" band, or at least for a 6. How do you get there? By familiarizing yourself with the types of essays you'll have to write and by following a few basic tips.

Understand the Prompt

Use your active reading skills to tear the prompt apart.

- What is the prompt *really* asking you to do? Understanding your task and maintaining a laser focus on it will keep you out of the swamp of inappropriate examples and unrelated arguments that populate the lower levels of the scoring scale.

- Does the prompt have broader implications? For example, if a quote in the argument essay prompt states that a government has a duty to protect its citizens, could carrying out that duty lead to undesirable limits on people's freedom? And protect citizens from what? Who says that's a government's duty? The key here is to demonstrate some depth of thought instead of simply taking the prompt at face value. Where does it lead you?

- Does the prompt contain any terms that you should define in order to keep your discussion on target? Broad, "fuzzy" concepts such as "justice" or "education" are prime examples. They mean different things to different people. Giving a precise explanation of how you understand the term *as it's used in the prompt* and how you intend to discuss it will help you avoid producing a vague, rambling essay.

Take a Position

No fence-sitting, no ambiguity, no neutral descriptive essays. The highest scoring essays take a definite position on the prompt topic and argue it convincingly. They use strong, relevant evidence to support the position and leave no doubt about where the essay writer stands.

Even in the rhetorical analysis essay you're expected to take a position: "This is the author's purpose, these are the three (or four, or five) most important techniques the author uses to achieve that purpose, and (very important) this is *how* each technique makes the purpose more effective." Another student might see a different purpose or highlight other techniques in the passage, but then that student would be taking a different position.

Manage Your Time

No one is going to tell you that your first 40 minutes are up and it's time to move on to the next essay. That's up to you. Since each essay has equal weight in the combined score, you should devote about the same amount of time to each one. A slightly better score on one essay will not make up for a bad score on another. Aim for the following breakdown within each 40-minute period:

- 3–5 minutes to think through the prompt and plan your essay

- 30–35 minutes to write

- 1–2 minutes to proofread

The more you practice writing each type of essay within 40 minutes, the more you'll gain a sense of how that block of time "feels" and the better you'll get at making occasional time checks to stay on track instead of engaging in distracting clock-watching that might only increase your anxiety.

Your school has likely given you sample essay prompts for practice. You can also find example prompts from several previous years on the AP website at https://apcentral.collegeboard.org/courses/ap-english-language-and-composition/exam.

Plan Your Response

Just getting into the car and starting to drive could land you anywhere, at a great waste of time and fuel. It's the same with just starting to write—you could easily spend 20 minutes and then realize you're seriously off track.

To make the best use of your 30–35 minutes of writing time, you first need to spend a few minutes planning where you want to end up and how you'll get there.

- Exactly what do you want to conclude about the topic of the synthesis prompt? Which three sources best support the points you want to make? In which order should you incorporate them into your discussion? Does one of the sources present a significant opposing argument that you should mention and then refute?

- In the rhetorical analysis passage, what is the writer's purpose? What techniques make that purpose clear and effective to you? In which order should you explain them?

- What position do you want to take about the topic presented for the argument essay? What evidence from your own experiences or reading could you use to support your position? How can you make your argument persuasive?

Organize Your Points

You're likely familiar with the five-paragraph essay model. While it's not the only method of organizing an essay, there's nothing wrong with using it on this exam if it's already a comfortable model for you. It goes like this:

Paragraph 1:

- An introductory sentence or two that capture the reader and announce, "This is going to be a great essay within your pile of boring, mediocre essays."

- The thesis that you intend to argue in your essay. A good thesis is debatable (that is, someone could possibly have a different opinion) and narrow enough to be covered adequately in a short essay.

- A brief list of the three pieces of evidence you'll use in the essay to prove your thesis

- A transition to the body of your essay

Paragraphs 2–4:

- One paragraph for each piece of evidence you listed in the first paragraph, in the same order as you listed them. Each piece of evidence should be linked directly to your thesis, with a clear explanation of *why* it supports your thesis. One of these paragraphs might describe a conflicting view which you then shoot down, or which supports an "only in certain circumstances" position in your thesis.

Paragraph 5:

- A conclusion that doesn't simply restate your thesis. You've developed your argument throughout the body of your essay, so it's now meatier and more convincing. The conclusion should remind the reader of your now-stronger position.

Of course, there's no rule that says you have to stop at three pieces of evidence; you might have four. Just don't take on more complexity and length than you can handle well in 40 minutes. And if you're familiar with another method of organizing an essay and feel more comfortable with it, then use it, as long as it provides a clear organizational framework for your points.

Get Off to a Strong Start

A great first impression goes a long way. Remember your audience of bored readers mired in stacks of mediocre essays? If you can wow them right off the top, you'll create an expectation that the rest of your essay belongs in the "effective" band, too. That initial glow of "finally—*finally*—a good essay!" can diminish the impact of later lapses in greatness.

Suppose the prompt for a rhetorical analysis essay quotes from a speech by Mayor Nellie Smith attributing her election victory to the many volunteers who worked on her campaign. You could clearly announce, "This is going to be a mediocre essay" by starting out with a sentence like, "This essay will describe how Mayor Nellie Smith uses rhetorical strategies to communicate the main point of her speech." Yawn. And do you have any clue what her main point is or what rhetorical strategies she uses? Even if you eventually do get to an insightful point later in the essay, chances are your opening has already caused the reader to tune out and miss it.

On the other hand, you could grab the reader's attention with an opening like, "Dedicated volunteers are the bricks and mortar of successful political campaigns. That's the overriding message of Mayor Nellie Smith's speech thanking them for their passionate support and acknowledging the key role they played. Through the skillful use of parallelism, repetition, and analogy, she makes her listeners feel that the victory is really theirs, likely winning their support after she takes office, too."

That stronger start doesn't take a lot of extra effort or time, but it shows the reader that you understand the mayor's purpose and rhetorical strategies, and can express your ideas with style and sophistication. You've just raised the reader's impression of your abilities, even if your essay tapers off to a more routine effort later on.

Express Your Ideas Clearly, Specifically, Concisely, Correctly, Smoothly, Persuasively, and with Flair

Oh yes, you *can* do that.

Be clear. You should know exactly what you want to say as a result of your initial planning and organizing. Imagine yourself on a clear path instead of stumbling around in the underbrush. If you find you're getting tangled up in long sentences or overlapping ideas, pause for a minute and think of *telling* someone right beside you what you mean to say. This strategy usually helps clarify your thoughts and language in your own mind. Now write down what you just "said."

Be concise. Making a vague statement such as, "The demand for subsidized housing increased a lot during the past few years (Source A)" isn't good enough if Source A actually referred to a study that proved demand grew by 65 percent between 2000 and 2010. Being as specific and concrete as possible will add credibility and impact to your words. Your argument will be clearer and more persuasive.

Be concise. That doesn't mean leaving out details that are essential to your argument. It means leaving out pointless repetition and padding. Say it once, precisely and with punch, and then move on.

Say it correctly. Use proper grammar. Essays with so many errors that the reader can't follow the argument are consigned to the bottom of the scoring scale.

Create correct paragraphs, too. Have you ever opened a book and seen nothing but very long paragraphs? Your next thought is probably, "Do I *really* have to read all of this?" That's exactly what readers think when they see an essay without paragraphs.

So create proper paragraphs—one main idea per paragraph, beginning with a topic sentence and ending with a smooth transition to the next paragraph—and make them obvious by leaving a space between or indenting them.

> Create a great first impression before the person scoring your essay even reads a word.
> - Write legibly.
> - Make sure readers can see the paragraphs at first glance.
> - Don't strike out too many things.
> - Make sure your work looks neat, organized, and clear.

Say it smoothly. Lead the reader through your argument with seamless transitions between your points and paragraphs. Transition words and phrases such as "on the other hand," "in addition," "therefore," and "nevertheless" will do the job.

Say it persuasively. These essays are all evidence-based writing, so you need strong evidence that supports each of your main points. Connect each piece of evidence clearly to the point it supports, and explain exactly how or why the evidence is relevant. Unrelated evidence and vague, weak explanations won't persuade anyone.

> The reader expects you to write like someone who is suffering through a tedious, nerve-racking exercise. If you write like someone who enjoys writing, the reader will enjoy reading your essay and reward you.

Say it with flair. Is there a punchier, more descriptive word you could use? Perhaps "shack" or "cabin" or "mansion" instead of "house." Can you make the phrasing of a sentence slicker? For example, instead of "The candidate's appearance was neat, and the boss gave him the job right away," let yourself get carried away and say, "The candidate's Armani suit and sleek silk tie captivated the boss, who slipped a contract across the table without comment or hesitation."

It doesn't take long to think of a more forceful word or a stronger way of saying something if you put your mind on that track, and even a few of these sprinkled throughout your essay can impress the reader with your ability to control language and use it to achieve your desired effect.

> Make it easy for the reader to give you a high score.
> - Understand the task in the prompt.
> - Think about where the prompt takes you.
> - Stake out a definite position.
> - Plan and organize your points before you start to write.
> - Be clear and specific.
> - Link each piece of evidence directly to your thesis.
> - Use correct grammar and paragraph construction.
> - Vary sentence length and structure.
> - Write legibly.

Proofread

You won't have time to revise, but leaving a couple of minutes to proofread allows you to fix minor errors you probably would not have made if you weren't writing in such a rush. And that, in turn, might just knock your essay up a notch on the scoring scale. You'll have to write your essay in dark blue or black pen—no pencils allowed on this section of the exam. However, you can strike out any errors you want the readers to ignore (they will) and then write in (neatly) your correction.

In Chapters 5–7, you'll get a closer look at the types of prompts on the exam, and find additional suggestions for responding to the three different types.

Summary

General Essay Information

o There are three essays: synthesis, rhetorical analysis, and argument.

o You have a total of 2 hours, 15 minutes—40 minutes for each essay plus 15 minutes to read the prompts and the sources for the synthesis essay.

o The three essays count for 55 percent of your total score. Each essay is worth an equal amount.

Essay Scoring

o Each essay is scored by a different reader on a scale from 0 to 9.

o The essays are scored "holistically" based on the reader's overall impression.

o The reader wants good essays that are easy to score.

o Essays that earn high scores show that the writer has thought deeply about the prompt, taken a clear position, supported that position with appropriate examples, and argued that position persuasively with sophisticated control of the language.

o Boring essays that do only an adequate job earn mid-range scores.

o Students who misunderstand the prompt, use inappropriate examples, and can't express their ideas clearly can expect low scores.

Presentation

o Make your essay look neat, clear, and well organized with legible writing, obvious breaks between paragraphs, and few strike-outs, if any.

Expression

- Capture the reader and create a great first impression with your opening paragraph.

- Vary your choice of words and sentence structure. A little extra effort will pay great dividends.

- Use correct grammar and paragraph construction.

Content

- Plan and organize your points before you start writing.

- Address the prompt. If you write a great essay that doesn't address the prompt, you will receive a low score.

- Develop your argument based on strong, relevant evidence. Connect each piece of evidence directly to the point it supports.

Chapter 5
How to Approach
the Synthesis Essay

SYNTHESIZE WHAT?

By "synthesis," the AP exam writers mean two things:

1. Using sources to develop your own position

2. Citing those sources accurately

High-scoring synthesis essays draw a clear connection between a source and a particular point in the writer's argument. The sources chosen are appropriate; the explanations are thorough and convincing. By the time you get down to a score of 5 (the bottom of the "adequate" band), the link is still apparent but "strained."

Also at the higher score levels, the essay writer cites the specific source being used (with a simple reference such as "Source A"; you're not expected to remember formal citation formats for this exam). Writers who score in the lower bands merely summarize a jumbled collection of points they've read in various sources, without citing a specific source and linking it to a particular point in their argument.

Your performance on the synthesis essay will help the readers (and yourself) predict how well you'll be able to handle college research assignments. In particular, your essay will show whether you can

- judge the best sources to back up your position

- incorporate other writers' claims or explanations into your *own* argument

- draw on sources in the order that develops your argument in the most logical, persuasive way

Steps to Choosing Sources

1. Analyze the prompt.

2. Decide which position you want to take.

3. Use active reading—what is the main point of each source?

4. Select three sources that provide the best support for your position.

How Many Sources?

The prompt will instruct you to use at least three sources, and in most cases that's a safe choice. Trying to use more than three might lead you into an unnecessarily complicated essay at best, and at worst, a pyramid of similar, superficially treated points piled up on top of each other. Using fewer than three will definitely knock your essay down into the "inadequate" scoring band.

Three sources are enough to show progress in your argument (for example, a more general or older source of support followed by increasingly specific or more recent claims, each one building upon the previous one). If you choose to argue a qualified position, three sources will give you, for instance, two authors who argue against something and one who is in favor of it in particular circumstances, supporting your qualified rejection of the claim.

Having a Conversation with Your Sources

Since your aim is synthesis, you need to weave the three sources into your own discussion of the prompt, using them to support and develop the position you've chosen to take. The exam writers offer a helpful image of how to do that. They call it having a conversation with your sources.

Imagine the creators of your chosen sources are sitting together in a living room discussing the topic of the prompt. Now you walk in and join the conversation. You wouldn't simply record each author's (or artist's) comments. That's the equivalent of just copying and pasting chunks from each source into your essay and stringing them together.

You would respond to each person's comments, build on them, and use them to enrich your own views about the topic. You would add something to the discussion your three authors are having, and they would add something to your own understanding of the topic. Then, if you had a conversation with each author individually, you would try to understand that author's position and add your own ideas to the discussion. That's what the test writers mean. They call the result a "source-informed" argument.

Direct Quote vs. Paraphrase

When you're drawing a source into your argument, you have a choice of paraphrasing (summarizing in your own words) what the author says, or quoting some of his or her words directly (within quotation marks, of course).

In many cases, paraphrasing makes it easier to incorporate someone else's ideas smoothly into your own. Several quotes, too, could make your essay appear to be more of a copy-and-paste exercise than a synthesis. However, if an author uses a particularly striking phrase or unusual wording that would be difficult to paraphrase accurately, then an occasional direct quote could make your essay more vivid.

SAMPLE ESSAY—HERE'S HOW IT'S DONE

Here's an example of a synthesis essay prompt. As you go through it, use your active reading skills to make sure you understand exactly what it's asking you to do.

The Directions

Question 1
Suggested reading and writing time—55 minutes.
It is suggested that you spend 15 minutes reading the question, analyzing and evaluating the sources, and 40 minutes writing your response.
Note: You may begin writing your response before the reading period is over.

(This question counts for one-third of the total essay section score.)

Artificial intelligence (AI) is hyped as the magic bullet for every challenge—from easing traffic congestion to providing medical care in remote locations, from protecting endangered species to rescuing hostages in dangerous settings. The common foundation is a conviction that AI operations will be faster, more effective, more accurate and sometimes cheaper than human operations, and—critically—will avoid human errors. But with their functional superiority and machine learning capabilities, will AI implementations also be able to evolve beyond human control? And is that necessarily a bad thing?

Carefully read the following seven sources, including the introductory information for each source. Then synthesize information from at least three of the sources and incorporate it into a coherent, well-written essay that addresses this question: Is artificial intelligence to be feared because of its potential independence from human control, or is it to be embraced due to its superior ability to deliver benefits that enhance our lives?

Use the sources to develop and explain your argument. Avoid merely summarizing the sources. Indicate clearly which sources you are drawing from, whether through direct quotation, paraphrase, or summary. You may cite the sources as Source A, Source B, and so forth, or by using the descriptions in parentheses.

Source A (Future)

Source B (Letter)

Source C (Frankenstein)

Source D (slides)

Source E (Third Offset)

Source F (Robots)

Source G (graph)

It's Time to Read

There's quite a lot of reading as you go through the sources for a synthesis essay question. In order to use your 15 minutes of reading time effectively, before you start you should already be clear on what the prompt is asking you to do and have some idea which position you want to take on the question you need to address. Do you want to argue that we should fear Artificial Intelligence (AI)? Welcome it? Or do you want to give a qualified answer? For example, "we should fear it unless… "or "we should welcome it except when …"

To show the depth of thought that pulls an essay up into the "effective" score band, you also need to consider implications that extend beyond the question in the prompt. In other words, use your active reading skills on the prompt. For instance, are fearing and embracing AI our only choices? Can we modify its current course of development? Stop it entirely? If AI is beyond our control, can we make sure we don't need to fear it?

Now you're ready to read through the sources with a fairly clear idea of what you're looking for. You want three sources that will enrich the position you've chosen, and will help you develop your own argument in a logical way. If two sources say essentially the same thing, you probably don't need both—which one is stronger? Which sources deal with the "beyond the prompt" questions you asked during your active reading? If you've chosen to take a qualified position, which source presents an opposing viewpoint that will support your "only in these circumstances" argument?

To help you locate supporting points later on while you're writing, underline a few key words and put a stroke through sources you don't want to use.

Then plan your essay: jot down a quick outline of the points you want to make, the order in which you'll explain them as you develop your argument, and the source you'll use (and cite) to support each of your points. A few minutes of planning will prevent you from going off track while you're writing.

Linear Graffiti

Underlining, circling, and making brief notes in the margins of the sources are all good practices, but don't get too carried away. The purpose of marking the passage is to make information easy to retrieve. A good rule of thumb is to underline no more than five words at a time. Anything longer should be marked with simple brackets.

The following is an excerpt from The Office of Science and Technology Policy's 2016 federal government report on the future of artificial intelligence in the U.S.

One area of great optimism about AI and machine learning is their potential to improve people's lives by helping to solve some of the world's greatest challenges and inefficiencies....Public- and private-sector investments in basic and applied R&D on AI have already begun reaping major benefits for the public in fields as diverse as health care, transportation, the environment, criminal justice, and economic inclusion.

At Walter Reed Medical Center, the Department of Veteran Affairs is using AI to better predict medical complications and improve treatment of severe combat wounds, leading to better patient outcomes, faster healing, and lower costs....Given the current transition to electronic health records, predictive analysis of health data may play a key role across many health domains like precision medicine and cancer research.

In transportation, AI-enabled smarter traffic management applications are reducing wait times, energy use, and emissions by as much as 25 percent in some places...

Some researchers are leveraging AI to improve animal migration tracking by using AI image classification software to analyze tourist photos from public social media sites. The software can identify individual animals in the photos and build a database of their migration using the data and location stamps on the photos....Other speakers described uses of AI to optimize the patrol strategy of anti-poaching agents, and to design habitat preservation strategies to maximize the genetic diversity of endangered populations.

Autonomous sailboats and watercraft are already patrolling the oceans carrying sophisticated sensor instruments, collecting data on changes in Arctic ice and sensitive ocean ecosystems in operations that would be too expensive or dangerous for crewed vessels....

The Administration is exploring how AI can responsibly benefit current initiatives such as Data Driven Justice and the Police Data Initiative that seek to provide law enforcement and the public with data that can better inform decision-making in the criminal justice system, while also taking care to minimize the possibility that AI might introduce bias or inaccuracies due to deficiencies in the available data.

Several U.S. academic institutions have launched initiatives to use AI to tackle economic and social challenges. For example, the University of Chicago created an academic program that uses data science and AI to address public challenges such as unemployment and school dropouts. The University of Southern California launched the Center for Artificial Intelligence in Society, an institute dedicated to studying how computational game theory, machine learning, automated planning and multi-agent reasoning techniques can help to solve socially relevant problems like homelessness. Meanwhile, researchers at Stanford University are using machine learning in efforts to address global poverty by using AI to analyze satellite images of likely poverty zones to identify where help is needed most.

Source B

"An Open Letter: Research Priorities for Robust and Beneficial Artificial Intelligence." *Future of Life Institute.* January 2015. Web. 21 January 2018.

The following open letter is an initiative of the Future of Life Institute in collaboration with the AI research community.

Artificial intelligence (AI) research has explored a variety of problems and approaches since its inception, but for the last 20 years or so has been focused on the problems surrounding the construction of intelligent agents—systems that perceive and act in some environment. In this context, "intelligence" is related to statistical and economic notions of rationality—colloquially, the ability to make good decisions, plans, or inferences. The adoption of probabilistic and decision-theoretic representations and statistical learning methods has led to a large degree of integration and cross-fertilization among AI, machine learning, statistics, control theory, neuroscience, and other fields. The establishment of shared theoretical frameworks, combined with the availability of data and processing power, has yielded remarkable successes in various component tasks such as speech recognition, image classification, autonomous vehicles, machine translation, legged locomotion, and question-answering systems.

As capabilities in these areas and others cross the threshold from laboratory research to economically valuable technologies, a virtuous cycle takes hold whereby even small improvements in performance are worth large sums of money, prompting greater investments in research. There is now a broad consensus that AI research is progressing steadily, and that its impact on society is likely to increase. The potential benefits are huge, since everything that civilization has to offer is a product of human intelligence; we cannot predict what we might achieve when this intelligence is magnified by the tools AI may provide, but the eradication of disease and poverty are not unfathomable. Because of the great potential of AI, it is important to research how to reap its benefits while avoiding potential pitfalls.

The progress in AI research makes it timely to focus research not only on making AI more capable, but also on maximizing the societal benefit of AI. Such considerations motivated the AAAI 2008–09 Presidential Panel on Long-Term AI Futures and other projects on AI impacts, and constitute a significant expansion of the field of AI itself, which up to now has focused largely on techniques that are neutral with respect to purpose. We recommend expanded research aimed at ensuring that increasingly capable AI systems are robust and beneficial: our AI systems must do what we want them to do. The attached research priorities document gives many examples of such research directions that can help maximize the societal benefit of AI. This research is by necessity interdisciplinary, because it involves both society and AI. It ranges from economics, law and philosophy to computer security, formal methods and, of course, various branches of AI itself.

In summary, we believe that research on how to make AI systems robust and beneficial is both important and timely, and that there are concrete research directions that can be pursued today.

The following is an excerpt from Mary Shelley's 1818 novel.

I trembled and my heart failed within me, when, on looking up, I saw by the light of the moon the dæmon at the casement. A ghastly grin wrinkled his lips as he gazed on me, where I sat fulfilling the task which he had allotted to me. Yes, he had followed me in my travels; …and he now came to mark my progress and claim the fulfilment of my promise.

As I looked on him, his countenance expressed the utmost extent of malice and treachery. I thought with a sensation of madness on my promise of creating another like to him, and trembling with passion, tore to pieces the thing on which I was engaged. The wretch saw me destroy the creature on whose future existence he depended for happiness, and with a howl of devilish despair and revenge, withdrew.…

Several hours passed, and I remained near my window gazing on the sea;…I felt the silence, although I was hardly conscious of its extreme profundity, until my ear was suddenly arrested by the paddling of oars near the shore, and a person landed close to my house.…

Presently I heard the sound of footsteps along the passage; the door opened, and the wretch whom I dreaded appeared. Shutting the door, he approached me and said in a smothered voice,

"You have destroyed the work which you began; what is it that you intend? Do you dare to break your promise? I have endured toil and misery; I left Switzerland with you; … I have endured incalculable fatigue, and cold, and hunger; do you dare destroy my hopes?"

"Begone! I do break my promise; never will I create another like yourself, equal in deformity and wickedness."

"Slave, I before reasoned with you, but you have proved yourself unworthy of my condescension. Remember that I have power; you believe yourself miserable, but I can make you so wretched that the light of day will be hateful to you. You are my creator, but I am your master; obey!"

"The hour of my irresolution is past, and the period of your power is arrived. Your threats cannot move me to do an act of wickedness; but they confirm me in a determination of not creating you a companion in vice.…"

The monster saw my determination in my face and gnashed his teeth in the impotence of anger. "Shall each man," cried he, "find a wife for his bosom, and each beast have his mate, and I be alone?…Beware, for I am fearless and therefore powerful. I will watch with the wiliness of a snake, that I may sting with its venom. Man, you shall repent of the injuries you inflict."

The following slides were used in a workshop presentation about Networking and Information Technology Research and Development Program's (NITRD) High Profile Technical Activities.

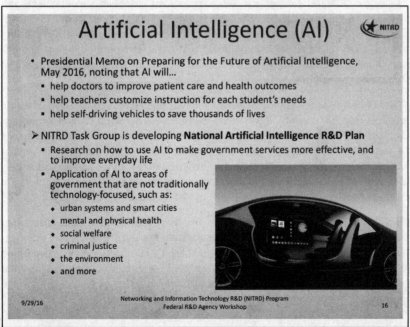

This is an excerpt from a publication by the U.S. Army Strategic Studies Institute. Note: "Third Offset" refers to "leap-ahead technologies and capabilities" that could give an advantage over an otherwise-equal opponent.

…There is a natural symbiosis between military and civilian innovation that, in the end, is driven by a need to solve problems and gain advantage. The challenges and realities of big data, complex networks and systems, uncertain environments, ubiquitous technology, and intense peer competition are drivers in both the commercial and military spaces and steer each toward a common set of solutions. The separation between self-driving automobiles and autonomous military air and ground systems is thin—and will grow thinner as deep and machine learning increasingly blur the separation between civilian or military applications. Once advanced AI is achieved, it will quickly spiral into almost every area of the commercial, governmental, and military domains.

The allure of science fiction-like capabilities will be a strong incentive for states and nonstates to pursue Third Offset technologies. These leap-ahead capabilities could be so game changing that the difference between finishing first and finishing next could mean years of decisive advantage in every meaningful area of warfare.

…The United States is rightfully concerned about the implications of many of the Third Offset technologies—but current policies and priorities are not reflective of the rapidly evolving technologies or the operational environment. As a result, the United States risks falling dangerously behind potential adversaries who are investing heavily in advanced technologies—and are doing so without self-imposed constraints which limit capabilities and fail to allow full exploitation of these technologies.

The DoD Directive 3000.09, *Autonomy in Weapons Systems*, establishes requirements and parameters for development and use of autonomous weapons systems (AWS). In short, Directive 3000.09 seeks to minimize the risk of unintended lethal engagements by requiring positive human interface for all semi-autonomous and AWS, and prohibiting autonomous lethal force against human targets. While this caution is understandable, the policy is out of step with the evolving battlefield.

Placing a "human in the loop" requirement on the development and employment of future weapons systems may inadvertently induce vulnerability into the system. Swarm technology has already exceeded the capability for any meaningful human control of individual agents and, as the technologies advance, swarms of tens or hundreds of thousands of individual agents will make human control—or even human understanding—of the actions and behaviors of the swarms impossible. In the future vague and uncertain environment, the decision to engage or not engage—to kill or not kill—may not be best made by a human.

…The battlefield of the next 30 years will likely evolve far differently (and much faster) than over the past 30 years. The legacy "big five" combat systems, even with version improvements and upgrades, may well be rendered outmatched and ineffective by AI-enabled unmanned autonomous systems, cyber dominance, and swarms. Continued incremental upgrades to current systems may address current readiness challenges, but could leave the Army ill-prepared to contend on a far different battlefield in the future.

The following is an excerpt from a blog post on the growing population of self-organizing "kilorobots."

In a lab at Harvard's Wyss Institute, the world's largest swarm of cooperative robots is building a star… out of themselves. There are 1024 of these inch-wide "Kilobots," and they can arrange themselves into different shapes, from a letter to a wrench. They are slow and comically jerky in their movements, but they are also autonomous. Once they're given a shape, they can recreate it without any further instructions, simply by cooperating with their neighbours and organising themselves.

The Kilobots are the work of Mike Rubenstein, Alejandro Cornejo and Radhika Nagpal, who were inspired by natural swarms, where simple and limited units can cooperate to do great things. Thousands of fire ants can unite into living bridges, rafts and buildings.…

"This is a staggering work," adds Iain Couzin, who studies collective animal behaviour at Princeton University. "It offers a vision of the future where robot groups could form structures on demand as, for example, in search-and-rescue in dangerous environments, or even the formation of miniature swarms within the body to detect and treat disease.…"

The tyranny of cost-efficiency meant that the team had to lose any sensors that might tell the robots their bearings or positions. They can't tell where they are, or if they're going straight.…

Fortunately, they have each other. A stuck Kilobot can't tell if it's stuck on its own, but it can communicate with its neighbors. If it thinks it's moving but the distances from its neighbors change, it can deduce that something is wrong.…

Every Kilobot runs on the same program. The team only has to give them a shape and nominate four of them as seeds. Once that's done, the rest slowly pour into the right pattern, in an endearingly life-like way. It takes them around 12 hours, but they do it all without any human intervention. And although the final shapes are always a little warped, that's life-like too. Fire ants don't have a Platonic ideal of what a bridge or raft should look like; they just work with their neighbours to get the job done.…

The next step will be to build robots that actually self-assemble by attaching to each other, says Marco Dorigo from the Free University of Brussels.…

Eventually, he also wants to get to a position where the robots can sense their environment and react accordingly, rather than just slide into some pre-determined shape. Like fire ants, when they get to a body of water, they wouldn't have to be fed the image of a bridge; they would just self-assemble into one. "That's a whole other level of intelligence, and it's not really understood how to do that in robotics," says Rubenstein. "But nature does it well."

"America's Wars Fact Sheet" and "American War
    and Military Operations Casualties: Lists and
    Statistics." *U.S. Department of Veterans Affairs
    and Congressional Research Service Report for
    Congress.* 13 July 2005 and May 2017. Web.
    21 January 2018.

*The following graph comparing battlefield fatalities in various historical conflicts is
derived from reports by the U.S. Department of Veterans Affairs and the Naval History
and Heritage Command. The timeline ends with the 1990-1991 Persian Gulf War.
The graph shows battlefield fatalities as a percentage of the number serving in each
conflict, so it offers an "apples-to-apples" comparison, even though the conflicts
differed in size.*

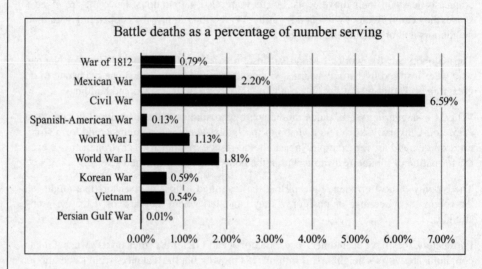

Battle deaths as a percentage of number serving

War of 1812 — 0.79%
Mexican War — 2.20%
Civil War — 6.59%
Spanish-American War — 0.13%
World War I — 1.13%
World War II — 1.81%
Korean War — 0.59%
Vietnam — 0.54%
Persian Gulf War — 0.01%

0.00% 1.00% 2.00% 3.00% 4.00% 5.00% 6.00% 7.00%

You Try It

Now you're ready to begin writing. Remember to plan your essay first and leave a couple of minutes at the end to proofread your work.

After you're finished writing your essay, take a look at the following page. This is a student essay that was written in the allotted 40 minutes. As you read it, evaluate how well it

- addresses the prompt

- ties each source clearly to one of the writer's points

- integrates the sources smoothly into the progression of the argument

- develops the writer's *own* argument

- expresses the writer's ideas

Then read the discussion of the student essay from a grader's viewpoint.

It's Not Me

Your essay will seem more professional and credible if you use third-person narrative instead of first person ("I think...").

A Student Essay

Some people see advances in artificial intelligence as leading to a frightening scenario where we can no longer control AI and therefore can't ensure that it doesn't harm us. Others imagine grand possibilities of AI making our lives easier, safer and less complex.

We are just now discovering the potential benefits of AI applications. Source A lists several benefits: better medical treatment, less traffic congestion and ways to address social problems. The same source suggests environmental benefits, too: protecting animal habitats and monitoring climate change in the Arctic. In general, Source A is optimistic about how AI can "improve people's lives" and "solve some of the world's greatest challenges and efficiencies."

Source B also mentions social benefits, such as autonomous vehicles and speech recognition. This source is even more ambitious than Source A, predicting that AI might be able to end poverty and disease entirely.

Many of these benefits depend on AI's ability to collect and analyze vast amounts of data that would be beyond human capability. Others allow us to learn about locations that would be too expensive or dangerous for human agents to enter.

Such characteristics suggest that AI will make us capable of doing more than we could do on our own. We must also consider the other side of the debate, though. By being able to do things we can't do, does AI also have the potential to master us, and will it always use its superior capabilities to help us?

Source B, while optimistic about the benefits AI can deliver, does raise this question. AI systems are going to grow more and more capable as research progresses. Therefore, we must focus the different AI research projects on the same goal: "our AI systems must do what we want them to do." AI must enhance and remain a tool of human intelligence, even if its abilities are superior to ours.

Source E raises a frightening scenario of AI research that does not prioritize the social benefits the other two sources describe. AI weapons systems, it says, could become so complex that we wouldn't even be able to understand them, let alone control them. Weapons that don't require a human to make them work should deliver the benefit of reducing war casualties, Source G does indicate that would be true. From World War II, when radio-controlled bombs were first directed by humans far away from the danger, to the automatic air defense systems of the Gulf War, the percentage of battlefield fatalities has been decreasing. Still, Source E's prospect of an autonomous weapon that can make its own decision to kill is frightening, especially since that same source draws a close connection between military and civilian developments. AI killers could roam our cities as well as our battlefields.

> As Source B suggests, it's too late now to stop AI develop-
> ment. Many different disciplines are already collaborating on a
> vast array of applications. As research results reach commer-
> cial success, there is an economic incentive to do more research
> and develop even more commercially viable applications. The genie
> can't be put back in the bottle now.
>
> AI, if not to be feared in the light of its potential benefits,
> must at least be viewed with caution and closely monitored
> because of its capacity to do harm. If we are to tame AI to do
> our bidding and to deliver only benefits, then everyone involved
> in AI research and development must have that same objective.
> How realistic is that?

What did you think? This essay has some strong points:

- The essay stretches beyond the question posed in the prompt to ask, "under what condition(s) would we *not* need to fear AI?"

- The writer does a good job of maintaining the high-level discussion initiated in the prompt. AI is such a broad topic that it would be easy to fall off the main track into a distracting consideration of one particular type of AI application.

- The writer's argument progresses smoothly, with points building on previous points and smooth transitions between them. For the most part, he shows good control of the language, expressing his ideas clearly and concisely.

- The writer does a decent job of incorporating a fourth source (the battle casualties graph) and outside knowledge (advances in developing weapons that don't require a human operator right beside them). He mentions both only briefly, and in the context of discussing one of his main sources (Source E). In general, though, your essay will exhibit better focus and demonstrate your research skills more effectively if you stick to three of the sources provided and avoid outside knowledge.

Did you pick up the weaknesses in this essay, too? They're significant.

- The sources—often summarized—dominate the writer's argument. He integrates them into the essay smoothly, and the progression of his argument is orderly and logical. However, the reader is left with an impression of sources strung together rather than an original argument supported by sources.

- The writer's position isn't evident until the end. This is a legitimate structure for an essay: build evidence that leads to a conclusion at the end instead of the more traditional structure of stating a thesis at the beginning, followed by evidence that proves it. However, the conclusion isn't stated clearly even at the end. The writer describes the condition under which we wouldn't need to fear AI (if everyone is aiming at beneficial applications) and then suggests that condition couldn't be reached ("How realistic is that?"). By implication, his conclusion is that we *do* need to fear AI.

- The opening isn't a strong one that would grab readers and make them want to keep reading. Instead, it basically restates information in the prompt, giving the reader (remember, there is a human grader for the AP essays) a first impression of an unoriginal, uninteresting essay.

This essay does an adequate job of addressing the question in the prompt, and would likely score a 6. The writer's ability to go beyond the prompt and his generally good control of the language elevate his score. However, the dominance of the sources over the writer's own original argument keep this essay from gaining a higher score.

By following our strategies and using the essays that you've seen as models, you can aim for—and achieve—higher scores.

Next, let's take a look at how to tackle the rhetorical analysis essay.

Chapter 6
How to Approach the Rhetorical Analysis Essay

FIRST THINGS FIRST: WHAT'S A RHETORICAL STRATEGY?

Authors use certain techniques, in both the language and the structure of the piece they're writing, to convey their messages effectively and to achieve the intended effect(s) on their audiences. Speakers use these techniques, too. Often they're trying to persuade their audiences to do something or to agree with their points of view.

In Chapters 8–11, you'll find explanations and examples of rhetorical strategies, plus questions so you can practice using them. Once you become familiar with rhetorical strategies and their effects, you'll probably start spotting them in your day-to-day life, too—in ads, in interviews given by politicians, or in instructions from your teachers, for instance.

YOUR TASKS IN THE RHETORICAL ANALYSIS ESSAY

The AP readers are looking for three main things in the rhetorical analysis essay.

- An understanding of the author's intended purpose

- The ability to identify the chief rhetorical strategies used to achieve that purpose effectively

- An analysis of *how* those strategies contribute to the development and effectiveness of the writer's argument, *supported by references to the text*

Of course, the readers are also assessing the usual skillful control of the language, clear expression, and smooth organization that they want to see in all three essays.

In the rhetorical analysis essay, the AP readers don't want a summary of the entire passage, or an argument for or against the author's main point. Your focus is strictly on what the author's purpose is, and what rhetorical strategies the author uses to achieve it effectively. Students typically find this essay the most challenging of the three, and straying from that focus is often where they go wrong.

Another common problem that lands essays in the lower score bands is being too general. An essay might describe the author's purpose right up front, in the first paragraph (a good idea, incidentally), and identify the three or four most important rhetorical strategies, but then fail to link each one to the author's purpose with a specific, thorough explanation of exactly how that strategy makes the message more effective. Direct references to the passage are a must, too, or the explanation runs the risk of being too general and oversimplified.

So your first task is to identify the author's purpose, which your active reading skills will enable you to do. After that, your task is to detect the main rhetorical strategies and build a convincing case for why and how each advances the author's purpose.

The Rhetorical Diamond

While you're reading the prompt and the passage, imagine—and try to flesh out—a baseball diamond with the following four points:

Diamonds Are an AP Student's Best Friend

Think of the four main aspects of a passage (author's message, context, purpose, and audience) in terms of a diamond. Understanding these main points will help you predict the rhetorical strategies being used in a text.

The passage represents an interaction among those points. Understanding them will help you recognize rhetorical strategies that an author might use to achieve his or her purpose for a specific audience and within a distinct context.

For example, you would expect a politician trying to win support from a mass audience at a rally to use different rhetorical techniques than a heart disease specialist writing the findings from a research study for publication in a professional, peer-reviewed journal. The politician, because of the verbal delivery and the diversity of the mass audience, would use simpler language, emotional appeals (pathos), and techniques such as repetition. The heart disease specialist, on the other hand, would use technical language and techniques to inspire respect for her qualifications and the thoroughness of her work (ethos).

The prompt will give you some of the information you need to describe the four points of the rhetorical baseball diamond. With a solid understanding of those points, you'll be able to predict at least some of the rhetorical strategies you can expect to find as you apply your active reading skills to the passage.

More Tips for Spotting Rhetorical Strategies

The author's main point will give you some clues about the rhetorical strategies you might find in the passage. Does it deal with a controversial topic, or with a "motherhood and apple pie" position that would create almost no opposition from anyone? Is it promoting a new, "fuzzy" concept that the audience would find hard to understand, or a topic that would be familiar to most people?

Trying to put yourself in the audience's shoes can also help you uncover rhetorical strategies. If you were part of that audience, at that time and in that context, would this piece of writing influence you? Why? Did it help you understand something through the use of examples, for instance? Did it make you feel the author sympathized with your concerns, perhaps through the use of anecdotes echoing your own experiences? Did it keep bringing you back to one central idea through the skillful use of repetition?

Now that you know your tasks and where you need to focus, let's look at a couple of rhetorical analysis prompts and passages.

A PERSUASIVE SPEECH EXAMPLE

The Directions

Question 2

Suggested time—40 minutes.

(This question counts for one-third of the total essay score.)

Susan B. Anthony delivered the speech below in 1873, after she was arrested for voting in the 1872 presidential election. She spoke throughout the county where her trial was to be held, aiming primarily at potential jurors and other women. Read the passages carefully. Then, in a well-developed essay, analyze the rhetorical strategies Anthony uses to persuade her audience that she did not commit a crime.

Analyzing the Prompt
As you're reading the prompt, look for how much it tells you about the four points on the rhetorical diamond.

- **Author**—Even if you've never heard of Susan B. Anthony (a leading 19th-century advocate for women's rights and co-founder of the National Woman Suffrage Association), the prompt gives you enough information to guess that she was an activist who deliberately defied a current law.

- **Purpose**—Sometimes the prompt will outline the author's purpose; sometimes it won't. In this case, you can guess that since Anthony is in conflict with legal authorities, she is probably giving a speech to present her side of the story in advance of her trial, and to convince her audience that her position is right.

- **Audience**—This prompt provides an unusual amount of information about the audience. Most of the time, you'll need to make inferences based on whatever details about the author and context you can squeeze from the prompt.

  In this case, since Anthony has been arrested but not yet tried, you could have guessed (even if the prompt didn't tell you) that the audience would include potential members of the jury pool. And since she felt strongly enough about her cause to risk arrest, you could guess that the audience would include a mix of supporters (who want to hear their champion) and people who are simply curious.

- **Context**—Anthony is giving a speech, so you can look for rhetorical strategies that you would expect to find in verbal delivery (such as simpler language, shorter sentences, repetition, and rhythm). And since she is facing a trial for following her beliefs, you could expect suggestions of urgency and passion.

Armed with the information you've gained from the prompt, you can now put your active reading skills into gear looking for Anthony's rhetorical strategies in the passage. Imagine you're in the audience listening to her speech. Does she convince you to agree with her? If so, how does she do it? If not, what would you need to hear in order to be convinced? As you identify each rhetorical strategy, keep asking yourself, "Why does she use this? How does it help her achieve her purpose?" because you'll need to answer those questions in your essay.

First try writing your own essay in 40 minutes. Remember to spend a few minutes planning your essay and support your points with direct references to the passage. Then read the sample student essay and assessment that follow the passage.

The Passage

Woman's Rights to the Suffrage
by Susan B. Anthony (1820–1906)
1873
[abridged]

The terms "bill of attainder" and "ex post facto law" in paragraph 5 refer to the power of the legislature to declare someone guilty (often without a trial), and to change, retroactively, the legal status of an action that occurred before the law was passed. The three people mentioned in paragraph 6 all published dictionaries.

Friends and Fellow Citizens: I stand before you tonight
under indictment for the alleged crime of having voted
at the last presidential election, without having a lawful
Line right to vote. It shall be my work this evening to prove to
5 you that in thus voting, I not only committed no crime,
but, instead, simply exercised my citizen's rights, guaranteed to me and all United States citizens by the National
Constitution, beyond the power of any State to deny.
The preamble of the Federal Constitution says:
10 "We, the people of the United States, in order to form a
more perfect union, establish justice, insure domestic tranquility, provide for the common defense, promote the general welfare, and secure the blessings of liberty to ourselves
and our posterity, do ordain and establish this Constitution
15 for the United States of America."
It was we, the people; not we, the white male citizens;
nor yet we, the male citizens; but we, the whole people,
who formed the Union. And we formed it, not to give the
blessings of liberty, but to secure them; not to the half of
20 ourselves and the half of our posterity, but to the whole
people—women as well as men. And it is a downright
mockery to talk to women of their enjoyment of the blessings of liberty while they are denied the use of the only
means of securing them provided by this democratic-
25 republican government—the ballot.
For any State to make sex a qualification that must ever
result in the disfranchisement of one entire half of the people is to pass a bill of attainder, or an ex post facto law, and
is therefore a violation of the supreme law of the land. By
30 it the blessings of liberty are for ever withheld from women
and their female posterity. To them this government has no
just powers derived from the consent of the governed. To
them this government is not a democracy. It is not a republic. It is an odious aristocracy; a hateful oligarchy of sex;
35 the most hateful aristocracy ever established on the face of
the globe; an oligarchy of wealth, where the right govern
the poor. An oligarchy of learning, where the educated
govern the ignorant, or even an oligarchy of race, where
the Saxon rules the African, might be endured; but this
40 oligarchy of sex, which makes father, brothers, husband,
sons, the oligarchs over the mother and sisters, the wife
and daughters of every household—which ordains all men
sovereigns, all women subjects, carries dissension, discord
and rebellion into every home of the nation.

45   Webster, Worcester and Bouvier all define a citizen to
     be a person in the United States, entitled to vote and hold
     office.
         The only question left to be settled now is: Are women
     persons? And I hardly believe any of our opponents will
50   have the hardihood to say they are not. Being persons, then,
     women are citizens; and no State has a right to make any
     law, or to enforce any old law, that shall abridge their priv-
     ileges or immunities. Hence, every discrimination against
     women in the constitutions and laws of the several States is
55   today null and void.

A Student Essay

Susan B. Anthony broke the law. For this, she was arrested and about to be tried. Before the trial took place, however, she wanted to prove that she didn't do anything wrong and to gain support for her innocence. So she gave this speech to convince people—potential jurors at her trial, other women and anyone who chose to listen—that it wasn't wrong for her to vote in the presidential election.

That would have been a radical assertion at the time. Anthony lived in an era when men and women had different rights, and the difference in their status was widely accepted as normal. While the audience likely included people who knew of Anthony and supported her position, others would have been shocked by the fact that she dared to challenge the accepted social order. She would have needed a strong argument to explain her action and win those people over.

Anthony bases her entire appeal on logos, or logic. "Are women persons?" she asks. If women are people, then they are also citizens and entitled to the "blessings of liberty" that the nation's Constitution guarantees, including the right to vote. She does not try to claim that she didn't break a state law. Instead, she argues that the law she broke is "null and void" because it denies her the status and the rights that the federal Constitution guarantees her.

In this appeal to reason and logic, Anthony is basically claiming that anyone who thinks she did something wrong by voting is also saying that she—or any woman—is not a person. In addition, anyone who thinks she committed a crime would also have to argue that a state law (which she did break by voting) outweighs the Constitution of the entire nation. Both positions would be hard to defend. By attributing these positions to her opponents, Anthony portrays people who don't agree with her—including everyone connected with her arrest and trial and with passing the law in the first place—as illogi-cal, unreasonable idiots. Such people couldn't possibly be right.

Not only are her opponents fools; Anthony claims they are more dangerous than that. They have created a "hateful aristocracy" and ensured that every family in the country is plagued by "dissension, discord and rebellion." The government is not a democracy, as the Constitution intended, she claims, but is instead controlled by a privileged few who are depriving her—and all women—of liberty. Her passion and hyperbole come through even more when she describes the government as "the most hateful aristocracy ever established on the face of the globe."

After this tirade, Anthony comes full circle back to her original point: women are citizens too, and therefore no state law (like the one preventing them from voting) can deny them the rights guaranteed by the country's Constitution. Through this passionate appeal to logic, Anthony achieves the purpose she clearly stated at the beginning: "to prove to you that in thus voting, I...committed no crime." It is as if she were a lawyer arguing her case at her upcoming trial, rather than the accused trying to drum up support and influence potential jurors. How could anyone disagree with her after listening to the logic of her argument?

The Assessment

This student makes a common mistake in responding to the rhetorical analysis essay question. Can you identify it? He focuses on *what* the author says rather than on *how* the author says it in order to achieve her purpose.

His discussion of Anthony's logical argument is accurate, although rather superficial. The trouble is, that's not what the prompt asked. The prompt instructed him to identify and analyze the *rhetorical strategies* the author uses. That task requires a focus not just on the author's message, but on the interaction among message, purpose, audience, and context. Different elements—for example, if Anthony were creating a written submission to the judge at her trial—would require different rhetorical strategies in order to achieve the author's purpose effectively.

This confusion between *what* the author says and *how* the author says it is one of the main reasons why test takers typically earn a lower score on the rhetorical analysis than on any of the other essay tasks. In this case, the essay would likely have received a score of 3 or 4 because the student misread the prompt and did not do an adequate job of analyzing Anthony's rhetorical strategies.

There are some good points in this essay. Although the first paragraph is simply an uninspiring restatement of the information provided in the prompt, the first sentence does turn out to be a good attention-getter. It makes the reader want to keep going to uncover more of the story, and creates a good first impression. The student also cites some evidence from the passage, which is essential to earning a good score. He conveys his thoughts clearly, leads the reader through his argument with transitions between points, and displays a good vocabulary and grasp of English language mechanics.

Let's look at some points this student could have covered in his essay to get a better score.

Although he correctly identifies Anthony's classical appeal to logos, or logic, the student doesn't catch her use of pathos—an appeal to the audience's values, to a sense of fairness in this case.

He does touch upon the likely makeup of the audience and the context of an era in which the restricted status of women was the norm. However, he connects these two elements only to the content of Anthony's message (the need for a strong argument), not to rhetorical strategies that would help her deliver that content more effectively to that audience in that era. For example, he could have discussed strategies such as identifying with the audience and establishing common ground (the wording of the Constitution, the desire for a peaceful home life) to make her action seem less alien to listeners who might initially find it shocking.

The student mentions "passion and hyperbole" but doesn't connect these rhetorical devices to Anthony's verbal delivery (can't you just hear the rising volume as she goes through that long "odious aristocracy" sentence?) or to her purpose of inflaming her audience to support her right to vote. And Anthony injects a bit of humour ("not we, the white male citizens") to give some relief to her impassioned plea for support.

He astutely notices that Anthony concludes her speech by returning to her starting point. However, again he fails to tie this rhetorical technique to the verbal delivery or to the mass audience she's addressing. Her listeners don't have a written version of her argument in front of them. In that context, she can achieve her purpose more effectively by reminding them of her main points and wrapping up her speech neatly by returning to the beginning.

The student also ignores some major rhetorical strategies used in speeches: repetition, cadence, and rhythm. Try to hear, for instance, the "...not to...but to..." rhythms of the fourth paragraph, or the repeated "an oligarchy of" descriptions in the fifth. Anthony also uses repetition in organizing her points, again in consideration of the verbal delivery and an audience that could well include people who are simply curious. She not only begins and ends with her main points (women are people, the nation's Constitution supersedes a state law, and therefore she did nothing wrong), but also refers to those points throughout the body of her speech.

The student misses the rhetorical technique of appeal to authority, too. Anthony claims she has no less authority on her side than the founding Constitution of the entire nation, and in case that isn't enough, she invokes Webster (of dictionary fame), Worcester, and Bouvier (who also published dictionaries). That technique would enhance her stature and credibility with listeners who might have regarded her as just some minor figure who was silly enough to challenge a state law.

Anthony also uses the tried-and-true politician's technique of identifying with her listeners in order to get them on her side. She addresses them as "Friends and Fellow Citizens," and tells them that she is fighting for them because the injustice she wants to overturn affects "every household."

Keep this student's mistake in mind when you reach the rhetorical analysis essay on the test. Don't simply discuss what the author says. Discuss how the author delivers the message in order to achieve his or her purpose with this particular audience in this particular context.

Here's another example for you to try, this time from a written work.

More AP Info Online!

We have put together even more goodies for a handful of AP Exam subjects. For short quizzes, high level AP course and test information, and expert advice, head over to www.princetonreview.com/college-advice/advanced-placement-resources.

AN EDUCATIONAL BOOK EXAMPLE

The Directions

Question 2

Suggested time—40 minutes.

(This question counts for one-third of the total essay score.)

In1880, nine years after he created "The Greatest Show on Earth," circus promoter P.T. Barnum wrote a short book about making money. He became wealthy himself, and believed that anyone could do the same if they would only follow the simple rules he had learned. Read the passages carefully. Then, in a well-developed essay, analyze the rhetorical strategies Barnum uses to convey his point of view.

Analyzing the Prompt

As you're reading the prompt, look for how much it tells you about the four points on the rhetorical diamond.

- **Author**—You may have heard of P.T. Barnum and the Barnum and Bailey Circus. The prompt reveals something about this successful businessman and promoter that you might not expect, though. He wants to share his secrets for making money—to help ordinary people become wealthy, too. That suggests a philanthropic quality and empathy for the kind of people who come to see his circus (and who, in the process, have helped him become a millionaire).

- **Purpose**—This prompt reveals a lot of information about the author's purpose. Anyone can get rich, he believes, and he wants to teach them how. And incidentally, he will be able to sell a lot of books to a mass audience if he really does provide helpful information geared to ordinary people. Readers who find his rules useful will tell their friends and relatives, who will buy the book and tell their friends and relatives, and so on.

- **Audience**—Barnum says his rules apply to anyone, not just financiers or businessmen. He is addressing the laborers and housewives of the era—people who don't have much money now, and who don't have a lot of formal education but hope for a better future.

- **Context**—This is a book for the masses, so it has to be useful to ordinary people or it won't sell. Look for rhetorical strategies that make the author's points easy to understand and remember. You can also expect efforts to identify with the audience; they won't listen to someone who thinks he is better than them and who "talks down" to them. He will want to convince his readers that he genuinely wants to help them get rich, and that they really can succeed if they follow his rules.

Armed with the information you've gained from the prompt, you can now use your active reading skills to look for Barnum's rhetorical strategies. In this excerpt, does he teach you any lessons that would help you improve your own financial situation? How does he do it? Does he explain his rules in a way that will help you remember them? Does he make you believe that his desire to help you is genuine, and that you, too, can become wealthy? As you identify each rhetorical strategy, keep asking yourself, "Why does he use this? How does it help him achieve his purpose?" because you'll need to answer those questions in your essay.

First, try writing your own essay in 40 minutes. Remember to spend a few minutes planning your essay and support your points with direct references to the passage. Then read the sample student essay and assessment that follow the passage.

The Passage

Excerpt from
The Art of Money Getting
or
Golden Rules for Making Money
by P.T. Barnum
1880

In paragraph 2, "Dr. Franklin" refers to Benjamin Franklin, the Founding Father who promoted the virtues of thrift and frugal living. "Mr. Micawber" is the chronic debtor in Charles Dickens' novel, David Copperfield. "Furbelows" signifies showy, basically useless ruffles on women's dresses. In paragraph 4, a "bung-hole" is a hole in a barrel (which might hold beer or whisky) capped with a cork called a bung. Punch was a popular satire magazine at the time.

In the United States, where we have more land than people, it is not at all difficult for persons in good health to make money. In this comparatively new field there are so
Line many avenues of success open, so many vocations which
5 are not crowded, that any person of either sex who is willing, at least for the time being, to engage in any respectable occupation that offers, may find lucrative employment.

Those who really desire to attain an independence, have only to set their minds upon it, and adopt the proper means,
10 as they do in regard to any other object which they wish to accomplish, and the thing is easily done. But however easy it may be found to make money, I have no doubt many of my hearers will agree it is the most difficult thing in the world to keep it. The road to wealth is, as Dr. Franklin truly
15 says, "as plain as the road to the mill." It consists simply in expending less than we earn; that seems to be a very simple problem. Mr. Micawber, one of those happy creations of the genial Dickens, puts the case in a strong light when he says that to have annual income of twenty pounds per
20 annum, and spend twenty pounds and sixpence, is to be the most miserable of men; whereas, to have an income of only twenty pounds, and spend but nineteen pounds and sixpence is to be the happiest of mortals. Many of my readers may say, "we understand this: this is economy, and we
25 know economy is wealth; we know we can't eat our cake and keep it also." Yet I beg to say that perhaps more cases of failure arise from mistakes on this point than almost any other. The fact is, many people think they understand economy when they really do not.
30 True economy is misapprehended, and people go through life without properly comprehending what that principle is. One says, "I have an income of so much, and here is my neighbor who has the same; yet every year he gets something ahead and I fall short; why is it? I know
35 all about economy." He thinks he does, but he does not. There are men who think that economy consists in saving cheese-parings and candle-ends, in cutting off two pence from the laundress' bill and doing all sorts of little, mean, dirty things. Economy is not meanness. The misfortune
40 is, also, that this class of persons let their economy apply in only one direction. They fancy they are so wonderfully

economical in saving a half-penny where they ought to spend twopence, that they think they can afford to squander in other directions. A few years ago, before kerosene oil
45 was discovered or thought of, one might stop overnight at almost any farmer's house in the agricultural districts and get a very good supper, but after supper he might attempt to read in the sitting-room, and would find it impossible with the inefficient light of one candle. The hostess, seeing
50 his dilemma, would say: "It is rather difficult to read here evenings; the proverb says 'you must have a ship at sea in order to be able to burn two candles at once;' we never have an extra candle except on extra occasions." These extra occasions occur, perhaps, twice a year. In this way the
55 good woman saves five, six, or ten dollars in that time: but the information which might be derived from having the extra light would, of course, far outweigh a ton of candles.

But the trouble does not end here. Feeling that she is so economical in tallow candles, she thinks she can afford
60 to go frequently to the village and spend twenty or thirty dollars for ribbons and furbelows, many of which are not necessary. This false connote may frequently be seen in men of business, and in those instances it often runs to writing-paper. You find good businessmen who save all the
65 old envelopes and scraps, and would not tear a new sheet of paper, if they could avoid it, for the world. This is all very well; they may in this way save five or ten dollars a year, but being so economical (only in note paper), they think they can afford to waste time; to have expensive parties,
70 and to drive their carriages. This is an illustration of Dr. Franklin's "saving at the spigot and wasting at the bung-hole;" "penny wise and pound foolish." Punch in speaking of this "one idea" class of people says "they are like the man who bought a penny herring for his family's dinner
75 and then hired a coach and four to take it home." I never knew a man to succeed by practising this kind of economy.

True economy consists in always making the income exceed the out-go.

A Student Essay

Circus promoter P.T. Barnum wanted to do more than entertain people at the Greatest Show on Earth. He wants to teach them how to make money and become wealthy, too. To do this, he uses some effective rhetorical strategies. He tells stories, he gives examples, he uses a comparison/contrast structure, he mentions authorities, he identifies with his readers, he uses the tone of a cheerleader and he uses simple language.

Telling stories is a good way to teach lessons. Barnum's readers are ordinary people, without much formal education. They will remember stories much more easily than if the author ordered them to follow a list of rules. For example, Barnum tells the story of the woman with the candle so vividly that readers could likely see her guest squinting, then finally giving up on

Simon Says

Try to use more varied verbs in your essay. Instead of constantly writing "The author says," how about "The author... claims, suggests, implies, states..."?

trying to read with such inadequate lighting. Then they could imagine the woman dashing around the village buying ribbons with the money she saved by only burning one candle.

Readers would also be more accepting of a lesson told in a story than they would of a rule ordered by a successful businessman. If Barnum just told them not to save money for buying foolish things, but to invest the money instead (in this case, in the knowledge she would gain by reading), readers might resent being ordered around. A story conveys the same rule in a friendlier way to this audience. They are reading Barnum's book because they want to learn, not be ordered around.

The author gives other examples so he can avoid delivering his lessons as rules and so readers will remember them better. He tells the story of the businessman who saves scraps of paper, but wastes the money he saved on parties and carriages. He gives the example of Mr. Micawber, who always spent more than he earned and therefore couldn't become wealthy. The author compares Mr. Micawber's practice with a contrasting habit of spending less than one earns, which leads to the ability to accumulate wealth.

Citing authorities that would be familiar to readers gives Barnum more credibility with his audience, and also strengthens his position as "one of them" rather than a remote, successful businessman they could never hope to become. Barnum reads Charles Dickens and the satire magazine Punch, too, just like his readers do. His statement, "many of my hearers will agree," reinforces his connection with the audience so they will accept his rules as advice from a friend rather than a route to something they could never achieve (wealth). The author needs to convince his readers that he really wants to help them become wealthy. Making them feel that he is "one of them" helps him achieve that goal.

He cheers them on and encourages them to follow his advice. It's "not at all difficult for persons in good health to make money," he assures them. Anyone can do it, even women (which would have been unusual at the time).

Barnum used simple language to convey simple lessons. There are no complex financial terms or concepts that would make his readers feel the book or Barnum's lessons were beyond their abilities. Spend less than you earn, and invest wisely instead of spending foolishly are his two main messages in this excerpt. The rhetorical strategies he chooses ensure that these important lessons are understood and remembered by ordinary readers.

The Assessment

In terms of the task given in the prompt, this student gets it to a large extent. Instead of simply rehashing the author's message, she focuses on the rhetorical strategies the author uses to help readers understand, remember, and accept his rules for gaining wealth. She gives evidence from the passage to support her points. It's obvious that she planned her response before she started writing, since her first paragraph contains a laundry list of rhetorical strategies that she then checks off in the following paragraphs.

That sense of checking items off a list makes her discussion adequate, landing this essay at a score of 6. It's the "analyze" part of the task where this student's essay falls short of a top score. Her explanations don't have the depth, sophistication, or conviction to elevate her work into the higher score range. A more effective, thorough analysis would explain how each of the author's rhetorical strategies fits into the interplay among purpose, audience, and context.

For example, plenty of authorities counsel thrift. Why was Benjamin Franklin a particularly good one for Barnum to cite? The student doesn't explore what the author gains with a mass audience by drawing on a trusted Founding Father: Barnum gains credibility for his message, legitimacy for his subject (the pursuit of wealth), and a connection to the concept of helping people build something.

As another example, the student misses the fact that Barnum uses different rhetorical strategies to achieve different purposes. Before he can successfully teach readers how to become wealthy, Barnum needs to convince them that his desire to help them is genuine and that they will benefit from his book. In order to achieve that initial purpose, he first gets his readers on his side with a rousing, encouraging "land of opportunity" opening. It's easy to make money in a country where there is so much land and so many jobs, he claims. An ordinary reader would likely feel, "I can actually do this, too, just like the famous Barnum did, and he really wants me to succeed." Next, the author identifies with his readers and demonstrates that he understands them: "I have no doubt many of my hearers will agree it is the most difficult thing in the world to keep it." Only then does he turn to his main purpose, launching into the stories that teach the difference between false economy (which does not lead to wealth) and true economy (which does).

In addition to the superficial analysis, another weakness in this essay occurs in the way the student expresses her ideas. No one expects a polished essay from a 40-minute effort. However, there is a choppy, disjointed quality to the way the student develops her points, and a weakness in her ability to control English mechanics (such as some confusion in verb tenses and some unclear pronoun antecedents). As a result, it's difficult to follow her argument in spots. A more in-depth analysis of the author's rhetorical strategies would have raised her score another notch, to a 7, but level 8 and 9 essays demonstrate a smoother, more controlled prose style than this student achieves. Understanding the task and citing evidence from the passage are both important in the rhetorical analysis essay, but so is the ability to express ideas clearly and effectively, with smooth transitions to guide the reader through the discussion.

In the next chapter, we move on to the argument essay.

Chapter 7
How to Approach
the Argument Essay

WHERE YOUR OPINION COUNTS

At last—a chance to make your own argument, without being limited by the source documents you're given and without having to focus on rhetorical strategies instead of the merits of what an author says. Here you get to take a stand and present your point of view on the topic in the prompt. This should be an essay you look forward to!

Even better, there is no "right" or "wrong" answer. All that matters is how effectively you argue and back up your position. If you like to debate, this is the part of the essay section where you can really shine.

The argument essay isn't a license to ramble on about your own personal views, though. To get a high score, you need to do three things.

1. Take a definite position, so no one would question where you stand on the topic of the prompt.

2. Develop an argument that builds and moves forward instead of simply repeating the same point several times in different ways.

3. Support the points in your argument with evidence drawn from your own knowledge, reading, experiences, and observations.

Argument Essay Checklist

Be sure to accomplish these three tasks in your argument essay!

Lower-scoring essays tend to simply summarize what the author says in the passage, or wander aimlessly through an impassioned list of the student's own beliefs without giving any evidence to support them. As in the synthesis essay, the concept of a conversation with the author is helpful. If you were talking with this author and either agreeing, disagreeing, or giving a "yes, but" (qualifying) opinion, how would you argue your position? What evidence would you offer to back it up?

Let's look at an example. We'll work through an analysis of the prompt and passage before you try writing your own essay in 40 minutes. Then read the student essay and evaluation that follow.

SAMPLE ESSAY #1—HERE'S HOW IT'S DONE

Here's a sample argument essay prompt.

The Prompt

Question 3

Suggested time—40 minutes.

(This question counts for one-third of the total essay section score.)

In *Utilitarianism*, John Stuart Mill promoted a theory of morality that postulated: "The creed which accepts as the foundation of morals, Utility, or the Greatest Happiness Principle, holds that actions are right in proportion as they tend to promote happiness, wrong as they tend to produce the reverse of happiness. By happiness is intended pleasure, and the absence of pain; by unhappiness, pain, and the privation of pleasure."

Mill argues that happiness is the foundation of morality, and that pursuing one's own happiness will necessarily lead to an ethical society for all. Write an essay that argues your position on the extent to which Mill's claims are valid. Use appropriate examples from your reading, experience, or observations to support your argument.

Analyzing the Prompt

If you've taken a lot of history courses, then you may have studied John Stuart Mill, and this would give you some information about context. If not, then the prompt still gives you rich material for a thoughtful argumentative essay.

Your first task is to identify the author's main point, so you can decide what position you want to argue. In this case, the author's main point is clearly stated: "actions are right in proportion as they tend to promote happiness, wrong as they tend to produce the reverse of happiness." In the next sentence, Mill defines happiness ("pleasure") and unhappiness ("pain or the privation of pleasure").

You still have terms to define when you write your own essay, though. Happiness may equal pleasure, but one person's pleasure may be a matter of complete indifference to another person. What does Mill mean by "pleasure"? How will you define it?

You can see why this particular example is tailor-made to take you beyond the prompt. Here you can really demonstrate that you've thought deeply about the topic. Is "pleasure" the same thing for everyone? What are the consequences of individuals pursuing a "pleasure" that doesn't mean the same thing to all of them? If everyone pursued pleasure, what consequences might result for society? Does one person pursuing pleasure mean someone else has to experience pain?

Whatever you decide to argue, make your position perfectly clear in the first paragraph of your essay.

As you think through those questions, what kind of evidence from your own experiences or reading pops into your mind? Which would be the strongest and the easiest to develop? That evidence should determine what stand you take on the argument. Remember that no reader knows or cares what you really think about an issue. You'll want to take the stand that's easiest for you to defend at that particular moment, based on the ideas that come to you. The most important things are that you have clearly decided how you feel about the issue and that you have the examples to back up your position.

> **I Remember When...**
> If you're describing your own experience or observation in the argument essay, you can use first-person narration.

Let's look at an essay that was written by a student under actual testing conditions.

A Student Essay

In John Stuart Mill's work <u>Utilitarianism,</u> the author advances a theory of morality that associates "the promotion of pleasure and the prevention of pain" with ethical correctness. While the pursuit of happiness can sometimes lead to a path of moral righteousness, Mill's claim is flawed in that it assumes hedonism will inherently bring positive results. By championing any action that produces pleasure, Mill condones humanity's greed, lust, and selfishness; three traits that are clearly immoral. As history and literature have demonstrated, pursuing goals motivated purely by self-interest does not lead to ethically responsible outcomes. Furthermore, the greatest achievements often arise when people readily eschew pleasure to attain a nobler end.

During the second half of the nineteenth century, a number of technological advances made the American economy blossom and helped to make the nation a world power. Eager to enjoy the pleasures made possible by great wealth, entrepreneurs and businessmen sought to increase profits and lower costs in any possible way. Workers were paid abysmally low wages, conditions were highly unsafe, and monopolies were commonplace. Though the heads of "Big Business" clearly adhered to Mill's "Greatest Happiness Principle," their actions were highly unethical. Their pleasure came at the expense of the poor and created a polarized society. In contrast, patriots seeking independence from England a century before, gladly relinquished the "absence of pain" afforded by accepting the status quo. Despite the great "privation of pleasure" brought about by the Revolutionary War, the patriots achieved their lofty goal of freedom, a morally desirable outcome. Evidently, seeking happiness does not necessarily entail finding "what is right and good."

F. Scott Fitzgerald's portrait of the Roaring Twenties, <u>The Great Gatsby</u>, examines hedonism and reaches a conclusion much different than Mill's. Jay Gatsby pursues pleasure in the form of rekindling a relationship with a former love, Daisy. Following utilitarian principles, seeking the desirable outcome should be an ethically sound choice. However, it instead leads Gatsby to engage in questionable business and to court a married woman, two clear violations of ethical standards. Clearly, morality based on pleasure is an unsound principle.

This essay is rather short. An additional example—perhaps from the student's own experience—would have made it stronger. However, it does the job quite well, and would likely earn a score of 7, at the bottom of the "effective" band.

The introduction is slightly long, but notice how well this student addresses the two tasks set forth. Right away, the student states the author's claim ("the author advances a theory of morality that associates the 'promotion of pleasure and the prevention of pain' with ethical correctness.") and takes a firm stand against it: "As history and literature have demonstrated, pursuing goals motivated by mere self-interest does not lead to ethically responsible outcomes." The student's clear definition of pleasure ("humanity's greed, lust, and selfishness") both explains and reinforces this stand.

The student gives the reader a roadmap for the rest of the essay by first mentioning history and then literature, and follows that roadmap in the same order.

Write in the Present Tense

This student does an excellent job of handling verb tenses. Particularly important is the use of the present tense when addressing the author, text and claim: "the author advances," "it assumes," "achievements often arise," and so on. The student uses the past tense only when presenting historical facts in the second paragraph.

One of the most common grammatical errors that students make in AP essays is using improper verb-tense shifts.

The conclusion is weak and seems tacked on. It would have been stronger if it reminded the reader of the evidence brought in to support the student's stand against Mill's claim.

What keeps this essay from scoring an 8 or 9 is the student's failure to follow the prompt where it leads. This essay simply takes the prompt at face value and doesn't examine the broader ethical questions it raises.

SAMPLE ESSAY #2—GIVING IT ANOTHER TRY

Let's try another one. Again, now that you're comfortable with the process for writing the argument essay, try writing this one on your own before you look at the student's essay.

The Prompt

Question 3

Suggested time—40 minutes.

(This question counts for one-third of the total essay section score.)

The former slave and abolitionist Frederick Douglass (1818–1895) wrote, "Once you learn to read, you will be forever free."

Write an essay that argues your position on the relationship between literacy and freedom in the world today. Use appropriate examples from your reading, experience, or observations to support your argument.

A Student Essay

Frederick Douglass once wrote, "Once you learn to read, you will be forever free" and this is true of the modern world. Though everyone in America can read, alot of people in the world can't read today and that's a serious problem for them. There are too many people in places like India and China who can't read and this iliteracy is holding them back. If we would have more programs to teach literacy to people in these Third World countries, then we we would have more literacy and therefore more freedom for all.

One reason I think there should be more literacy is that you need to educate children early on in their educational experience, otherwise, they will not learn what they need to succeed. Once the children in a given country achieve literacy, then the country can also improve the quality of life and the children can teach there parents how to read when they return home from school. This would help the parents to find better jobs and allow for more financial freedom for the family. Also, if the people in China and India learned English, they could get jobs using their new skills in English.

Another reason why I think literacy increases freedom is because literacy is the key concept to the development of political freedom. When Frederick Douglass was a slave in America, black people were enslaved and deprived of literacy. When the slave owners didn't teach their slaves to read, they were holding them back from the freedoms they deserved; including the right to read. If the slaves learned to read,

> though, they would have been more free and this would have threatened the slave masters. So with slaves having been deprived of literacy, the owners could keep control of them.
>
> In conclusion, literacy is the key to freedom around the world. As the examples of India and slavery have demonstrated, freedom is possible for people who have a chance to read the way we do.

This essay has significant flaws in both content and style and would not score above a 5. The most serious problem is the absence of a strong connection between literacy and freedom. This is not an easy concept and many students would struggle to find good, specific examples to bridge a connection between these ideas. While literacy in the Third World and in American slavery could be excellent examples, they are not made specific or relevant in this essay. In the discussion of slavery, for example, the student wrote

> If the slaves learned to read, though, they would have been more free and this would have threatened the slave masters. So with the slaves having been deprived of literacy, the owners could keep control of them.

What does this mean? How would literacy have made slaves "more free"? How did illiteracy help slave owners "keep control of them"? Good essays on the AP English Language and Composition Exam develop specific examples and then carefully connect them to the issue at hand. They also demonstrate a depth of thought and complexity that is mostly absent in this essay. As you write your own essays, be sure to have a clear, stable definition of the essential terms (in this case, "literacy" and "freedom") in mind and don't be afraid to talk about how complex the terms can be.

The style of this essay did not help. It is not necessary, for example, to repeat the quote verbatim in the first sentence: The grader already knows what Frederick Douglass said. Also, the first paragraph does not really contain a thesis or any clear statement about how literacy allows people to be more free. Throughout, the student makes some awkward errors in style and diction, which detract from the overall effect.

But, in spite of these flaws, the essay does provide some examples and at least attempted to address the relationship between literacy and freedom, so it would receive a score of 3 or 4.

Now let's take a look at a more successful essay, which was also written by a student under time constraints.

A Student Essay

Literacy is something we take for granted in America. Most children learn to read at an early age and receive formal education until they are eighteen years old. During this time, they develop a deep understanding of their own language, both in its written and spoken forms. I remember when I first learned to read and how it made me feel so empowered over my younger sister, who hadn't learned yet. As my teachers encouraged me in elementary school, I grew to enjoy reading adventure stories and then much harder books. In my AP English class this year, my teacher Mrs. Lasko assigned extremely challenging books, such as <u>Paradise Lost</u>, <u>Gulliver's Travels</u>, and <u>Lord of the Flies</u>. In all these cases, literacy empowered me to feel more and more intellectually free and to explore new ideas through reading.

But literacy does more that just free our minds: it is the key to bringing about political and economic freedom for ordinary people. There are many times in history when increasing literacy allowed people to experience a new kind of political freedom. For example, during the Protestant Reformation, ordinary people began to read because the printing press allowed books to be printed quickly rather than copied by hand. As the people began to read the Bible for themselves, they developed their own interpretations about theology and they challenged the teachings of the Catholic Church. People also read political pamphlets and were empowered to overthrow the leaders in power during that time. These kinds of political pamphlets, which only work when the majority of the population can read, have formed the basis of many political movements in the modern era.

In women's history, too, increasing literacy has brought about an increase in political freedoms. For centuries, few women could read or write and thus they were denied freedoms we now consider basic: the freedom to vote, the freedom to hold political office, the freedom to represent oneself in court. When we think of the movement for women's suffrage a century ago, how could the suffragettes have succeeded if they did not have a largely literate population of women to support them. As women learned to read in large numbers, they began to develop the political tools necessary to fight for their own freedom. In this way, literacy was a prerequisite to real political freedom for millions of women around the world.

When Frederick Douglass wrote of literacy and freedom, he was speaking of real freedom from the bondage of slavery. For him, the power to read and write played a role in his abolitionist activities. But as I have discussed in this essay, literacy can bring about more than just freedom from slavery: it can free us to think for ourselves, determine our own theologies, and fight for real political freedom. And whether it is African Americans, children, the poor, or just ordinary people, reading can transform the lives of those with less power. Literacy is thus a direct cause of freedom, both in the distant historical past and in the future of our constantly evolving world.

This essay is an obvious success and would score very highly (probably an 8) on the real AP. Not only did the student specifically answer the question at hand, she offered a nuanced assessment of the relationship between literacy and freedom. In fact, she took pains to define multiple senses of the word freedom (intellectual, political, etc.) throughout the paper. The examples were specific, detailed, and relevant to the topic at hand.

The student begins by briefly recounting her own history of literacy and how it empowered her as she developed her reading skills. The first body paragraph then explicitly connects increasing literacy with newfound political and religious freedom during the Protestant Reformation. Notice how the student takes her time in introducing each example and then adds as much relevant, specific information as possible. The next body paragraph is equally effective and shows yet another dimension of the complex link between literacy and freedom.

The student also helped her score by creating fluid prose and elegant transitions from one paragraph to the next. The range of vocabulary was good, but not exceptional—it never needs to be to get a high score on this test. Offer the readers as wide a range of vocabulary as you can, but focus on writing a good essay as you design, develop, and execute your response.

COMING UP...

In this chapter and the two preceding chapters, you've seen a range of essay examples. In the next part of this book, you'll learn (or review) the important aspects of formal training in rhetoric and composition that will prepare you to craft essays that equal—or exceed—the ones that you've examined so far.

Study Break!
You're about halfway through your review! Before you dive into Part V, be sure to give yourself some downtime to let your brain absorb the information you've been studying.

REFLECT

Think about what you've learned in Part IV, and respond to the following questions:

- How long will you spend on multiple-choice questions?

- How will you change your approach to multiple-choice questions?

- What is your multiple-choice guessing strategy?

- How much time will you spend on the first essay? The second? The third?

- What will you do before you begin writing an essay?

- How will you change your approach to the essays?

- Will you seek further help, outside of this book (such as a teacher, tutor, or AP Students website), on how to approach multiple-choice questions, the essays, or a pacing strategy?

Part V
Terms and Modes Review for the AP English Language and Composition Exam

HOW TO USE THE CHAPTERS IN THIS PART

You may need to come back to the following chapters more than once. Your goal is to obtain mastery of the content, and a single read of a chapter may not be sufficient. At the end of each chapter, you will have an opportunity to reflect on whether you truly have mastered the content of that chapter.

Chapter 8: Words and Their Use

This chapter introduces you to the most important terminology that appears on the AP English Language and Composition Exam. If you have heard the words "diction," "syntax," and "rhetoric," but you're not really sure what they mean, this chapter will finally help you figure them out. In addition, it covers the entire vocabulary of rhetorical and literary devices that appear most commonly on the exam.

Chapter 9: Rhetorical Fallacies

This brief chapter introduces you to the kinds of faulty reasoning that commonly appear in student writing. The errors may even be lurking in the background of the passages you have to analyze on the AP English Language and Composition Exam.

Chapter 10: Basic Rhetorical Modes

"Rhetorical modes" refers to the ways that writers organize their arguments. What is the difference between an illustration and a classification? Why do some authors structure their essays around comparisons and contrasts? This brief chapter will help you identify these structures quickly on the multiple-choice passages.

Chapter 11: Complex Rhetorical Modes

This chapter expands on the content of the previous chapter and goes much deeper into analyzing how authors conceptualize their evidence and arguments. If you are running low on time, you can skim through this chapter and jump right to Practice Test 2.

Chapter 8
Words and
Their Use

THE GOOD NEWS AND THE BAD NEWS ABOUT THE AP ENGLISH LANGUAGE AND COMPOSITION EXAM

The Good News

While the title of this exam allows people to differentiate between this test and the AP English *Literature* Exam, it's still somewhat misleading. The AP English *Language* Exam is not a language exam—at least not in the sense that you may think. For example, it is possible not to know the difference between a gerund and a present participle—or even a gerund and a giraffe—and still score a 5 on this exam.

In the multiple-choice section of the exam, test writers will attempt to evaluate your ability to analyze how writers use language to explain or to argue; in the free-response, or essay, section they will expect *you* to use language to explain or to argue. Naturally, you should avoid making egregious errors in grammar or usage on the test, but don't get hung up on the rules of language as you study. If you're considering taking the AP exam, your language skills are probably sufficient for the task. Now, you may be wondering what *is* tested on the exam. The answer is *composition,* and we'll spend Chapters 9 through 11 of this book reviewing all you need to know about composition to be fully prepared for the test.

The Bad News

Now for the bad news. Despite the test's lack of emphasis on the rules of language, there are some aspects of language that we must examine here to make sure you're ready for test day. We'll start by discussing diction, syntax, style, tone, and point of view. We'll move on to rhetoric and the many types of figurative language, and then discuss circumlocution and euphemism. Finally, we will review irony and satire.

DICTION

The basic definition of **diction** is "word choice." Generally, the diction questions you'll see on the test will ask you to evaluate why an author's choice of words is particularly effective, apt, or clear. However, as we explained in the chapters on the multiple-choice section, more often than not it is the test writer's diction that you have to crack. While knowledge of grammar and usage is almost irrelevant for this exam, a broad vocabulary is a necessity.

Vocabulary is important for both the multiple-choice section AND the essays. Start creating flashcards: write down any unfamiliar words from this book and look up their definitions and write them down on index cards. There is a good chance you will see many of these words on your test!

1. The style of the first paragraph on the previous page can best be described as

    (A) pedantic
    (B) lyrical
    (C) terse
    (D) ludic
    (E) edifying

While it's possible that none of the answers stands out to you as the correct choice, you could rule out "pedantic" if you know that it means narrowly, stodgily, and often ostentatiously learned. Likewise, an AP test and lyricism (intense, intimate display of emotion) make for an unlikely pair, so you can use POE to get rid of that choice too. The test writers slipped "ludic" (pertaining to game, playful) in there in case you wanted to misremember some Latin (*ludus*). Finally, "terse" (concise, without superfluous detail) shows up regularly on this exam but probably doesn't describe the writing in this book very well. Given that the last choice can mean both enlightening and informative, (E) is the best answer.

But as you can see, if you knew none of these words, the question may as well have read as follows:

2. The style of the paragraph above can best be described as

    (A) pompom
    (B) banana
    (C) dog
    (D) tire iron
    (E) Susan

And then which would seem like the correct answer? Obviously, vocabulary is important, so start that vocabulary journal.

SYNTAX

Tactics for Syntax

Syntax is simply another way of talking about grammar and sentence structure.

Syntax is another language term that you should be familiar with for the AP English Language and Composition Exam. Syntax is the ordering of words in a sentence; it describes sentence structure. Syntax is not a topic that excites many high school students—or teachers—and therefore is not discussed very much. However, *syntax* is a word that finds it way onto AP English Language and Composition Exams on a regular basis. Don't worry: you don't need to be an expert on this subject, but you should know how manipulating syntax can enhance an author's meaning, tone, or point of view. Let's look at an example from *Candide,* taken from the famous opening of Chapter 3.

> Never was anything so gallant, so well outfitted, so brilliant, and so finely disposed as the two armies. The trumpets, fifes, reeds, drums, and cannon made such harmony as never was heard in Hell.

The first sentence poses as a fairly simple sketch of a glorious battle scene. The second begins in the same fashion, but its words are arranged in a way that maximizes the effect of surprise that comes at the end of the sentence. The cannons are slipped in as the final member of a list of military musical instruments; the formation of the list creates an expectation that the final element will fit nicely into the set. It doesn't, but we don't have time to register our surprise because we're immediately distracted by a new setup with the phrase "such harmony as never was heard…." We expect harmony to be something beautiful, and we already begin to supply the final word (Earth? Heaven?) when—surprise—we are jolted by the word that Voltaire chose instead: hell. The syntax in this sentence is brilliant.

Here's another slightly different example. In the following example, Candide asks about the proper etiquette for greeting the King of Eldorado through his servant and sidekick, Cacambo.

> When they drew near to the royal chamber, Cacambo asked one of the officers in what manner they were to pay their respects to His Majesty; whether it was the custom to fall upon their knees, or to prostrate themselves upon the ground; whether they were to put their hands upon their heads, or behind their backs; whether they were to lick the dust off the floor; in short, what was the usual ceremony for such occasions.

The syntax of this long sentence is very carefully constructed; Voltaire uses all of the parallel clauses that begin with "whether" to achieve great comic effect. At first, the text is fairly straightforward—after all, going down on one's knees before a king would have been fairly standard for a European reader of the 18th century; however, with each clause, the groveling etiquette becomes more extreme, and the final image—of licking the dust off the floor—pushes the concept beyond the believable. The syntax of this sentence is structured in a way that allows us to see the absurdity of *all* forms of ceremonial deference. In fact, in this story, the enlightened King of Eldorado simply embraces both Cacambo and Candide.

Related to syntax are style, tone, and point of view. As you will read in the next section, these elements work together with syntax to create a "profile" of the speaker that tells us how the speaker or author feels about the subject at hand.

STYLE, TONE, AND POINT OF VIEW

You can count on seeing some combination of the terms *style*, *tone*, and *point of view* in both multiple-choice and essay questions on this exam, so let's make sure you're familiar with their definitions.

> **Style** is the manner of expression. It describes how the author uses language to get his or her point across (e.g., pedantic, scientific, and emotive).
>
> **Tone** is the attitude, mood, or sentiments revealed by the style. Tone describes how the author seems to be feeling (e.g., optimistic, ironic, and playful).
>
> **Point of view** is the stance revealed by the style and the tone of the writing. The author's point of view expresses his or her position on the topic discussed. Point of view can be tricky—sometimes, especially in works of fiction, it is difficult to determine point of view, and, thus, you may be left with nothing more to say than "first-person narrator" or "third-person omniscient narrator."

Consider this excerpt.

> Our left fielder couldn't hit the floor if he fell out of bed! After striking out twice (once with the bases loaded!), he grounded into a double-play. My grandmother runs faster than he does! In the eighth inning, he misjudged a routine fly ball, which brought in the winning run. What a jerk! Why didn't the club trade him last week when it was still possible? What's wrong with you guys?

The *style* is simple, direct, unsophisticated, truculent, and even crass. The style helps evoke a simple sentiment: anger. The *tone* is angry, brash, emotional, and even virulent.

The *point of view* is clear; the author appears to be a disgruntled spectator who doesn't like the player at all and wants the team to get rid of him.

Now let's try a sample question with an excerpt from Fyodor Dostoyevsky's *Notes from Underground*.

> The long and the short of it is, gentlemen, that it is better to do nothing! Better conscious inertia!

3.   The tone of the speaker is best characterized as

   (A)   ironic
   (B)   nihilistic
   (C)   reflective
   (D)   optimistic
   (E)   accusatory

You probably immediately eliminated (C) and (D) because the passage did not sound particularly reflective or optimistic. The author is not accusatory, so eliminate (E) as well. Choice (B) may have confused you a bit; nihilism refers to a belief in nothing. (Again notice the importance of vocabulary!) The speaker's tone can indeed be described as more "nihilistic" (referring to nothing) than "ironic," so the correct answer is (B).

RHETORIC AND FIGURATIVE LANGUAGE

Rhetoric is the art of speaking or writing effectively. **Figurative language** is strictly defined as speech or writing that departs from literal meaning to achieve a special effect or meaning. The terms covered later in this section are terms you should know cold before taking the exam. Multiple-choice questions may use them in answer choices, and you are certainly expected to use them in your essays.

Rhetoric

First of all, what *is* rhetoric? It is often referred to as the stylistic devices an author uses to appeal successfully to a specific audience and is usually persuasive in nature. Before we get into the nitty gritty of figurative language and how it's used, let's review the three classical rhetorical appeals—methods of persuasion—you should know for the exam.

Classical Appeals

Aristotle identified three methods of appealing to an audience in order to persuade them to your point of view: *logos*, *pathos*, and *ethos*.

Logos is an appeal to reason and logic. An argument that uses logos to persuade needs to provide things like objective evidence, hard facts, statistics, or logical strategies such as cause and effect to back up its claim. (*Logos* is the root of our word "logic," which is a good way to remember which of the appeals this is!)

Ethos is an appeal to the speaker's credibility—whether he or she is to be believed on the basis of his or her character and expertise. For example, the prosecution in a murder trial might put a renowned psychiatrist on the stand to testify that the defendant is able to identify right and wrong and is thus capable of standing trial. Their argument would be using an appeal to *ethos* to persuade the jury (their audience) that the testimony of this expert is to be trusted. (*Ethos* is related to our word "ethics"—the principles of conduct that govern people and organizations and give them the authority to speak on certain topics.)

Pathos is an appeal to the emotions, values, or desires of the audience. Aristotle felt that, although ideally people would be persuaded by appeals to logic (*logos*, remember?), they would probably most often be persuaded by their emotions and beliefs instead. This is why, in that same murder trial, a defense attorney might tell the jury about the lonely childhood and difficult life of the defendant—he would be appealing to the *pathos* of the audience to convince them that his client should not be convicted. (*Pathos* is also the root of "pathetic," a word we use to describe something that is, shall we say, *suffering* from inferiority.)

Also preparing for the SAT? Check out *Essential SAT Flashcards*, 2nd Edition to help you improve your vocabulary for both tests.

Figurative Language

As we stated at the beginning of this chapter, you don't need to be an expert in rhetoric to ace the AP English Language and Composition Exam; however, you do need to have some understanding of how language works. With the exception of technical manuals (like the one that helped you assemble your entertainment center), few texts are written such that all of their language is meant to be taken literally. Take, for example, the end of one of Abraham Lincoln's inaugural speeches.

> With malice toward none, with charity for all, with firmness in the right as God gives us to see the right, let us strive on to finish the work we are in, to bind up the nation's wounds, to care for him who shall have borne the battle and for his widow and his orphan, to do all which may achieve and cherish a just and lasting peace among ourselves and with all nations.

Are we supposed to take "to bind up the nation's wounds" literally? Of course not. Lincoln has personified our country to make the suffering of particular individuals relatable to all the people of the nation. And what about "him who shall have borne the battle"? Clearly, Lincoln is using the singular (a man) to represent the collective mass of soldiers, and when he adds "his widow and his orphan," we understand that "shall have borne the battle" really means "shall have died in battle." Lincoln personalizes the suffering of this group of people by instead speaking of individual sacrifice, which he knows is far more likely to strike a profound emotional chord in his listeners.

Despite the effectiveness of Lincoln's speech, you should keep in mind that many other perfectly convincing arguments and explanations are conveyed primarily through literal language. On this exam, there's no need for you to strain yourself attempting to use figurative language in the free-response section. But it will be very helpful for you to review the common terms associated with figurative language that we've listed below because you will be obliged to analyze texts that contain figurative language on this test.

With all this in mind, here is a list of some common terms related to figurative language; we've put them in order of their decreasing relevance to the test.

Imagery

For the purposes of this exam, you may consider **imagery** to be synonymous with figurative language. However, in a more restricted sense, imagery is figurative language that is used to convey a sensory perception (visual, auditory, olfactory, tactile, or gustatory).

Hyperbole

Hyperbole is overstatement or exaggeration; it is the use of figurative language that significantly exaggerates the facts for effect. In many instances, but certainly not all, hyperbole is employed for comic effect. Consider the following example.

If you use too much figurative language in your essays, the AP readers will crucify you!

Clearly, this statement is a gross exaggeration; while the readers may give you a poor grade if you use figurative language that doesn't suit the purposes of your essay, they will not kill you.

Understatement

Understatement is figurative language that presents the facts in a way that makes them appear much less significant than they really are. Understatement is almost always used for comic effect.

> After dinner, they came and took into custody Doctor Pangloss and his pupil Candide, the one for speaking his mind and the other for appearing to approve what he heard. They were conducted to separate apartments, which were extremely cool and where they were never bothered by the sun.

Taking the last sentence literally would lead you astray. The understatement in this case ("They were conducted to separate apartments, which were extremely cool and where they were never bothered by the sun") should be taken to mean that the poor men were thrown into horribly dark, dank, and cold prison cells.

Simile

A **simile** is a comparison between two unlike objects, in which the two parts are connected with a term such as *like* or *as*. Here's an example of a simile:

> The birds are like black arrows flying across the sky.

You can easily identify a simile—and distinguish it from a metaphor—because of the use of *like* or *as*.

Metaphor

A **metaphor** is a simile without a connecting term such as *like* or *as*. Here's an example of a metaphor.

> The birds are black arrows flying across the sky.

Birds are not arrows, but the commonalities (both are long and sleek, and they travel swiftly through the air—and both have feathers) allow us to easily grasp the image.

Extended Metaphor

An **extended metaphor** is precisely what it sounds like—it is a metaphor that lasts for longer than just one phrase or sentence. A word of caution for the exam, however; do not use extended metaphors in your own AP essays, for many scholars (and many AP graders) believe that the extended metaphor is a poor expository or argumentative technique. Consider this example:

> During the time I have voyaged on this ship, I have avoided the cabin; rather, I have remained on deck, battered by wind and rain, but able to see moonlight on the water. I do not wish to go below decks now.

As surprising as this may seem, this passage is not about nautical navigation. The ship's voyage is the central metaphor (representing the course of life); the writer extends the metaphor by relating elements of figurative language: cabin, deck, wind and rain, moonlight, water, and decks. The cabin is a safe place, but it's a place where you can't experience much; on deck, you're exposed to the elements, but you can experience beauteous sights. Having made the difficult, dangerous, but rewarding choice of staying on deck, it would be a personal defeat, a kind of surrender to wish for the safety, comfort, and limited horizons of the cabin later in life.

Symbol

A **symbol** is a word that represents something other than itself. Here's an example:

> The Christian soldiers paused to remember the lamb.

In this case, the rough, tough soldiers did not stop to think about the actual animal; the lamb is a traditional Christian symbol for Jesus Christ.

Denotation and Connotation

Denotation refers to a word's primary or literal significance, while **connotation** refers to the vast range of other meanings that a word suggests. Context (and at times, author's intent) determines which connotations may be appropriate for a word. An author will carefully pick a particular word for its connotations, knowing or hoping a reader will make an additional inference as a result. Some literary critics argue that it is impossible to distinguish between denotation and connotation. Who, they ask, is to determine which meaning to assign as a primary significance? Let's move on and look at an example.

> I am looking at the sky.

The denotation of the underlined word should be as clear as a cloudless sky (the space, often blue, above the earth's surface). However, there can be connotations associated with the word. The sky is often associated with heaven; it can also evoke the idea of freedom or vast openness. Because of connotation, one can't help but believe that the sky evokes in the writer a sense of longing for freedom from work, the computer, or the AP English Language and Composition Exam.

Metaphors vs. Symbols

Sometimes, it is difficult to distinguish between metaphor and symbol. Remember that a metaphor always contains an implied comparison between two elements. Recall the metaphorical image of the birds and the arrows: the birds remain birds, and the arrows remain arrows—and the metaphor serves to give us an image of the flight of the birds by suggesting a visualization of arrows. However, in the case of a symbol, the named object really doesn't count. There is no lamb; *lamb* is merely an object that's meant to conjure up another object or element.

Oxymoron

In an oxymoron, two seemingly contradictory words (or sometimes brief phrases) are paired together. However, the two elements only appear to contradict each other. Look deeper, and the contradiction can be resolved.

One common example is "jumbo shrimp." Since "shrimp" is an edible creature as well as a term meaning "small," there is really no contradiction. The oxymoron describes a large version of an edible creature.

What does an oxymoron add to a written work? Look at some other common examples: open secret, civil war, freezer burn, old news, deafening silence. How about the title of George Romero's zombie film, *Night of the Living Dead?* Or Juliet's "Parting is such sweet sorrow" in the first balcony scene from Shakespeare's *Romeo and Juliet?*

As these examples show, oxymorons give authors a couple of tools: a way to describe a new or unusual thing, and economy of expression. For instance, the oxymoron "cold comfort" describes an unusual case in which something (perhaps a friend's comment) that one would expect to be warm and helpful has the opposite effect instead. Notice how many words it just took to describe that concept, compared with the vivid image economically conveyed by the oxymoron "cold comfort."

By using an oxymoron, an author can also jolt readers into paying attention if they've been skimming through the work on autopilot. Something doesn't sound quite right; they go back to reread the seemingly contradictory words and try to figure out what those words mean. Perhaps the readers then pay more attention to the next few paragraphs or pages.

Don't Be a "Moron"!

Oxymorons and paradoxes both involve contradictions, but there are two main differences.

1. The contradiction in an oxymoron is only apparent; it can be resolved. In a paradox, it cannot.

2. Oxymorons almost always involve only words or brief phrases, whereas paradoxes (in written work) involve statements.

Paradox

A paradox contains two elements which cannot both be true at the same time (although usually each one could be true on its own).

The classic example is the Cretan Liar Paradox, attributed to the sixth-century BC philosopher and poet Epimenides. He was from Crete, and his famous paradox says, "All Cretans are liars."

Think about it. He's a Cretan; therefore (if his statement is true), he must also be a liar. But if he's a liar, he can't be making a true statement, so the statement must be false. As you can imagine, many philosophers and logicians have puzzled over how to resolve Epimenides's paradox.

Here's another ancient Greek example, this time from Socrates, the 5th-century BC philosopher: "One thing only I know, and that is that I know nothing." Well if it's true that he knows nothing, then it can't also be true that he knows even that one thing. And if he knows that one thing, it can't be true that he knows nothing.

A great real-life example comes from the 17th-century witch trials. If a woman passed the test, thereby proving she was not a witch, she could live and go free. Failing the test proved she was, indeed, a witch and she was burned at the stake. So far, so good. But here's the test—and the paradox. The suspect was bound, attached to a large rock and thrown into a nearby deep body of water. If she sank to the bottom, that meant the water (symbolizing baptism) accepted her and that she was not a witch. However, since she would have drowned in the process of passing the test and proving her innocence, she could hardly live and go free. If you're innocent, you live but you're dead.

What's the point of putting a paradox in a piece of writing? It depends on the author's purpose and point of view—both of which you should have identified as you were reading the passage.

Perhaps the writer is describing a world—or advancing an argument—where things are not always what they seem. A paradox is a good way to encourage readers to look at familiar things in new ways, or to question their assumptions. The writer might also be asking readers to suspend logical reasoning and use intuition or a more spiritual type of perception instead. Or, quite simply, the author might just be trying to jolt readers out of a habitual, absorption-type mode of reading—to make them think and return to reread and analyze the paradoxical statement.

Whatever the specific reason, the writer is trying to get your attention by using a paradox. You need to figure out why.

Personification

Personification is the figurative device in which inanimate objects or concepts are given human qualities. It can enhance our emotional response because we usually attribute more emotional significance to other humans than to things or concepts. Consider this example of personification:

> He had been wrestling with lethargy for days, and every time that he
> thought that he was close to victory, his adversary escaped his hold.

This figurative wrestling match, in which lethargy is personified as the opponent to the author of this sentence, brings the struggle to life—human life. If you don't believe this, think about the literal alternative: He tried to stop being lethargic, but he was not successful. This doesn't sound very lively.

Anthropomorphism is a specific type of personification wherein animals are given human qualities, i.e., the Fox in Aesop's fables.

Rhetorical Question

A **rhetorical question** is a question whose answer is obvious; these types of questions do not need to be answered—and usually aren't. Rhetorical questions attempt to prove something without actually presenting an argument; sometimes they're used as a form of irony, in which something is stated, but its opposite is meant.

> With all the fast food restaurants in the United States, is it any wonder obesity is on the rise? (no irony)

Since it has already been determined that you agree (even if you don't), the writer need not substantiate this remark.

> Aren't AP exams great fun? (with irony)

Here, there is an assumption that you would answer in the negative, although there is no way for you to respond—unless you write a letter. Rhetorical questions allow a writer to make a point without further support, whether it's a straightforward remark or one with a touch of irony.

Bombast

Bombast (adjective = bombastic) is language that is overly rhetorical (pompous), especially when considered in context. Generally speaking, graduation speeches contain bombast; pedantic people (those who use their learning ostentatiously) tend to use bombast. Occasionally, a passage on the AP English Language and Composition Exam will contain bombast.

We are here in these hallowed halls, accompanied by
genial kin and erudite mentors, surrounded by Corinthian
columns and the three wisdoms of the ages, to celebrate
Line the conjunction of fare thee well and many happy returns
5 and to proffer advice worthy of Athena to these prodigal
sons and daughters as they depart our august institution.
You happy survivors are not graduates, but champions who
have been assailed on all sides by demons of mathematics,
dragons of science, and inhuman beasts of humanities, but
10 who have emerged victorious from each and every battle.
In this respect, one is reminded of Thucydides, who writes:
"So long as a vessel was coming up to charge another boat,
the men on the decks rained darts, arrows, and stones upon
her, but once alongside, the heavy infantry tried to board
15 each other's vessel, fighting hand to hand. In many quarters
it happened, because of the restricted space, that a vessel
was charging an enemy on one side and being charged
herself on another, and that two or even more ships were
entangled all around one, obliging the helmsmen to attend
20 to defense here, offense there, not to one thing at a time,
but to many things on all sides, while the huge commotion
caused by the number of ships crashing together not only
spread terror, but also made the orders of the boatswains
inaudible." I urge you to remember Attica, and to remem-
25 ber the Spartan way.

This passage is marked by pretentious and inflated speech; it is a perfect example of bombast.

Pun

A **pun** is a play on words. In general, a pun either plays on the multiple meanings of a word or replaces one word with another that is similar in sound but very different in meaning. Puns are almost always used for comic effect.

In *Star Wars*, why did the Empire leave the Catholic nuns alone? Force of habit.

If you know anything about the significance of "the Force" in *Star Wars* and about the double meaning of "habit," you'll get the play on words here.

Metonymy and Synecdoche

Both *metonymy* and *synecdoche* are terms that mean the use of figurative language in which characteristics are substituted for the things with which they are associated.

In **metonymy,** one term is substituted for another term with which it is closely associated. Consider this example:

The sailors drank a glass of hearty red.

Red is a color; sailors cannot drink it. However, metonymically, the color represents wine (red wine), which sailors over the age of twenty-one may drink.

Synecdoche is a form of metonymy that's restricted to cases in which a part is used to signify the whole. Here's an example of synecdoche:

All hands on deck!

The hands (part of each sailor) represent the sailors (the whole).

If you have an aversion to learning rhetorical terms, then for the purposes of this exam you can feel free to forget the definition of synecdoche; you can get away with using the term *metonymy* for any situation in which a characteristic of a certain thing is used to represent the thing.

Meto-WHAT?

Don't worry! Metonymy and synecdoche are tested very rarely on the AP English Language and Composition Exam, but you should be familiar with these definitions anyway.

Theme

A **theme** is a general idea contained in a text; the theme may be stated explicitly or only suggested. A theme is not just an idea; it is *an idea that is developed,* often over the course of a chapter or an entire book. Usually, one can identify a central theme and several minor ones. Sometimes both are overtly stated, as in the example that follows:

Many scholars agree that the central theme in *The Adventures of Huckleberry Finn* is the conflict between nature and civilization. But clearly, the book contains other themes, such as the worth of honor and the voyage of self-discovery.

Read the following passage, and see if you can identify a central theme.

We now touch on civilization's most sensitive spot; it is an unpleasant task to raise one's voice against the folly of the day, against chimeras that have caused a downright
Line epidemic.
5 To speak against the absurdities of trade today means to expose oneself to anathemas, just as much as if one had spoken against the tyranny of the popes and the barons in the twelfth century. If it were a matter of choosing between two dangerous roles, I think it would be less dangerous
10 to offend a sovereign with bitter truths than to offend the mercantile spirit that now rules like a despot over civilization—and even over sovereigns!
And yet a superficial analysis will prove that our commercial systems defile and disorganize civilization and that
15 in trade, as in all other things, we are being led further and further astray.
The controversy on trade is barely half a century old and has already produced thousands of books, and yet the participants in the controversy have not seen that the trade
20 mechanism is organized in such a way that it is a slap in the face to all common sense. It has subordinated the whole of society to one class of parasitic and unproductive persons: the merchants. All the essential classes of society—the proprietor, the farmer, the manufacturer, and even the gov-
25 ernment—find themselves dominated by a non-essential, contingent class, the merchant, who should be their subordinate, their employed agent, removable and accountable, and who, nevertheless, directs and obstructs at will all the avenues of circulation.

It should not surprise you that the title of the essay that this passage is excerpted from is "On Trade." In his essay, the French socialist Charles Fourier develops a central theme: merchants, through trade, have both corrupted society and become its tyrant.

Many of the passages in the multiple-choice and free-response sections of the AP exam are long enough to permit you to identify at least one central theme, and you will almost certainly be asked to do so.

Aphorism

An **aphorism** is a concise, pithy statement of an opinion or a general truth.

> Life is short, the art [of medicine] is long, opportunity fleeting, experimentation dangerous, reasoning difficult.

That aphorism is attributed to Hippocrates, the "Father of Medicine." Note that his statement is more sophisticated than the "commonplace wisdom" of a saying like "Haste makes waste."

Malapropism

Malapropism is the unintentional use of a word that resembles the word intended but that has a very different meaning.

> He was a man of great statue.

The AP English Language and Composition readers often collect malapropisms to share with friends and colleagues as they read through the free-response essays; it isn't in your best interest to provide them with any good laughs, so try to avoid them.

There are several literary terms that have similar meanings. The AP will not test you on the minute differences among the terms but rather on your familiarity with them.

Aphorism: "Power tends to corrupt, and absolute power corrupts absolutely." (Lord Acton)

Adage/Proverb: "Nothing ventured, nothing gained."

Maxim: "Where there's life, there's hope."

Motto: "All the news that's fit to print." *(The New York Times)*

CIRCUMLOCUTION AND EUPHEMISM

Circumlocution has two meanings, and you should be familiar with both of them. For the purposes of this exam, we'll say that one meaning of circumlocution is "talking around a subject" and that the other is "talking around a word."

It is entirely possible that you have used circumlocution when addressing your parents. For instance, instead of simply asking them straight out if you may borrow the car, have you ever said something such as, "I understand that you guys are going to stay in tonight and watch a DVD, right? If so, since I've already seen that movie, I was thinking about maybe going downtown. It's a nice summer evening and all that, but it's still too far to walk, and I'll be with Nina, anyway, and she'd never agree to walk downtown. We were thinking that she could drive, but, unfortunately, Nina's parents are going out, so she can't take their car. I know that I forgot to put gas in your car the last time that I drove to the mountains, but I learned my lesson. That won't happen again." You may even have gone on speaking for longer. You might never have gotten to the point where you actually asked to borrow the car, but your parents understood what you wanted and put you out of your misery by saying something such as, "We already told your sister that she could use the car tonight."

On the AP English Language and Composition Exam, you're more likely to encounter the second type of circumlocution—"talking around a word"—that is, using several words or a phrase in place of a specific word (or specific words). You may have noticed that sometimes it is more effective to be wordy than to be precise. For example, some people consider their automobiles cars, and, not surprisingly, they refer to these objects just as cars. Other people, however, use evocative circumlocutions when referring to their heap of metal—one of which is "cruisin' machine" (and the other of which is "heap of metal"). The point is that circumlocution is often an effective means for communicating points of view. Take a look at the following sentence.

> Candide was court-martialed, and he was asked which he liked better, to run the gauntlet six and thirty times through the whole regiment, or to have his brains blown out with a dozen musket-balls.

In this sentence, we read that in a spirit of compassion and justice, the military court is giving Candide a choice: He may choose to be either beaten to death or executed by firing squad. The wording of the second choice, in particular, provides a wonderful example of the evocative power of well-used circumlocution. While using the phrase "execution by firing squad" would have allowed both the author and the reader to remain distant from the event and dispassionate, the circumlocution that the author employed with "to have his brains blown out with a dozen musket-balls" vividly describes the horror and brutality of the event. In this sentence, Voltaire succeeds in relating his feelings about the court-martial without commenting on it.

A **euphemism** is a word or words that are used to avoid employing an unpleasant or offensive term. Again, you probably (hopefully) use euphemisms all the time. In both fiction and nonfiction, the most common euphemisms have to do with sex. In these cases, the author knows what he or she means, you know what he or she means, and the author knows that you know what he or she means. Let's look at another example from Voltaire's *Candide*. In this passage, Voltaire uses euphemism for comic effect.

> One day when Mademoiselle Cunégonde went to take a walk in a little neighboring wood that was called a park, she saw—through the bushes— the sage Doctor Pangloss giving a lecture in experimental philosophy to her mother's chambermaid, a little brown wench, very pretty and very accommodating.

Voltaire knows that his readers know what is really going on here. This particular example of euphemism is used for comic effect rather than direct avoidance of the word *sex*. One may expect Pangloss to limit his sagacity to philosophical matters, but clearly his "lecture in experimental philosophy" is most prosaic.

IRONY AND SATIRE

When reading the passages on the AP English Language and Composition Exam, you cannot always take what you see at face value; in fact, when reading, you must always be on the lookout for slightly or very veiled meanings behind the words.

Isn't It Ironic?

Irony: Most people use the term without really knowing its definition. Alanis Morissette's 1996 song about irony didn't help the situation. If you don't believe this, ask one of your friends to define irony and see what kind of answer you receive. The two basic types of irony that you'll need to be familiar with for this test are verbal irony and situational irony.

Verbal Irony

Verbal irony refers to the process of stating something but *meaning* the opposite of what is stated. Verbal irony can refer to irony that's used in spoken language as well as in print. In spoken language, intonation is often a clue to ironic intent; however, in writing, it is not possible to imply things through intonation, so there's always a danger that the irony may be missed; in essence, the writer who employs irony risks communicating the exact opposite of what is intended. For example, let's say that you write, "This Princeton Review book is really interesting." Unless your listener or reader hears your remark in context, he or she won't know if this is high praise for this book, or if you're bored silly and have chosen to express your sentiment more forcefully by using verbal irony.

Consider the following excerpt, again from *Candide*. The philosopher Pangloss has just given a rather personalized history of venereal disease, a veritable uncontrollable—and uncontrolled—plague in 18th-century Europe.

> "O sage Pangloss," cried Candide, "what a strange genealogy is this! Is not the devil at the root of it all?"

> "Not at all," replied the great man, "it was unavoidable, a necessary ingredient in the best of worlds."

The student Candide shows sincere respect for Pangloss when he addresses him as "sage Pangloss"; Candide has no ironic intent. However, the same cannot be said of the narrator—who for all intents and purposes is Voltaire. In *Candide,* one of Voltaire's principal aims is to excoriate (to censure scathingly) the "philosophers of optimism," of whom Pangloss is a caricature. He does this through the frequent use of verbal irony; in the passage above, his use of "great man" is ironic—even though Candide's tone is not. After all, neither the narrator nor the careful reader views Pangloss as a great man—he is just the opposite.

Rain on Your Wedding Day

Irony is not mere misfortune. It is a set of circumstances that wind up the opposite of how the reader would expect them to turn out or how the characters had planned.

In essence, to fully appreciate the passage, we must read in stereo, simultaneously picking up on Candide's serious tone and the narrator's ironic tone. This is a pretty complicated case of verbal irony.

Sarcasm is simply verbal irony used with the intent to injure. It's often impossible to discern between irony and sarcasm, and, more often than not, sarcasm is in the mind of the beholder. Let's say that your close friend and soccer teammate missed a wide-open goal from ten feet away, and you smiled and shouted, "Nice shot!" Presumably your friend, used to your jests, would interpret your quip as playful irony. If the opposing team's goalie said the same words, however, it is far more likely that your friend would take the remark as sarcasm—and reply with a not-so-kind word or two. In written form, irony and sarcasm can be considered to be fairly synonymous—but just think of sarcasm as malicious. Here is an example from Henrik Ibsen's *Hedda Gabbler*.

Brack: There's a possibility that the appointment may be decided by competition—

Tesman: Competition! By Jove, Hedda, fancy that!

Hedda: [*motionless in her chair*] How exciting, Tesman.

Of course, it is easier to see the sarcasm when you are familiar with the play, but it is sufficient for you to know that Tesman is the rather boring, plodding husband and that Hedda is an unfulfilled wife. The stage direction ("motionless in her chair") helps us see that her words are at least full of irony; if you add the bitter, malignant intent, which the husband misses but we do not, then you have sarcasm.

Situational Irony

Situational irony refers to a circumstance that runs contrary to what was expected.

Suppose you live in Seattle during the rainy season and plan a vacation to sunny Phoenix. While you are in Phoenix, it rains every day there, but is sunny the entire week in Seattle. This is situational irony.

Situational Irony

A simple example of situational irony can be found in the classic tale "The Gift of the Magi." Jim and Delia are a poor couple who have no money to buy each other gifts for Christmas. Jim sells his watch to buy Delia a comb for her hair. Delia sells her hair to buy Jim a watch-chain. Both gifts wind up useless to their respective recipients—the ultimate in irony.

Satire

In **satire,** something is portrayed in a way that's deliberately distorted to achieve comic effect. Implicit in most satire is the author's desire to critique what is being mocked. Voltaire's *Candide* is principally a satire of optimism, the philosophy that, given that the first "cause" was perfect (God's creation of the world), all causes and effects must naturally be part of this original perfect plan. The French satirist takes on many other causes, however, and one of his favorite targets is the part of religion that he considers no more than fanatical superstition. Here is what happens after Candide and Pangloss are caught in the infamous earthquake of Lisbon, Portugal.

After the earthquake, which had destroyed three-fourths of the city of Lisbon, the sages of that country could think of no better manner to preserve the kingdom from complete
Line ruin than to entertain the people with an *auto-da-fe,* it hav-
5 ing been decided by the University of Coimbra that burning a few people alive over low heat and with great ceremony is an infallible way to prevent earthquakes.

 In consequence, they had seized a Biscayan for marrying his godmother and two Portuguese for taking out the bacon
10 of a larded chicken they were eating; after dinner, they came and took into custody Doctor Pangloss and his pupil Candide, the one for speaking his mind and the other for appearing to approve what he heard. They were conducted to separate apartments, which were extremely cool and
15 where they were never bothered by the sun. Eight days later, they were each dressed in a *sanbenito* and their heads were adorned with paper *mitres.* The *mitre* and *sanbenito* worn by Candide were painted with upside down flames and with devils that had neither tails nor claws, but Doctor
20 Pangloss's devils had both tails and claws, and his flames were right side up. In these clothes they marched in the procession and heard a very pathetic sermon, which was followed by an anthem accompanied by bagpipes. Candide was flogged to the beat of the music while the anthem was
25 being sung; the Biscayan and the two men who would not eat bacon were burned, and Pangloss was hanged, which is not a common custom at these solemnities. The same day there was another earthquake, which created the most dreadful havoc.

After the real earthquake of 1755, there were real *auto-da-fes* ("acts of faith"), during which "evil" inhabitants of Lisbon were sacrificed to appease God, who, ostensibly (to all outward appearances), had provoked the earthquake to punish the city. The "evils" that are being punished say more about the ridiculous prejudices of the persecutors than they do about the so-called evil victims. The two Portuguese who refrained from eating the bacon are guilty of nothing—but they are taken for Jews; the man who married his godmother, who, presumably, is not tied to him by blood, is guilty of no more than infringing on a technicality of the religious code (Catholicism, in this case).

Note that the satire is heightened by Voltaire's use of verbal irony ("the sages"), situational irony (right after the ceremony there is a second earthquake), and a comical circumlocution ("burning a few people alive over low heat and with great ceremony" is a circumlocution for *auto-da-fe*). Satire can be effective in both fiction and nonfiction, and *Candide,* a philosophical story that combines both, is thought to be one of the most brilliant satires of all.

The following terms are similar, but not identical. Know the differences.

Satire: A social or political criticism that relies heavily on irony, sarcasm, and often humor

Parody: Imitation for comic effect

Lampoon: Sharp ridicule of the behavior or character of a person or institution

Caricature: A ludicrous exaggeration of the defects of persons or things

Most critics, however, relegate satire—and satirists—to a secondary sphere in the universe of writing; satire makes for good entertainment, but mocking others does not measure up to the conviction of cogent writing. Had Voltaire been nothing more than a satirist, he would not have been remembered as a brilliant *philosophe,* but as a clever joker—if he were remembered at all. Although Voltaire's satire in *Candide* is quite brilliant, some other examples of satire are a little easier to figure out. Let's look at a sample question based on a passage from Jonathan Swift's *Gulliver's Travels.*

> For about seventy moons past there have been two struggling parties in this empire, under the names of *Tramecksan* and *Slamecksan,* from the high and low heels
> *Line* of their shoes, by which they distinguish themselves. It is
> 5 alleged, indeed, that the high heels are most agreeable to our ancient constitution; but, however this be, his majesty has determined to make use only of low heels in the administration of the government, and all offices in the gift of the crown, as you cannot but observe; and particularly that his
> 10 majesty's imperial heels are lower at least by a *drurr* than any of his court (*drurr* is a measure about the fourteenth part of an inch). The animosities between these two parties run so high, that they will neither eat, nor drink, nor talk with each other. We compute the *Tramecksan*, or high
> 15 heels, to exceed us in number; but the power is wholly on our side. We apprehend his imperial highness, the heir to the crown, to have some tendency towards the high heels; at least we can plainly discover that one of his heels is higher than the other, which gives him a hobble in his gait.

4. The above passage is an example of

   (A) an analysis of court customs
   (B) a satire of British footwear
   (C) a study of British eccentricities
   (D) a satire of the British court
   (E) a nonsensical account of life at court

Well, the correct answer must be either (B) or (D) because this section is all about satire. The correct answer is (D). The passage serves to satirize the Whig-Tory discord (the Whigs dominated politics during much of the 18th century) and the relationship of the "parties" (the Whigs and Tories were not really political parties as we know them today) and the king. Unless you recognize that the passage is satirical, you will not have a good grasp of what is going on—which will lead to major problems with all of the multiple-choice questions on that passage.

REFLECT

Respond to the following questions:

- For which topics discussed in this chapter do you feel you have achieved sufficient mastery to answer multiple-choice questions correctly?

- For which topics discussed in this chapter do you feel you have achieved sufficient mastery to discuss effectively in an essay?

- For which topics discussed in this chapter do you feel you need more work before you can answer multiple-choice questions correctly?

- For which topics discussed in this chapter do you feel you need more work before you can discuss them effectively in an essay?

- What parts of this chapter are you going to re-review?

- Will you seek further help, outside of this book (such as a teacher, tutor, or AP Students website), on any of the topics in this chapter—and, if so, on which ones?

Chapter 9
Rhetorical Fallacies

THE RHETORICAL FALLACY TRAP

Have you ever seen commercials or billboard ads showing a happy, carefreecrowd walking on a blissful beach at a 5-star resort? Don't they always seem to be enjoying a wonderful vacation, enticing you to want to also take a vacation at that same resort?

Ads like this rely on rhetorical fallacy: a way to persuade you to buy into what they are selling. They don't explain the advantages of the resort. Instead, they promote the resort by showcasing a fun-loving couple on the beach. The people in the ad might not be anything like you; their lives might be completely different from yours. Who's to say your experience would be the same if you were to visit the same resort? This is a prime example of how rhetorical fallacy is used in everyday life.

A rhetorical fallacy is basically faulty reasoning leading to a conclusion the advertiser, author, or speaker wants you to make. They pop up often—in ads, in statements by politicians, in appeals from charities, in arguments from your own friends and family. Skilled communicators such as political speech writers use them deliberately. Others use them unconsciously—the conclusion seems so obvious to them that "everybody else has one" sounds like irrefutable evidence. You might have used rhetorical fallacies subconsciously, too.

Rhetorical fallacies also pop up on the AP English Language and Composition Exam, since this test covers how language works and how it is used. A rhetorical fallacy uses (or rather, *mis*-uses) language in order to trick you into accepting the author's conclusion. This conclusion appears to be truth at first but the evidence supporting it crumbles when your active reading or listening skills kick in. You then ask yourself, "*why* should I do or believe this?".

> On the test, you might find rhetorical fallacies lurking in the passages for the multiple-choice questions or in the sources provided for the synthesis and analysis essays. You need to be able to recognize them so you won't be led astray in your answers. You also need to avoid them in your own essays.

Spotting and Avoiding Rhetorical Fallacies

Think of a rhetorical fallacy as "fake evidence." It seems to support a conclusion that the author wants the reader to accept, but—on close examination—it doesn't really lead to that conclusion.

You can identify rhetorical fallacies (and avoid them in your own work) by following this process:

1. Identify the conclusion. What position does the author want you to accept? What action does the author want you to take? What inference does he or she want you to draw?

2. Identify the evidence. How does the author lead you to that conclusion? What does the author present as evidence that the conclusion is correct?

3. Examine the evidence. Is it
    a. relevant to the conclusion?
    b. accurate?
    c. credible?
    d. logical?
    e. complete?

If it's not, then you've likely encountered a rhetorical fallacy.

Common Rhetorical Fallacies

Let's look at some common types of rhetorical fallacies so you can understand how they try to mislead you. The name of each specific fallacy is given, but what's most important for the exam is being able to recognize faulty reasoning when you see it, and avoiding it in the essays you write.

Emphasizing the Person

In this class of rhetorical fallacies, the evidence focuses on the person who supports a conclusion, not on the merits of the conclusion itself.

Ad Populum or **"bandwagon":** A certain political candidate is ahead in the polls. Since most people are going to vote for him, you should, too. Otherwise you'll just be wasting your vote.

The happy crowd on the beach described at the beginning of this chapter is another instance of the "bandwagon" fallacy. All of these people are having a great vacation at this resort; you should go there and you'll have fun, too.

The conclusion is an action the author (or the advertiser) wants you to take—vote for this candidate, book a vacation at this resort. No support is provided to explain *why* the candidate is the best choice, or *why* the resort is better than others. The very thin evidence is only that others are doing it.

Argument from Authority: Dr. X recommends this medication to his patients, or well-known musician Y always drives this brand of car. Are they being paid by the manufacturers to endorse those products, or do the products have attributes that really make them superior? You'll never know. This rhetorical fallacy focuses solely on the credentials or fame of the person recommending the product, without saying anything about the product itself.

And watch those credentials – is Dr. X really a recognized specialist in the illness the medication is intended to treat? What does musician Y know about cars?

Ad Hominem: This rhetorical fallacy turns to the other side of the coin and points out negative characteristics of the person who promotes an idea or action. By implication, the action is as negative as the person who endorses it. The mayor was caught plagiarizing an essay in college and was accused of embezzlement by a former employer. Therefore, his claim that municipal taxes must increase to cover necessary road repairs has to be a lie and an attempt to steal taxpayers' money. Nothing is said about the actual condition of the roads.

Dogmatism: The conclusion must be correct because the author or speaker says it is and she can't possibly be wrong. After all, she is an internationally recognized authority on the subject, or she is the CEO of the most profitable company on the planet. She wouldn't have risen to that position if she were ever wrong. No other reasons are presented to support the conclusion, and no opposing viewpoints are even considered.

Presenting Only Part of the Truth

Equivocation: This type of fallacy leaves out facts that a reader or listener would need in order to make a thorough assessment of the conclusion. Equivocation often relies on ambiguous definitions of words.

For example, your home insurer might say that for an extra $50 premium, you'll be covered for $100,000 in water damage. Look at the "definitions" section of your policy, though, and you might see that the insurer considers "water damage" to be damage caused by a sewer backup. "Overland flooding" or "ice dams on roof" are separate categories that are not covered. You probably assumed those events would all result in "water damage," and the insurer is counting on that to lead you to the conclusion that it's worth spending the extra $50.

> In the movie *Pink Panther*, Inspector Clouseau enters a quaint European hotel and, upon spying a cute little dog, asks the owner, "Does your dog bite?" The manager responds, "No," and Clouseau attempts to pet the dog, which growls and bites him. "You told me that your dog does not bite!" exclaims Clouseau. "That's not my dog," responds the owner.

Sentimental Appeals: Charities often use this tactic when they ask for donations. Poor, starving children living in deplorable surroundings, or clear-cut hillsides that were once covered by beautiful forests—these scenes appeal to your emotions rather than your intellect. This rhetorical fallacy omits rational explanations about why the charity deserves your donation. What has it achieved recently to right the wrong it presents? How much of your donation is used for its programs, and how much goes into executive salaries or "team-building" events? How much is it spending in order to raise the donations it's seeking?

You're My Hero— or Not

"Argument from Authority" is really "*Ad Hominum*" turned upside down.

Arousing Fear

Slippery Slope: It may seem minor now, but the end result will inevitably be a catastrophe. According to this rhetorical fallacy, if you eat at a fast-food takeout once, pretty soon you'll never want to eat healthy, nourishing home-cooked meals again. Therefore, you can never allow yourself to eat at a fast-food takeout, not even once. The author uses the fear of the disaster waiting at the bottom of the slippery slope to trick the reader into agreeing that the first action must not be allowed to occur.

Scare Tactics: Here the speaker or author is trying to frighten you into agreeing with him. If you don't commit to a two-year contract, your monthly rate won't be protected and prices are going to go through the roof in the next couple of years. Who says? On what evidence does he make that prediction?

Weakening an Opposing Argument

These rhetorical fallacies present an opposing view in such a weak light that almost nobody would agree with it. Readers would, instead, accept the author's apparently stronger conclusion.

Red Herring: Instead of addressing the key issues of an opposing argument, a red herring fallacy focuses attention on an insignificant or irrelevant factor. For instance, you should avoid eating green vegetables (the conclusion) because of the risk of salmonella contamination (the red herring). This fallacy avoids the main points of the opposing argument in favor of green vegetables (such as nutritional content and health benefits).

Straw Man: The writer creates a straw man—something that's easy to knock down and tear apart—as the opposing viewpoint. The straw man could be either an over-simplification of an opponent's position, or a completely fictitious argument. In contrast, the writer's conclusion seems strong and reasonable.

For instance, suppose the mayor wants taxpayers to fund a new bridge that will lead directly to a large new subdivision. People who oppose this expense, she says, don't believe the new bridge is necessary because subdivision residents can simply spend an extra half hour driving downtown, across the existing bridge and back up the other side of the river to the new subdivision. That opposing viewpoint is pretty easy to knock down if you live, work, or shop in the new subdivision, so of course you favor a new bridge.

Making Inaccurate Connections

Faulty analogy: One thing is compared to a second thing, but the comparison is exaggerated or misleading or unreasonable. Nevertheless, that comparison colors the reader's impression of the first thing. "Hiking on that trail is like descending into a dungeon of horrors from which you might never return." Perhaps it's just a challenging trail that leads through thick woods and would give you a good workout. But not many people would try it after hearing the speaker's comparison.

Faulty causality (also called *Post hoc ergo propter hoc*): This type of fallacy assumes that because one event happened shortly before another, the first event must have caused the second. (That's what the long Latin name refers to, by the way). "She wore her old Brand X runners instead of her new Brand Y runners, therefore she lost the race." Well, maybe. But perhaps she lost the race because she hadn't trained sufficiently, or because her knee was sore that day, or because others were simply faster. No evidence is presented to prove that the first event caused the second.

Twisting the Language

Begging the Question: In this rhetorical fallacy, an assumption which is not proven is used as evidence that the conclusion is correct. For instance, "high-altitude skiing is such a dangerous sport (the evidence) that no one under the age of 18 should be allowed to do it (the conclusion)." That might be a logical argument if the writer had proven—with statistics or with specific examples—that high-altitude skiing is dangerous for young people in particular. But he doesn't. He states that assumption as if it were a proven fact and then uses the assumption to prove his conclusion.

Circular Argument: This fallacy says essentially the same thing in both the conclusion and in the evidence that allegedly supports it. For example, someone might say that Sally cares about other people (the conclusion) because she is always willing to help them (the evidence). Someone who is always willing to help others obviously cares about them. Both the conclusion and the evidence describe the same idea. If the speaker had given specific examples of times when Sally helped someone else, and other actions that show she cares about others, he would have provided more credible proof for his conclusion.

Rhetorical fallacies in this category can be tough to spot, particularly when you're reading quickly under pressure. You need keen active reading skills to be able to say, "wait a minute, how do you know that piece of evidence is true?" or "didn't your evidence and your conclusion just say the same thing in different words?".

Mismatch Between Evidence and Conclusion

Missing the point: The author offers evidence that supports a conclusion—it's just not the same conclusion that the author reaches. Imagine a presenter with gorgeous slides of meadows and grasslands in the northern plains, dense forests and subarctic tundra—the preferred habitats of grizzly bears. She cites research that reveals the grizzly population is declining and being pushed into smaller and smaller territories as humans take over the bears' habitats for their own uses. As a result, she continues, we should experiment with relocating small groups of grizzlies to see if they can adapt to habitats where they won't get so much competition from humans for use of the land. She suggests wetlands and high up on western mountains.

Her evidence does support the conclusions that we should take steps to protect the remaining grizzly population and should be more conscious of the impact our land use has on other creatures. However, it doesn't lead to a radical relocation scheme that ignores factors such as food sources, climate, and the bears' likely reaction.

Non Sequitur: This Latin term means, "it doesn't follow." In this rhetorical fallacy, the conclusion is not logically related to the evidence that preceded it. "Violent crime in this city has increased by 10 percent year over year for the past five years. Adding to the police force hasn't improved the situation. Therefore, we should build more private schools."

What do private schools have to do with the violent crime rate? Perhaps more than half of violent crimes occur around schools, private schools have the money for much better security measures, and the existing private schools all have long waiting lists. The author doesn't explain that, though; he has left serious gaps in the connection between his evidence and his conclusion.

It's easy to fall into this fallacy in your own work when the conclusion seems obvious to you. Think about your readers, though—would they need a few more steps before they could follow you to your conclusion?

Unstated Assumptions

Conclusions in this class of rhetorical fallacies rest on assumptions that the author doesn't even state, let alone prove. These, too, can be tough to spot in a pressure-cooker exam setting.

False Dichotomy: This rhetorical fallacy assumes a black-and-white world in which there is no middle ground, no other alternative. "If we don't launch a preemptive attack and destroy the enemy first, they will destroy us." No consideration is given to other possibilities, such as a diplomatic solution or a small-scale limited strike.

Hasty Generalization: Here the author or speaker assumes that a limited experience foreshadows the entire experience. The result is insufficient evidence to support the conclusion. "I could tell from the first few minutes that the movie was going to be unbearably boring, so I left rather than waste any more of my time." Maybe the director deliberately starts off slowly in order to intensify viewers' reactions to the terrifying monster that is about to appear.

Non-testable hypothesis: In this rhetorical fallacy, anything that has not been proven false is assumed to be true; the author doesn't need to prove it's true. For example, suppose an environmental group claims that average temperatures across the entire North American continent would fall by 1° Celsius if we switched completely to renewable energy. Since we have never abandoned fossil fuels entirely, it's impossible to prove that the group's claim is false. Therefore, the argument assumes it must be true.

You Can't Prove I'm Not Right

The absence of evidence to the contrary does not, in fact, prove anything.

Drill – Catch the Rhetorical Fallacies

The following examples are similar to parts of passages you might encounter in the multiple-choice section of the AP English Language and Composition Exam, or to parts of the sources given in the essay questions. Before you read the explanation that follows each selection, try to identify how the author is misleading you into reaching the conclusion he or she wants you to accept. Remember to look for the claim or action or belief that the author is endorsing. Then find and assess the evidence the author presents. And think about how your answer on the exam might be different depending on whether you noticed the rhetorical fallacy or not.

(Hint: One example does not contain a rhetorical fallacy. See if you can identify that one, too.)

In this selection, a detective is questioning a woman in order to gather evidence about a crime he is investigating.

> … it is on me that all this weight lies. If the police begin investigations they come close upon the fact that I went there to meet a man whom my husband has forbidden me to meet. Any little turn of evidence that involves me, any little accident that obliges me to admit it, and I am lost,"—her voice thrilled and pleaded.

> "It is you who are lost," he echoed dully. "I can understand how you feel. If I can ease your burden or lessen the anxiety you suffer from, you may depend upon me, Mrs. Wilder. This matter is a dark road where I, too, walk blind, not knowing the path I follow, but, at least, I can give you my word that under no circumstances shall I be led to mention your name. You can be sure of that, Mrs. Wilder. If I can add your trouble to my own burden I shall not feel its weight, …

> Excerpt from *The Pointing Man: A Burmese Mystery*
> by Marjorie Douie, 1920

Now suppose a multiple-choice question asks:

> What technique does the detective use to try to gain Mrs. Wilder's confidence?
>
> (A) Deceit
> (B) Sympathy
> (C) Threats
> (D) Empathy
> (E) Begging

What conclusion is Mrs. Wilder supposed to reach?—that it's safe to answer the detective's questions. He won't tell anyone who gave him the information, so Mr. Wilder won't find out that his wife met the forbidden man. What evidence does the detective offer to support that conclusion? None. Mrs. Wilder can count on him keeping her name out of the investigation because she can depend on him (circular argument). She should believe him because he understands how she feels (non-testable hypothesis) and because he says she can (dogmatism).

Choices (C) and (E) are clearly not supported in the passage. If you didn't notice the rhetorical fallacies, though, you might be tempted to choose (D) or perhaps (B), both of which are incorrect. If you spotted the faulty evidence, you'd know the correct choice is (A). The detective's only objective is to get answers to his questions, and he'll tell this frightened woman whatever she needs to hear before she'll answer them.

This paragraph appears in "Maintenance and Safety of Hybrid and Plug-In Electric Vehicles," a resource from the U.S. Department of Energy's Vehicle Technologies Office. It is the type of source you might find in the synthesis essay question.

Safety Requirements

HEVs [hybrid electric vehicles], PHEVs [plug-in hybrid electric vehicles], and EVs [all-electric vehicles] have high-voltage electrical systems that typically range from 100 to 600 volts. Their battery packs are encased in sealed shells and meet testing standards that subject batteries to conditions such as overcharge, vibration, extreme temperatures, short circuit, humidity, fire, collision, and water immersion. Manufacturers design these vehicles with insulated high-voltage lines and safety features that deactivate the electrical system when they detect a collision or short circuit. EVs tend to have a lower center of gravity than conventional vehicles, making them more stable and less likely to roll over.

Suppose the synthesis prompt asked you to defend, challenge, or qualify the claim that electric vehicles are unsafe. How would you evaluate this excerpt when you're choosing sources for your essay? Is it a strong, reliable source, or does it contain faulty reasoning that misleads you into accepting a conclusion?

Start by identifying the conclusion: electric vehicles are safer than you might think because of the safety features designers have built into them. Now what evidence does the author give to support that conclusion? The selection lists specific examples of safety features (such as sealed cases and automatic shutoff) intended to shield people from the dangers of high voltage. It also describes a design feature (low center of gravity) that helps prevent instability and rollovers. And it acknowledges the high voltage instead of trying to hide the danger.

This author gives relevant, specific, logical evidence supporting the conclusion, and does not resort to rhetorical fallacies. This would be a good choice as one of your sources.

The following excerpt from a mobile app's End User License Agreement (EULA) illustrates the type of source you might see in the analysis essay question, for which you're asked to identify the strategies an author uses to achieve his or her purpose.

Bazaar Bonanza is a free, powerful, user-friendly tool to get you to the best deals on things that will make your life easier, more fulfilling and just plain more fun. Millions of users are saving money and time on products they want and need with Bazaar Bonanza. We take your privacy very seriously, and are committed to providing you with choice and transparency. We'd like you to know about the benefits you'll gain when you create an account and download our app.

In order to make sure you never miss a great deal, we track your location and maintain a database of your favorite places and the times and days you usually visit them. We also access your contacts, your messages and your emails because we know you'll want to share amazing bargains with your friends and family members. Since you'll want to return to the same shops that offered outstanding deals in the past, we track and store data about all of the purchases you make via a mobile payment service. Over time, we build a complete profile of your travel and shopping habits. So we can provide you with an ever-expanding universe of wonderful products and services at unbelievable prices, we share your profile with other companies that may be of interest to you. We also give those companies access to your reviews and endorsements so they can share them with other users who may be looking for similar deals.

What rhetorical strategies is this author using to achieve her purpose of gaining new users? Are rhetorical fallacies among those strategies?

This excerpt is full of rhetorical fallacies. First is the bandwagon ("millions of users") and then dogmatism—there's no evidence that the company values the privacy of its users or that it is offering them any choice. It's true because the company says it's true. The commitment to transparency is actually well supported, though, in the extensive list of data the company collects and descriptions of what it does with that data. Next comes a scare tactic (missing a great deal). Then there are a few *non sequiturs*—for instance, if you want to share information about bargains with your friends, why does it follow that the app needs access to your contacts and messages? Throughout the entire excerpt is the unstated assumption that your desire to find a deal outweighs your desire to protect your personal information.

This is the type of prompt you might see in the argument essay question:

In order to save time, reduce costs, and avoid security risks, many companies are encouraging their employees to substitute technology (such as video conferencing) for business trips that can involve long absences, expensive travel, and potentially dangerous locations. In contrast, some executives and sales professionals claim there's no substitute for the personal relationships they can develop through meeting someone face to face or attending an industry event in person. Political leaders often seem to agree, traveling halfway around the world for a meeting that might last only an hour or two.

Think about the trade-off between savings and security on the one hand, and the gains that can result from an in-person meeting on the other. Then write an essay explaining your position on whether travel is worth the costs and risks. Use appropriate evidence from your reading, experience, or observations to support your argument.

Before you read the suggestions below, consider what position you would take on this question. Then think about the conclusions you'll need to persuade readers so they can follow your argument and eventually agree with it.

You could argue for using technology, for in-person travel or—most likely in this case—for a combination of the two. You might say, for example, that travel is justified for an initial meeting or two in order to establish a personal relationship, but after that, little more would be gained from the expense and potential risks of traveling to meet in person. Electronic communication or phone calls would serve the purpose.

To lead readers to agree with this argument, you'll need to get them to concede that travel is expensive, time-consuming, and depending on the destination, can be dangerous. They'll have to acknowledge the importance of saving money, saving time, and avoiding risks. They also need to accept that an in-person relationship can form a foundation that leads to a better outcome in later long-distance dealings.

Now what evidence can you use to support each of those conclusions? And how can you avoid rhetorical fallacies in presenting that evidence? This prompt is particularly vulnerable to fallacies that emphasize the person or group instead of the merits of an idea, to fallacies that arouse fear, and to mismatches between the evidence and the conclusion.

Under the time pressure of the exam, you won't have time to do a thorough assessment of your evidence for each conclusion. But as you're writing, you can ask yourself if you're really addressing the conclusion itself, or only the people who would advocate that course of action. Are you trying to frighten readers by describing the consequences that might result from not following your recommendation? Have you left any gaps in the evidence that leads to your conclusion? Are you covering the key issues and most relevant aspects of the topic?

> Don't let clever rhetorical fallacies lead you down the wrong path!

Rhetorical fallacies can be very convincing. They're also easy errors to make in your own writing, particularly when you have a strong opinion about a subject, when you're making broad claims or when you're experiencing stress during an exam. By training yourself to think in terms of relevant, complete, logically presented evidence, you can avoid falling into the trap of believing—or creating—rhetorical fallacies.

Another Course? Of Course!

If you can't get enough AP English Language and Composition and want to review this material with an expert, we also offer an online Cram Course that you can sign up for here: www.princetonreview.com/college/ap-test-prep.

REFLECT

Respond to the following questions:

- Do you understand how rhetorical fallacies work? How they can trick people?

- Are there any types of rhetorical fallacies that you are particularly susceptible to believing?

- Are there any types of rhetorical fallacies that you tend to use automatically when you're trying to convince a listener or reader to agree with your argument?

- What are the characteristics of valid evidence?

- What techniques could you use to avoid rhetorical fallacies in your own work?

- How can you avoid rhetorical fallacies when you're writing essays under the time pressure of the AP English Language and Composition Exam?

- For which topics in this chapter do you feel you need more practice or more examples?

Chapter 10
Basic Rhetorical Modes

WHAT ARE RHETORICAL MODES?

The rhetorical modes (or patterns) contained in this chapter are worth studying for two reasons. First, they will provide you with ready-made approaches for writing your essays on the exam, and second, the multiple-choice questions on the test also often include some of the rhetorical mode terminology.

As you prepare for the exam by taking practice tests, you'll see that 40 minutes is not much time in which to write a sophisticated essay, and the shortcuts you'll learn in this chapter will be invaluable in helping you write a great essay in the allotted time. However, you do not need to cram and memorize all the material in this section. If you read and understand the explanations and just make sure you retain the basics, you'll be comfortable enough with the process to do well on the exam.

Another important point to remember is that, more often than not, rhetorical modes are used in combination. Breaking them up into individual components is a somewhat arbitrary process—but for our purposes, it makes the material easier to understand. Let's begin.

EXAMPLE OR ILLUSTRATION

Our first rhetorical mode consists of using specific examples to illustrate an idea. Now, this may seem like a pretty simple idea, but one of the most common mistakes students make when writing their AP English Language and Composition essays is to use poor examples. Remember that all examples are not created equal. If you use poor illustrative examples, your ideas will be communicated much less clearly and effectively than if you'd used solid, appropriate ones. In writing these essays, your principal goal is clarity.

Read the following student essay based on *Candide*, and as you do so, evaluate the effectiveness of the examples that it uses.

> Pangloss is correct when he claims that everything is for the best in the best of all possible worlds. First of all, we are seeing more and more technological innovation every year. Computer technology, in particular, has helped us in many ways, and break-throughs in medicine have helped raise the life expectancy significantly. Furthermore, in most cities, there are bustling restaurants and great nightlife. Finally, travel has become affordable for most people, and paradises like Aruba and Hawaii await us all!

Surely you agree that the examples are not convincing, but you should also understand that they are not even relevant. Implicit in the examples chosen is the reduction of the best of all possible worlds to the writer's own tiny corner. A better approach would be something as follows:

> Pangloss is correct when he claims that everything is for the best in the best of all possible worlds. First of all, the

challenges that we have faced or are facing have inspired some of our most important scientific advances. Great famines have led scientists to exciting new agricultural discoveries, such as drought-resistant crops; great droughts have inspired engineers to develop cost-effective desalination plants. In essence, the evils in the world have been necessary stimulants for changes for the better. Furthermore, advances in medicine are no longer restricted to the wealthy nations of the world, and there is reason to hope that coordinated efforts to help developing countries will become more effective; take, for example, the international relief efforts to help the people whose homes were destroyed by the recent tsunami. Not only will the victims have better and safer homes now, but also the cooperation among the developed nations will translate into a better, safer world. Indeed, everything is for the best.

While the second essay may be naive, at least it does its best to substantiate an untenable position. Without any doubt, the examples in the second passage are much more appropriate for the argument than those that were used in the first passage.

Just as it is important to choose relevant, convincing examples to substantiate your own ideas, it is essential to constantly evaluate the examples that others use in their attempts to explain or to convince.

Tricksters, dogmatists, and charlatans usually illustrate their positions with scanty, inappropriate details. Be critical.

Laundry List for Example (Illustration)

- Use examples that your reader (the person who reads your essays) will identify with and understand. Do not assume that the AP reader has seen the latest teen cult film or knows any pop culture icons younger than Britney Spears.

- Draw your examples from "real life," "real" culture (literature, art, classical music, and so on), and well-known folklore.

- Make sure the example really does illustrate your point. Don't use a fancy example just to show off your knowledge; find ones that really work!

- Introduce your examples using transitions, such as *for example, for instance, case in point,* and *consider the case of.*

- A single example that is perfectly representative can serve to illustrate your point.

- A series of short, less-perfect (but still relevant) examples can, by their accumulation, serve to illustrate your point.

- The ideal approach is to construct a well-developed, representative example supported by several shorter examples.

- Remember that you are in control of what you write. As you brainstorm, discard examples that may disprove your point. Your AP essays will have little or nothing to do with your beliefs or with a balanced examination of an issue. You will be defending a point of view (argumentative essay) or explaining something (expository essay)—don't feel as if you have to be fair to all sides of an argument; your aim is to get your point across.

- Quality is more important than quantity; poorly chosen examples detract significantly from your presentation.

Sample Question for Using Examples

Write a thoughtful and carefully constructed essay in which you use specific examples to defend, challenge, or qualify the assertion that Hollywood movies are a reflection of a decaying society.

Drill: Reflect on How You Could Use Examples to Address the Following Topics

As you read each of the topics listed below, make a list of five examples you could use to support them. Are your examples all relevant? Do they support just this side of the argument? Treat each as the basis for your thesis statement in a practice free-response question.

TOPIC 1: High schools unwittingly encourage students to cheat.

TOPIC 2: Studying the humanities is important.

TOPIC 3: A person's attitude towards diversity reveals much about that person.

CLASSIFICATION

How do you classify things? Well, you probably start by dividing up whatever you have into groups according to certain characteristics. For example, if you wanted to explain "new music" to someone, you might divide the artists into groups by type (female vocalists, male vocalists, and bands) and classify the groups by genre (heavy metal, punk rock, alternative, and so on). This would make the material easier for someone to understand because it would be organized. In other words, *We classify to more easily analyze and explain.*

When you place things into categories on the AP English Language and Composition Exam, avoid creating classifications that overlap. For example, it would not make sense to classify your favorite foods in the following way: sweets, barbecued meats, vegetables, and chocolates; logically, the last group is a smaller subset of the first group.

All of this boils down to the following: classification is nearly the same thing as organization. And organization is important. As you know by now, the directions in the free-response section of the AP English Language and Composition Exam request that you write "a well-organized essay." It may seem obvious that the test writers would request this of you—but then you'd be surprised how poorly organized many of the AP essays that students write are. Classify before you write.

> There is almost always more than one way to classify things. Right now, you may group your teachers as being either cool or uncool. Later, it's more likely that you'll classify them according to what they helped you learn: the new categories may be teachers who inspired you, teachers who taught you the most, teachers who taught you about life, and teachers who should not have been teachers.

Aristotle liked to classify, and he did so quite often. Some of his classifications have stood the test of time, including the one below, which is the beginning of Part 6 of an essay entitled "Categories."

Quantity is either discrete or continuous (…). Instances of discrete quantities are number and speech; instances of continuous quantities are lines, surfaces, solids, and,
Line besides these, time and place.
5   In the case of the parts of a number, there is no common boundary at which they join. For example: two fives make ten, but the two fives have no common boundary, but are separate; the parts three and seven also do not join at any boundary. Nor, to generalize, would it ever be possible in
10   the case of number that there should be a common boundary among the parts; they are always separate. Number, therefore, is a discrete quantity.
     The same is true of speech. That speech is a quantity is evident: for it is measured in long and short syllables.
15   I mean here that speech which is vocal. Moreover, it is a discrete quantity for its parts have no common boundary. There is no common boundary at which the syllables join, but each is separate and distinct from the rest.
     A line, on the other hand, is a continuous quantity, for it
20   is possible to find a common boundary at which its parts join. In the case of the line, this common boundary is the point; in the case of the plane, it is the line, for the parts of the plane have also a common boundary. Similarly you can find a common boundary in the case of the parts of a solid,
25   namely either a line or a plane.
     Space and time also belong to this class of quantities. Time, past, present, and future, forms a continuous whole. Space, likewise, is a continuous quantity; for the parts of a solid occupy a certain space, and these have a common
30   boundary; it follows that the parts of space also, which are occupied by the parts of the solid, have the same common boundary as the parts of the solid. Thus, not only time, but space also, is a continuous quantity, for its parts have a common boundary.

Here, Aristotle's division of quantity into two categories (discrete and continuous) makes sense. The examples that he uses to illustrate the nature of his categories reveal a great deal about his interests: time, space, language, and mathematics. This is a well-organized passage; the categories are well-defined and Aristotle clearly explains how the members of each category have been classified.

Laundry List for Classification

- When you're asked to analyze and explain something, classification will be very useful.

- Make sure you have a central idea (thesis).

- Sort your information into meaningful groups. Are there enough elements in each group to allow you to write a convincing, useful paragraph? Sometimes you'll find that you need to combine categories.

- Make sure you have a manageable number of categories—three or four. Remember that you have only about 40 minutes to plan and execute each essay.

- Make sure the categories (or the elements in the categories) do not overlap.

- Before writing, make sure the categories and central idea (thesis) are a good fit. Sometimes you'll want to modify your thesis statement based on the categories that you've found.

- As you write, do not justify your classification unless this is somehow necessary to address a very bizarre free-response question. Justify your thesis, not your categories.

Sample Classification Question

Write a short essay in which you analyze the different methods a teacher uses to convey information to his or her class. In your essay, be sure to use classification to organize your ideas. Once you've written your essay, show it to your AP teacher or tutor. You might want to show it to a fellow AP student for peer review.

Drill: Reflect on How You Could Use Classification to Address the Following Topics

As you read each of the topics, think about how you would organize your essay in terms of classification. Come up with a possible thesis (central idea), and plan how you could categorize the information you have on these topics into three or four meaningful divisions.

TOPIC 1: Television commercials

TOPIC 2: Movies

TOPIC 3: Students

TOPIC 4: Cars

ANALOGY

Although analogies are not that useful in argumentative writing, they *are* useful in expository writing—this means that analogies will be useful when you write your expository essay for this test.

Analogies are sometimes used to explain things that are difficult to understand by comparing them with things that are easier to understand. Let's say that you want to explain how a well-run corporation works. You might explain that it functions like a football team. In both cases there are owners or stockholders. In the corporation, there's a CEO, who is similar to the coach of a football team. The CEO directs the managers (or vice presidents), just as the coach directs the assistant coaches; these work directly with the employees—the players. When an employee doesn't heed directions, the success of the enterprise is put at risk, just like when a player fails to execute a block or a tackle. The most important thing about using analogies is that you choose one that will be readily understood by your audience.

> Think of an **analogy** as a comparison used to explain something.

In this case, if the reader knows nothing about football, this analogy may do more harm than good.

You can also use an analogy to explain something that's abstract by comparing it with something that's concrete. Throughout history, people have used analogies to explain their god or gods. Christians explain God, for example, through analogy. They say that God is like a father who loves his children and, thus, both punishes and rewards them. The only difference is that they consider God's judgment to be perfect. They believe that God is like a father in that both are good, but that the difference is that God is *perfectly* good.

The most famous philosophical analogy serves as the basis for Plato's "allegory of the cave." The analogy purportedly evolved from a conversation between Socrates and Glaucon.

> Imagine human beings living in an underground cave;
> here they have been from their childhood, and they have
> their legs and necks chained so that they cannot move and
Line can only see before them, being prevented by the chains
> 5 from turning round their heads. Above and behind them,
> a fire is blazing at a distance, and between the fire and the
> prisoners there is a raised way; and there is a low wall built
> along the way, like the screen which marionette players
> have to hide them and over which they show the puppets.
> 10 Men are passing along the wall (and screened by the
> wall) and are carrying all sorts of things and animals made
> of wood and stone and various materials that appear over
> the wall. Some of them are talking, others are silent.
> Like ourselves, they see only their own shadows, or the
> 15 shadows of one another, or the shadows of the things and
> animals, which the fire throws on the opposite wall of the
> cave.
> And if the human beings were able to converse with one
> another, would they not suppose that they were naming
> 20 what was actually before them (even though they were
> seeing only shadows of those things)?
> And suppose further that the prison had an echo which
> came from the other side, would they not be sure to fancy
> when one of the passers-by spoke that the voice which they
> 25 heard came from the passing shadow?
> To them, I said, the truth would be literally nothing but
> the shadows of the images.

This is only part of the analogy, but you probably get the idea. Socrates uses this analogy to explain that we think that we see things just as they really are in our world, but that we are seeing only reflections of a greater truth, an abstraction that we fail to grasp. The cave is our world; the shadows are the objects and people that we "see." We are like the prisoners, for we are not free to see what creates the shadows; the truth, made up of ideal forms, is out in the light.

Laundry List for Analogy

- Use analogy for expository writing (explanation).

- Do not use analogy for argumentative writing (argumentation).

- Use analogy to explain something that is abstract or difficult to understand.

- Make sure your audience will readily understand your "simple" or concrete subject.

Sample Analogy Question

Write an essay in which you explain the process of applying to college. Use analogy when appropriate. Once you've written your essay, show it to your AP teacher or tutor. You might want to show it to a fellow AP student for peer review.

Drill: Reflect on How You Could Use Analogy to Address the Following Topics

As you read each topic, think of it as the basis for the thesis of an expository essay. Come up with a simpler subject that you can use as an analogy for this more complex topic. Write down a basic plan for an essay.

TOPIC 1:   The way your school functions

TOPIC 2:   The benefits of honesty

MOVING ON...

In this chapter we discussed three rhetorical modes: example, classification, and analogy. Make sure you are familiar with the laundry lists in this chapter. If you get into good habits now when using these rhetorical modes, you'll be much better off on test day!

Further proving how useful these modes will be, we guarantee that both your expository and argumentative essay questions will fit into some combination of these modes.

Of course, remember to plan your essay before you begin writing. It often helps to write your thesis statement along with this plan so that you can keep in mind whether the parts of your plan are relevant to your central idea. This will ensure that you write the best organized, most coherent essay you can.

Now that we've covered the three basic rhetorical modes, let's move on to review a few complex modes in the next chapter.

REFLECT

Respond to the following questions:

- For which topics discussed in this chapter do you feel you have achieved sufficient mastery to answer multiple-choice questions correctly?

- For which topics discussed in this chapter do you feel you have achieved sufficient mastery to discuss effectively in an essay?

- For which topics discussed in this chapter do you feel you need more work before you can answer multiple-choice questions correctly?

- For which topics discussed in this chapter do you feel you need more work before you can discuss them effectively in an essay?

- What parts of this chapter are you going to re-review?

- Will you seek further help, outside of this book (such as a teacher, tutor, or AP Students wesbite), on any of the topics in this chapter—and, if so, on which ones?

Chapter 11
Complex
Rhetorical Modes

In this chapter, we'll discuss a few more—and more complex—rhetorical modes, including process analysis, cause and effect, definition, description, narration, and induction and deduction. As was the case with the rhetorical modes you learned about in the last chapter, it will be extremely beneficial to you to know all you can about these modes on test day. It will not only help you recognize when these modes are used in the sample passages, but also enable you to use them in your essays.

So let's jump right in.

PROCESS ANALYSIS

Process analysis is a rhetorical mode that's used by writers when they want to explain either how to do something or how something was done. When your science teacher hands you instructions for a lab, she is giving you a rather dry sheet of process analysis that says, "first do this; then do that; then examine the data; then explain such-and-such." When you write your lab report, you're also indulging in process analysis, saying, "first we did this; then we did that; then we examined the data; then we determined such-and-such." If you like to follow recipes when you cook, then you've already been exposed to process analysis. However, process analyses used in writing generally aren't as dry as recipes or how-to manuals; they usually have a few examples to spice them up a little.

Process analysis can be an effective way of relating an experience. Take, for example, this excerpt from "On Dumpster Diving" from *Travels with Lizbeth* by Lars Eighner.

> I learned to scavenge gradually, on my own. Since then I have initiated several companions into the trade. I have learned that there is a predictable series of stages a person
> Line goes through in learning to scavenge.
> 5   At first the new scavenger is filled with disgust and self-loathing. He is ashamed of being seen and may lurk around, trying to duck behind things, or he may try to dive at night. (In fact, most people instinctively look away from a scavenger. By skulking around, the novice calls attention
> 10   to himself and arouses suspicion. Diving at night is ineffective and needlessly messy.)
>   Every grain of rice seems to be a maggot. Everything seems to stink. He can wipe the egg yolk off the found can, but he cannot erase the stigma of eating garbage out of his
> 15   mind.
>   That stage passes with experience. The scavenger finds a pair of running shoes that fit and look and smell brand-new. He finds a pocket calculator in perfect working order. He finds pristine ice cream, still frozen, more than he can eat
> 20   or keep. He begins to understand: people do throw away perfectly good stuff, a lot of perfectly good stuff.
>   At this stage, Dumpster shyness begins to dissipate. The diver, after all, has the last laugh. He is finding all manner

Mnemonics
If you're having trouble remembering rhetorical modes, make some flashcards and memorize them like vocabulary words.

186 | Cracking the AP English Language and Composition Exam

of good things which are his for the taking. Those who
25 disparage his profession are the fools, not he.

He may begin to hang onto some perfectly good things
for which he has neither a use nor a market. Then he begins
to take note of the things which are not perfectly good but
are nearly so. He mates a Walkman with broken earphones
30 and one that is missing a battery cover. He picks up things
which he can repair.

At this stage he may become lost and never recover.
Dumpsters are full of things of some potential value to
someone and also of things which never have much intrin-
35 sic value but are interesting. All the Dumpster divers I have
known come to the point of trying to acquire everything
they touch. Why not take it, they reason, since it is all free.

Here's a good example of process analysis in writing. Although the material is organized in chronological stages, the author inserts explanatory examples and personal
commentary that make the passage more lively. In this passage, the author is not
instructing the reader on how to scavenge for food in Dumpsters; rather, he is
explaining the psychological evolution of a homeless scavenger—based on his own
experience—and illustrating the excesses of a consumerist society.

> Remember that process analysis is a rhetorical mode that serves to organize
> something in a step-by-step manner, and it can serve both scientific and
> literary needs.

Laundry List for Process Analysis

- Sequence is chronological and usually fixed—think of recipes.

- When you use this device, make sure the stages of the process are clear, by
  using transitions (e.g., *first, next, after two days, finally).*

- Make sure your terminology is appropriate for the reader. For example, the
  person who will read your essays probably does not know much about the
  embryonic development of frogs, so you should avoid using too-specialized
  terms like *Spemann organizer* or *Nieuwkoop center.*

- Verify that every step is clear; an error or omission in an intermediate step
  may make the rest of the process analysis very confusing. Let's say you were
  describing how to braid hair, and wrote the following instructions: "First,
  comb or brush your hair so that it is untangled and manageable to work with.
  Next, take the far-right section of hair and put it over the middle section and
  under the far-left section." This could be confusing to your reader because
  you never said to divide the hair into three sections before starting the actual
  braiding process.

Sample Process Analysis Question

Write a short essay in which you describe the process of how you selected the colleges to which you applied (or are going to apply to). Once you've written your essay, show it to your AP teacher or tutor. You might want to show it to a fellow AP student for peer review.

Drill: Reflect on How You Could Use Process Analysis to Address the Following Topics

Try making a numbered list with a few examples. Make sure you have included all the necessary steps and have used appropriate language and terminology for your reader. Remember to use transition words when you write the essay.

TOPIC 1:   How decisions are made at your school

TOPIC 2:   How to get through high school successfully

TOPIC 3:   How to choose and keep close friends

CAUSE AND EFFECT

You just saw how process analysis is a useful rhetorical mode for explaining how to do things or how things were done; the rhetorical mode known as **cause and effect** explains *why things should be done* or *should have been done*. In a sense, cause and effect explains the processes responsible for the process.

Some cause-and-effect relationships are easy to describe. For instance, read the example below from *Candide*'s Dr. Pangloss.

> "It is demonstrable," said Pangloss, "that things cannot
> be otherwise than as they are; for as all things have been
> created for some end, they must necessarily be created
> *Line* for the best end. Observe, for instance, the nose is formed
> 5 for spectacles; therefore we wear spectacles. The legs
> are visibly designed for stockings; accordingly we wear
> stockings. Stones were made to be hewn and to construct
> castles; therefore My Lord has a magnificent castle, for the
> greatest baron in the province ought to be the best lodged.
> 10 Swine were intended to be eaten; therefore we eat pork all
> the year round."

In this passage, Pangloss is using a series of cause-and-effect relationships to prove his point, that "things cannot be otherwise than as they are." This rhetorical mode is everywhere, however. You see examples of this rhetorical mode all around you.

On this exam, the causes and effects that you choose to explore will depend on what you're asked to explain. You may have to use cause and effect in your essays, possibly in combination with one or more other rhetorical modes; you may also see a few questions in the multiple-choice section that deal with how the author uses cause and effect to make a point. When making critical decisions, writers will often consider both the immediate and the long-term effects; when analyzing an important event, writers will often examine both the immediate and the underlying causes.

Laundry List for Cause and Effect

If you were writing about the poor average of AP English Language and Composition test scores at your school, you could go about it in two ways. First, you could examine some *immediate* causes: Ms. What's-Her-Name retired and was replaced by a teacher who had no experience teaching and no background in English, we didn't have a good review book for the exam, or the exam is administered in Room Z during school band practice. Alternatively, you could examine some *underlying* causes for the poor exam scores: The superintendent of schools changed hiring policies (so a terrible teacher was hired); last year, funds for buying books were diverted to buying new lockers for the football team (so we had no good review book); and the room that the school band normally practices in was flooded when a pipe broke.

- Do not confuse the relating of mere circumstances with a cause-and-effect relationship. For example, it is not logical to assume that socialism in Chile necessarily caused socialism in Argentina.

- Turn your causal relationships into causes and effects by using carefully chosen examples. Remember that not all causal relationships are causes and effects. However, careful use of evidence and examples can turn causal relationships into causes and effects.

- Make sure to carefully address each step in a series of causal relationships; if you don't, you risk losing your reader. Imagine the attendance secretary when she hears, "I'm sorry I'm late. We had a fire, so I had to find my cat." A better (clearer) explanation would have been as follows: "I'm sorry I'm late. This morning at 4:00 A.M. there was an electrical fire in the garage; fortunately, there was an alarm that woke my dad, who put out the fire, but when he opened the garage door, my cat ran outside. I think it was frightened so it ran up a tree. I decided to climb up the tree and get the cat but I fell, and my mother had to take me to the emergency room." Although this explanation is longer, it is far more detailed and answers any questions your reader may have.

Sample Cause-and-Effect Question

Write an essay in which you examine the possible causes and effects of violence in the United States today. Once you've written your essay, show it to your AP teacher or tutor. You might want to show it to a fellow AP student for peer review.

Drill: Reflect on How You Could Use Cause and Effect to Address the Following Topics

In a T-chart, compare the possible causes and affects of the topics below. Then for at least one topic, make sure to give examples to back up your claims.

    TOPIC 1:   Academic dishonesty in high schools

    TOPIC 2:   The fear of domestic terrorism in the United States

    TOPIC 3:   The changing face of ethnic America

DEFINITION

You are probably familiar with definitions; you see them every time you look up a word in the dictionary. Hopefully when you write, you try to make sure your reader understands the words that you use.

When writing your essays for the AP English Language and Composition Exam, if you happen to leave a key term unexplained or explained vaguely, even a carefully crafted essay will fall apart. This is especially true of very specialized terminology and obscure words. For example, if you are explaining a wonderful new tradition at your school and define it by synonym, you may write, "Basically, it's a Mexican *feis*." If your readers are Irish, this would be all right; if your readers were from just about anywhere else, you would need to define *feis* by putting it into a **category**

> For the AP exam, we have to consider *definition* in its meaning as a rhetorical mode.

(defining it in terms everyone will understand): "a *feis* is a competition for Irish dance, song, and instrumental music." Then, you could explain your project: "We want to do the same thing with traditional Mexican dance, song, and music."

In this case, a paragraph—or an entire essay—is devoted to the definition of a term. Here, for example, is a paragraph that defines *feis* (pronounced "fesh").

> A *feis* is a day of competition in Irish dancing, music, and song. Perhaps you were wondering where all the Irish dancers from *Lord of the Dance* came from. All first performed at a *feis* and honed their skills through competitions

Line 5   at various levels. A *feis* is a living legacy of Irish culture;
       it is where beginners, trying to remember their left from
       right, unknowingly dance the ancient steps of Ireland and
       pass this legacy on to the next generation. On the more
       practical side, a *feis* is to Irish performers what a soccer
  10   game is to athletes the world over. Competitions are orga-
       nized by ability (Beginner, Advanced Beginner, Novice,
       Open, Preliminary Championships, and Championships)
       and by age (Under 6, Under 7, etc). At a typical *feis*, there
       might be as many as 2,500 dancers.

The passage begins with a straightforward definition, but the definition is extended and rhetorical modes are mixed. You noted, I'm sure, the *analogy* to a soccer game; then, there is an inchoate (imperfectly formed) stab at *classification* (the divisions in the competition). You could even argue that the mention of *Lord of the Dance* serves as a kind of *example*. The rhetorical mode of *definition* can be used simply to explain a word or concept, but typically the author using it also wants to interest the reader in what's being explained.

Let's take a look at another good example of definition.

       The *Palio* is a horse race that's held twice each year
       in Siena, Italy: on July 2nd in honor of the Madonna
       of Provenzano, and on August 16th in honor of the
Line   Assumption of the Virgin. But saying that the Palio is just
  5   another horse race would be like calling the Superbowl
       just another football game. The Palio is not just a race. It is
       blood, sweat, and tears; it is part competition and part festi-
       val. According to some, it is the world's craziest horse race;
       according to others, it is Italy's most honored tradition. One
  10   thing is clear to everyone, however: the Palio represents the
       tradition, culture, and soul of Siena. The actual race lasts
       only about a minute, but those moments represent an entire
       year's worth of anticipation and preparation.

Again, the passage begins with a simple definition; but here, too, we have an example of another rhetorical mode—analogy (to the Super Bowl).

However, the author of this passage uses an important additional tactic, known as *definition by negation*. You should be aware of this rhetorical device and use it where appropriate. In the passage above, the negation is partial—the Palio is, indeed, a race, but it is not "just a race." Most negations work in that manner; definition by negation is usually used to impress upon the reader the importance of the item under discussion or create a distinction between the item under discussion and the item with which it is being "negatively" compared. For instance, you may write, "Madonna is not a pop singer; she's a phenomenon, a true diva, a multi-talented musical ambassador, and savvy businesswoman." Perhaps this statement is true, but she's still a pop singer.

You may be able to use definition as a mode in your free-response essays, but most likely, you will see definition used in the passages in the multiple-choice sections.

For example, you may be asked to answer a question that deals with how an author uses definition to analyze a topic.

Laundry List for Definition

- Keep your reason for defining something in mind as you're writing.

- Define key terms according to what you know of your audience, in other words, the readers of the essays; you don't want to bore your reader by defining terms unnecessarily, nor do you want to perplex your reader by failing to define terms that may be obscure to your audience. Keep in mind that for you, your readers are the AP English Language and Composition Exam graders.

- Explain the background (history) when it is relevant to your definition.

- Define by negation when appropriate.

- Combine definition with any number of other rhetorical modes when applicable.

Sample Definition Question

Write an essay in which you use definition to analyze the role of integrity in your life. Once you've written your essay, show it to your AP teacher or tutor. You might want to show it to a fellow AP student for peer review.

Drill: Reflect on How You Could Use Definition to Address the Following Topics

First define each word by category; then, define each word by negation.

WORD 1: Hip-hop

WORD 2: Success

WORD 3: Love

WORD 4: Cool

Objective:
Based on facts

Subjective:
Based on feelings or opinions

DESCRIPTION

Description can help make expository or argumentative writing lively and interesting and hold the reader's interest, which is vital, of course. Think of how many essays those test graders have to read every day; as we mentioned in the techniques chapters, a large part of scoring well on the free-response section is keeping your audience interested.

Oftentimes description serves as the primary rhetorical mode for an entire essay—or even an entire book. It's typically used to communicate a scene, a specific place, or a person to the reader. Although writers tend to concentrate most on the visual aspects of descriptions, descriptions can be used to appeal to any of the reader's senses.

It is important to keep in mind that sometimes description can be objective; in these cases, the author is not describing something in a sentimental or otherwise subjective way—he or she is merely stating the facts. As an example of this, take a look at Charles Darwin's depiction of Valparaíso, the chief seaport in Chile, in *Voyage of the Beagle.*

> The town is built at the very foot of a range of hills,
> about 1,600 feet high, and rather steep. From its position, it
> consists of one long, straggling street, which runs paral-
> Line lel to the beach, and wherever a ravine comes down, the
> 5 houses are piled up on each side of it. The rounded hills,
> being only partially protected by very scanty vegetation,
> are worn into numberless little gullies, which expose a sin-
> gularly bright red soil. From this cause, and from the low
> whitewashed houses with tile roofs, the view reminded me
> 10 of St. Cruz in Tenerife. In a northwesterly direction there
> are some fine glimpses of the Andes, but these mountains
> appear much grander when viewed from the neighboring
> hills: the great distance at which they are situated can then
> more readily be perceived.

This type of objective description tends to be drier than more subjective descrip-tion. The degree of objectivity exhibited above probably doesn't thrill you—nor will it thrill the AP readers.

Fortunately, unlike most other rhetorical modes, description allows for a signifi-cant degree of subjectivity. In most descriptions, the writer attempts to communi-cate personal impressions of something someone. To do so, it is necessary to draw on the powers of figurative writing; simile, metaphor, and personification are the most common.

Here is another description of a city: Nathaniel Hawthorne's impressions of Florence. The description comes not from one of Hawthorne's novels, but from one of the notebooks that he kept during his travels in Europe.

> By and by, we had a distant glimpse of Florence, show-
> ing its great dome and some of its towers out of a sidelong
> valley, as if we were between two great waves of the tumul-
> Line tuous sea of hills, while, far beyond, rose in the distance
> 5 the blue peaks of three or four of the Apennines, just on the
> remote horizon. There being a haziness in the atmosphere,
> however, Florence was little more distinct to us than the
> Celestial City was to Christian and Hopeful, when they
> spied at it from the Delectable Mountains.
> 10 Florence at first struck me as having the aspect of a
> very new city in comparison with Rome; but, on closer
> acquaintance, I find that many of the buildings are antique
> and massive, though still the clear atmosphere, the bright
> sunshine, the light, cheerful hues of the stucco, and—as
> 15 much as anything else, perhaps—the vivacious character

of the human life in the streets, take away the sense of its
being an ancient city.

    As we returned home over the Arno River, crossing the
Ponte di Santa Trinitá, we were struck by the beautiful
20 scene of the broad, calm river, with the palaces along its
shores repeated in it, on either side, and the neighboring
bridges, too, just as perfect in the tide beneath as in the air
above—a city of dream and shadow so close to the actual
one. God has a meaning, no doubt, in putting this spiritual
25 symbol continually beside us.

    Along the river, on both sides, as far as we could see,
there was a row of brilliant lamps, which, in the far
distance, looked like a cornice of golden light; and this
also shone as brightly in the river's depths. The lilies of
30 the evening, in the quarter where the sun had gone down,
were very soft and beautiful, though not so gorgeous as
thousands that I have seen in America. But I believe I must
fairly confess that the Italian sky, in the daytime, is bluer
and brighter than our own, and that the atmosphere has a
35 quality of showing objects to better advantage. It is more
than mere daylight; the magic of moonlight is somehow
mixed up with it, although it is so transparent a medium of
light.

This is a much more personal vision of a city. Hawthorne uses one simile to give us
a better visual image of the countryside around Florence ("as if we were between
two great waves of the tumultuous sea of hills") and another to communicate the
effect of the gas lamps ("like a cornice of golden light"); and he employs a metaphor ("a city of dream and shadow") to evoke his impression of the reflections in
the river. In fact, virtually all of the description serves to communicate or explain
Hawthorne's impressions of the city; here, the writer wishes to evoke and is not
interested in scientific exactitude.

Keep in mind that this rhetorical device allows you a certain amount of freedom
of language, but it also allows you certain liberties in organization. In Hawthorne's
passage, for example, the author put down in writing his impressions in whatever order they came to him. In more objectively written descriptions, however, it
often makes sense to think spatially when writing a visual description. You might
describe a scene from left to right or front to back, for example; you might start a
description of a person with the head (and end with the feet).

In the following passage, Fyodor Dostoyevsky gives us both a spatial description
and a barrage of sensory impressions.

    In the first place, on entering this house, one passes into
a very bare hall, and thence along a passage to a mean
staircase. The reception room, however, is bright, clean,
Line and spacious, and is lined with redwood and metalwork.
5 But the scullery you would not care to see; it is greasy,
dirty, and odoriferous, while the stairs are in rags, and
the walls so covered with filth that the hand sticks fast
wherever it touches them. Also, on each landing there is a
medley of boxes, chairs, and dilapidated wardrobes; while

10 the windows have had most of their panes shattered, and
everywhere stand washtubs filled with dirt, litter, eggshells,
and fish bladders. The smell is abominable. In short, the
house is not a nice one.

As to the disposition of the rooms, I have described
15 it to you already. True, they are convenient enough, yet
every one of them has an atmosphere. I do not mean that
they smell badly so much as that each of them seems to
contain something which gives forth a rank, sickly sweet
odor. At first the impression is an unpleasant one, but a
20 couple of minutes will suffice to dissipate it, for the reason
that everything here smells—people's clothes, hands, and
everything else—and one grows accustomed to the rank-
ness. Canaries, however, soon die in this house. A naval
officer here has just bought his fifth. Birds cannot live long
25 in such an air. Every morning, when fish or beef is being
cooked, and washing and scrubbing are in progress, the
house is filled with steam. Always, too, the kitchen is full
of linen hanging out to dry; and since my room adjoins that
apartment, the smell from the clothes causes me not a little
30 annoyance. However, one can grow used to anything.

Note that Dostoyevsky's description first takes us through the ground floor and leads us up the staircase. Unlike the previous passages, this one appeals to our tactile ("so covered with filth that the hand sticks") and, even more prominently, olfactory senses. Choice of detail is important, and the choice of fish bladders, for example, conveys wonderfully the disgusting sights and smell. This is great writing—not only is the description effective, it's also humorous, thanks to the short comment at the end of each paragraph.

Laundry List for Description

- When possible, call on all five senses: visual, auditory, olfactory (smell), gustatory (taste), and tactile.

- Place the most striking examples at the beginnings and ends of your paragraphs (or essay) for maximum effect.

- Show, don't tell, using anecdotes and examples.

- Use concrete nouns and adjectives; nouns, not adjectives, should dominate.

- Concentrate on details that will convey the sense you're trying to get across most effectively. (Remember the fish bladders!)

- Employ figures of speech, especially similes, metaphors, and personification, when appropriate.

- When describing people, try to focus on distinctive mannerisms; if possible, you should go beyond physical appearance.

- Direct discourse (using dialogue or quotations) can be revealing and useful.

- A brief illustrative anecdote is worth a thousand words. Instead of simply using a general statement ("My friend Kai is a very generous person"), use an example ("My friend Kai is known for his generosity; the whole school knows about the time that he spent an entire weekend volunteering at a homeless shelter").

- To the extent possible, use action verbs. You could write, "The delightful aroma of chocolate chip cookies baking in the oven *crept around the corner and filled the den* with its sweetness" instead of just "The baking chocolate chip cookies *smelled* sweet."

Sample Description Question

Write an essay in which you describe your local shopping mall. Remember that you are not limited to physical descriptions. Once you've written your essay, show it to your AP teacher or tutor. You might want to show it to a fellow AP student for peer review.

Drill: Reflect on How You Could Use Description to Address the Following Topics

First decide the general feeling you'd like to convey, and second begin to list some specifics; don't forget examples or anecdotes. When describing people, go beyond just the physical.

TOPIC 1:   A party

TOPIC 2:   Your parents

TOPIC 3:   A natural disaster (seen from personal experience or on television)

TOPIC 4:   Your favorite place to relax

TOPIC 5:   The campus of your school

NARRATION

A narrative is a story in which pieces of information are arranged in chronological order. Narration can be an effective expository technique. Decades after her experience in a Japanese internment camp, Jeanne Wakatsuki Houston decided to narrate her experiences before, during, and immediately after imprisonment. She did not want to tell the story just for the story's sake; she wanted to relay her experience to the public to exorcize personal demons and to raise public awareness about this period in history. Here is a passage from this personal narrative. The passage describes the period after the Wakatsuki family had lost their house in Ocean Park, California, when they were forced into detention.

> My own family, after three years of mess hall living,
> collapsed as an integrated unit. Whatever dignity or feeling
> of filial strength we may have known before December
> *Line* 1941 was lost, and we did not recover it until many years
> 5 after the war, not until after Papa died and we began to
> come together, trying to fill the vacuum his passing left in
> all our lives.

The closing of the camps, in the fall of 1945, only aggra-
vated what had begun inside. Papa had no money then and
10 could not get work. Half of our family had already moved
to the East Coast, where jobs had opened up for them. The
rest of us were relocated into a former defense workers'
housing project in Long Beach. In that small apartment
there never was enough room for all of us to sit down for
15 a meal. We ate in shifts, and I yearned all the more for our
huge round table in Ocean Park.

Soon after we were released I wrote a paper for a
seventh-grade journalism class, describing how we used to
hunt grunion before the war. The whole family would go
20 down to Ocean Park Beach after dark, when the grunion
were running, and build a big fire on the sand. I would
watch Papa and my older brothers splash through the
moonlit surf to scoop out the fish, then we'd rush back to
the house where Mama would fry them up and set the siz-
25 zling pan on the table, with soy sauce and horseradish, for
a midnight meal. I ended the paper with this sentence: "The
reason I want to remember this is because I know we'll
never be able to do it again."

You may be asked to use personal narrative when writing your essays on the AP
English Language and Composition Exam; and you will certainly be asked to
analyze narratives that employ this rhetorical mode.

In the following passage, Booker T. Washington uses narrative to explain how his
view on education developed. Watch for changes between the first- and third-
person style of narration.

When a mere boy, I saw a young colored man, who had
spent several years in school, sitting in a common cabin in
the South, studying a French grammar. I noted the poverty,
Line the untidiness, the want of system, and thrift that existed
5 about the cabin, notwithstanding his knowledge of French
and other academic subjects. Another time, when riding on
the outer edges of a town in the South, I heard the sound of
a piano coming from a cabin of the same kind. Contriving
some excuse, I entered and began a conversation with the
10 young colored woman who was playing, and who had
recently returned from a boarding-school, where she had
been studying instrumental music among other things.
Despite the fact that her parents were living in a rented
cabin, eating poorly cooked food, surrounded with poverty,
15 and having almost none of the conveniences of life, she had
persuaded them to rent a piano for four or five dollars per
month. Many such instances as these, in connection with
my own struggles, impressed upon me the importance of
making a study of our needs as a race, and applying the
20 remedy accordingly.

Some one may be tempted to ask, Has not the negro
boy or girl as good a right to study a French grammar and
instrumental music as the white youth? I answer, Yes, but
in the present condition of the negro race in this country
25 there is need of something more. Perhaps I may be forgiven
for the seeming egotism if I mention the expansion of my

own life partly as an example of what I mean. My earliest
recollection is of a small one-room log hut on a large slave
plantation in Virginia. After the close of the war, while
30   working in the coal-mines of West Virginia for the support of my mother, I heard in some accidental way of the
Hampton Institute.

When I learned that it was an institution where a black
boy could study, could have a chance to work for his board,
35   and at the same time be taught how to work and to realize
the dignity of labor, I resolved to go there. Bidding my
mother good-by, I started out one morning to find my way
to Hampton, though I was almost penniless and had no
definite idea where Hampton was. By walking, begging
40   rides, and paying for a portion of the journey on the steam-
cars, I finally succeeded in reaching the city of Richmond,
Virginia. I was without money or friends. I slept under a
sidewalk, and by working on a vessel next day I earned
money to continue my way to the institute, where I arrived
45   with a surplus of fifty cents. At Hampton I found the opportunity—in the way of buildings, teachers, and industries
provided by the generous—to get training in the class-room
and by practical touch with industrial life, to learn thrift,
economy, and push. I was surrounded by an atmosphere of
50   business, Christian influence, and a spirit of self-help that
seemed to have awakened every faculty in me, and caused
me for the first time to realize what it meant to be a man
instead of a piece of property.

While there I resolved that when I had finished the course
55   of training I would go into the far South, into the Black Belt
of the South, and give my life to providing the same kind of
opportunity for self-reliance and self-awakening that I had
found provided for me at Hampton.

Notice that in the first paragraph, the narration slips briefly into the third person—
Washington is telling the story of the girl, not his own. Likewise, Washington presents the story of the boy studying French from his point of view. In these two
instances, Washington switches from first to third person with ease, so that the
transition is optimally effective and unnoticeable. The second paragraph effortlessly
transitions to a personal anecdote, which is continued in the third paragraph. The
final paragraph justifies the narrative: Washington's life story leads to his commitment to establish his own institute—called the Tuskegee Normal and Industrial
Institute—deep in the South.

Laundry List for Narration

- When possible, structure the events in chronological order.

- Make your story complete: make sure you have a beginning, middle, and end.

- Provide a realistic setting (typically at the beginning). Notice how Booker T. Washington provides a setting in this passage with just a few details: "a young colored man," "a common cabin in the South," "the poverty, the untidiness, the want of system, and thrift that existed about the cabin."

- Whenever possible, use action verbs; for example, write "the fighters *tumbled* to the ground," rather than "there *were* fallen soldiers on the ground."

- Provide concrete and specific details.

- Show, don't tell. This is another way of saying that you should use anecdotes and examples whenever possible.

- Establish a clear point of view—if it's clear who is narrating and why, then it will be easier to choose relevant details.

- Include appropriate amounts of direct discourse (dialogue or quotations).

Sample Narration Question

"A college education is not necessary for success." Relate an experience of someone you know (directly or indirectly) that defends, challenges, or qualifies this statement. Once you've written your essay, show it to your AP teacher or tutor. You might want to show it to a fellow AP student for peer review.

Drill: Reflect on How You Could Use Narration to Address the Following Topics

Think of a personal experience (or an experience of someone you know) that pertains to the topic. Determine how you would best describe this experience. Come up with a few anecdotes or examples.

TOPIC 1: Danger when eating becomes an obsession

TOPIC 2: Hardship is a necessary part of our education

INDUCTION AND DEDUCTION

Induction:
PART to WHOLE

Deduction:
WHOLE to PART

You will probably find that the rhetorical modes of induction and deduction are most useful when you're writing the argument essay, although they will be helpful on the rhetorical analysis essay too.

Induction is a process in which specific examples are used to reach a general conclusion. If you took the AP European History Exam and did not like the experience, and then took the AP Calculus BC Exam and did not like the experience, you might arrive at the following general conclusion: AP exams are always an unpleasant experience. If, when you were young, you found that you didn't like broccoli, asparagus, or cabbage, your parents might have concluded that you didn't like vegetables. In both cases, the conclusion would be of questionable value because there is not enough evidence to justify the generalization.

Assume that you want to argue that your English teacher is in a bad mood every time the Boston Red Sox lose a game to the New York Yankees. You could substantiate that generalization by recalling certain tantrums that he or she threw and comparing those days with the dates of Red Sox losses. This would substantiate your claim but not prove it, especially if you didn't even know whether your teacher saw the games. After all, what if something else happened to coincide with the games and was the real cause of his or her bad temper, such as traffic jams on the way home from school?

We tend to believe in generalizations arrived at through induction, whether or not they can actually be proved. The Food and Drug Administration, for example, has to follow the inductive reasoning of scientists; just because a certain drug produced the desired results—and didn't produce an undesirable result, such as death—20,000 experimental cases does not prove that the same results will occur when 20,000,000 people take the drug.

Deduction involves the use of a generalization to draw a conclusion about a specific case. For example, if you read in the morning paper that all schools in your county would be closed that day because of inclement weather, you could conclude that you won't have to go to school. You just used deductive reasoning.

Laundry List for Induction and Deduction

- Induction proceeds from the specific to a generalization. For example, your classmate Ricky plays on the school's football and basketball teams, and he has ice hockey posters all over his bedroom at home. You could conclude that Ricky likes all sports in general.

- Make sure you have sufficient evidence to support your claim.

- Deduction is the process of applying a generalization to a specific case. For example, your cousin Jennifer told you that she hates dancing and loud music. From this, you could safely say that she probably wouldn't want to come with you to the hot new nightclub opening this weekend.

- Make sure your generalization has sufficient credibility before applying it to specific cases. For example, it would be an unfair generalization to assume that all baseball players use or have used anabolic steroids.

Sample Induction and Deduction Question

Write a short essay in which you analyze the following statement using induction or deduction: *Contemporary films are a reflection of today's values.* Once you've written your essay, show it to your AP teacher or tutor. You might want to show it to a fellow AP student for peer review.

Drill: Reflect on How You Could Use Induction to Substantiate the Following Theses

THESIS 1: Academic honesty is alive and well.

THESIS 2: High schools don't really care about their mission to educate.

THESIS 3: Computer games have beneficial effects.

THESIS 4: Children generally demonstrate more wisdom than their parents.

In this chapter we looked at a few more rhetorical modes that will be extremely useful to you on test day. Remember that these can be used in combination with each other *and,* further complicating matters, in combination with the modes in the previous chapter. Hopefully, these modes have given you some ideas about how you can structure your essays into coherent works that the test readers will understand and maybe even enjoy.

Here we are at the end of the review section of the book. You are now ready to take the second practice test; depending on how you did on the first one, you may have been dreading this moment, but we know that once you begin, you'll see that you know a lot more than you think you do! If you've worked through the book up to this point and complete these practice exams, you'll certainly be ready for test day.

Good luck!

REFLECT

Respond to the following questions:

- For which topics discussed in this chapter do you feel you have achieved sufficient mastery to answer multiple-choice questions correctly?

- For which topics discussed in this chapter do you feel you have achieved sufficient mastery to discuss effectively in an essay?

- For which topics discussed in this chapter do you feel you need more work before you can answer multiple-choice questions correctly?

- For which topics discussed in this chapter do you feel you need more work before you can discuss them effectively in an essay?

- What parts of this chapter are you going to re-review?

- Will you seek further help, outside of this book (such as a teacher, tutor, or AP Students website), on any of the topics in this chapter—and, if so, on which ones?

Part VI
Practice Test 2

Practice Test 2

AP® English Language and Composition Exam

SECTION I: Multiple-Choice Questions

DO NOT OPEN THIS BOOKLET UNTIL YOU ARE TOLD TO DO SO.

At a Glance

Total Time
1 hour

Number of Questions
55

Percent of Total Grade
45%

Writing Instrument
Pencil required

Instructions

Section I of this examination contains 55 multiple-choice questions. Fill in only the ovals for numbers 1 through 55 on your answer sheet.

Indicate all of your answers to the multiple-choice questions on the answer sheet. No credit will be given for anything written in this exam booklet, but you may use the booklet for notes or scratch work. After you have decided which of the suggested answers is best, completely fill in the corresponding oval on the answer sheet. Give only one answer to each question. If you change an answer, be sure that the previous mark is erased completely. Here is a sample question and answer.

<u>Sample Question</u>

Chicago is a
(A) state
(B) city
(C) country
(D) continent
(E) village

<u>Sample Answer</u>

Ⓐ ● Ⓒ Ⓓ Ⓔ

Use your time effectively, working as quickly as you can without losing accuracy. Do not spend too much time on any one question. Go on to other questions and come back to the ones you have not answered if you have time. It is not expected that everyone will know the answers to all the multiple-choice questions.

Many candidates wonder whether or not to guess the answers to questions about which they are not certain. Multiple-choice scores are based on the number of questions answered correctly. Points are not deducted for incorrect answers, and no points are awarded for unanswered questions. Because points are not deducted for incorrect answers, you are encouraged to answer all multiple-choice questions. On any questions you do not know the answer to, you should eliminate as many choices as you can, and then select the best answer among the remaining choices.

GO ON TO THE NEXT PAGE.

This page intentionally left blank.

ENGLISH LANGUAGE AND COMPOSITION
SECTION I
Time—1 hour

Directions: This part consists of selections from prose works and questions on their content, form, and style. After reading each passage, choose the best answer to each question and completely fill in the corresponding oval on the answer sheet.

Note: Pay particular attention to the requirement of questions that contain the words NOT, LEAST, or EXCEPT.

Questions 1–11. Read the following passage carefully before you choose your answers.

This passage is from an eighteenth-century biography of Sir Thomas Browne.

His exuberance of knowledge, and plenitude of ideas, sometimes obstruct the tendency of his reasoning and the clearness of his decisions: on whatever subject he employed
Line his mind, there started up immediately so many images
5 before him, that he lost one by grasping another. His memory supplied him with so many illustrations, parallel or dependent notions, that he was always starting into collateral considerations; but the spirit and vigour of his pursuit always gives delight; and the reader follows him, without reluctance,
10 through his mazes, in themselves flowery and pleasing, and ending at the point originally in view.
   "To have great excellencies and great faults, '*magnæ virtutes nec minora vitia*,' is the poesy," says our author, "of the best natures." This poesy may be properly applied to
15 the style of Browne; it is vigorous, but rugged; it is learned, but pedantick; it is deep, but obscure; it strikes, but does not please; it commands, but does not allure; his tropes are harsh, and his combinations uncouth.
   He fell into an age in which our language began to lose
20 the stability which it had obtained in the time of Elizabeth; and was considered by every writer as a subject on which he might try his plastick skill, by moulding it according to his own fancy. Milton, in consequence of this encroaching license, began to introduce the Latin idiom: and Browne,
25 though he gave less disturbance to our structures in phraseology, yet poured in a multitude of exotick words; many, indeed, useful and significant, which, if rejected, must be supplied by circumlocution, such as commensality, for the state of many living at the same table; but many superfluous,
30 as a paralogical, for an unreasonable doubt; and some so obscure, that they conceal his meaning rather than explain it, as arthritical analogies, for parts that serve some animals in the place of joints.
   His style is, indeed, a tissue of many languages; a
35 mixture of heterogeneous words, brought together from distant regions, with terms originally appropriated to one art, and drawn by violence into the service of another. He must, however, be confessed to have augmented our philosophical diction; and, in defence of his uncommon words and
40 expressions, we must consider, that he had uncommon

sentiments, and was not content to express, in many words, that idea for which any language could supply a single term.
   But his innovations are sometimes pleasing, and his temerities happy: he has many "verba ardentia" forcible
45 expressions, which he would never have found, but by venturing to the utmost verge of propriety; and flights which would never have been reached, but by one who had very little fear of the shame of falling.

1. The reader can infer from the first paragraph that some critics have

   (A) chastised Browne for his inability to reason
   (B) lauded Browne's frequent linear explanations
   (C) complained about Browne's lack of clarity
   (D) compared Browne with Shakespeare
   (E) compared the author of the passage with Browne

2. In context, "poesy" (line 13) most nearly means

   (A) poetry
   (B) inspiration for writing
   (C) sentimental thoughts
   (D) flowery writing
   (E) poetic dreaming

3. In context, the phrase *magnæ virtutes nec minora vitia* (lines 12–13) most nearly means which of the following?

   (A) Poetry is best when it embodies both excellence and failure.
   (B) Great excellencies are impossible without great faults.
   (C) Both excellence and weakness are often found in great people.
   (D) Our best nature is found in poesy.
   (E) Browne's style is both vigorous and rugged.

GO ON TO THE NEXT PAGE.

4. In the second paragraph, the author

   (A) is openly critical of Browne's style
   (B) hints that Browne's writing is pedantic
   (C) justifies the strength of Browne's style
   (D) argues in favor of a reexamination of Browne's style
   (E) suggests that Browne's writing is too facile

5. The author modifies the strict parallelism of "it is vigorous, but rugged; it is learned, but pedantick; it is deep, but obscure; it strikes, but does not please; it commands, but does not allure; his tropes are harsh, and his combinations uncouth" (lines 15–18) to

   (A) better define his point of view
   (B) keep the reader off balance
   (C) maintain a sense of imbalance
   (D) show more respect for Browne's accomplishments
   (E) obfuscate his real opinions

6. According to the author, Browne lived at a time of significant

   (A) linguistic experimentation
   (B) literary conservatism
   (C) linguistic stability
   (D) metaphorical license
   (E) impoverishment of the English language

7. In lines 24–33 ("Browne, though he gave less disturbance...in the place of joints"), the author classifies Browne's diction in a manner that proceeds from

   (A) interesting, to captivating, to intriguing
   (B) appropriate, to inappropriate, to superfluous
   (C) interesting, to intriguing, to disappointing
   (D) useful, to unhelpful, to deleterious
   (E) appropriate, to inappropriate, to intriguing

8. The author posits that Browne's unusual diction can be tied to his desire to

   (A) mystify his readers
   (B) develop English phraseology
   (C) enrich the English language
   (D) set himself apart from other authors of his time
   (E) express exactly his unusual thoughts

9. According to the author, Browne's style is marked by

   (A) heteroclite diction
   (B) homogeneous words
   (C) mundane vocabulary
   (D) humorous phrases
   (E) heterogeneous tropes

10. Which of the following best summarizes the passage?

   (A) An impartial reconsideration of Browne's style
   (B) A scathing critique by a rival
   (C) A manifesto by one of Browne's colleagues
   (D) A comparative study of Milton and Browne
   (E) A virulent polemic

11. The author's tone in this passage is best described as

   (A) sarcastic and doctrinaire
   (B) analytical and scholarly
   (C) expository and harsh
   (D) indulgent and condescending
   (E) capricious and sentimental

GO ON TO THE NEXT PAGE.

Questions 12–20. Read the following passage carefully before you choose your answers.

This passage is excerpted from an essay about the author George Eliot that was first published in 1919.

But is it upon the heroines that we would cast a final glance. "I have always been finding out my religion since I was a little girl," says Dorothea Casaubon. "I used to pray
Line so much—now I hardly ever pray. I try not to have desires
5 merely for myself." She is speaking for them all. That is their problem. They cannot live without religion, and they start out on the search for one when they are little girls. Each has the deep feminine passion for goodness, which makes the place where she stands in aspiration and agony the heart
10 of the book—still and cloistered like a place of worship, but that she no longer knows to whom to pray. In learning they seek their goal; in the ordinary tasks of womanhood; in the wider service of their kind. They do not find what they seek, and we cannot wonder. The ancient consciousness
15 of woman, charged with suffering and sensibility, and for so many ages dumb, seems in them to have brimmed and overflowed and uttered a demand for something— they scarcely know what—for something that is perhaps incompatible with the facts of human existence. George
20 Eliot had far too strong an intelligence to tamper with those facts, and too broad a humour to mitigate the truth because it was a stern one. Save for the supreme courage of their endeavour, the struggle ends, for her heroines, in tragedy, or in a compromise that is even more melancholy. But their
25 story is the incomplete version of the story that is George Eliot herself. For her, too, the burden and the complexity of womanhood were not enough; she must reach beyond the sanctuary and pluck for herself the strange bright fruits of art and knowledge. Clasping them as few women have ever
30 clasped them, she would not renounce her own inheritance— the difference of view, the difference of standard—nor accept an inappropriate reward. Thus we behold her, a memorable figure, inordinately praised and shrinking from her fame, despondent, reserved, shuddering back into the arms of
35 love as if there alone were satisfaction and, it might be, justification, at the same time reaching out with "a fastidious yet hungry ambition" for all that life could offer the free and inquiring mind and confronting her feminine aspirations with the real world of men. Triumphant was the issue for
40 her, whatever it may have been for her creations, and as we recollect all that she dared and achieved, how with every obstacle against her—sex and health and convention—she sought more knowledge and more freedom till the body, weighted with its double burden, sank worn out, we must lay
45 upon her grave whatever we have it in our power to bestow of laurel and rose.

12. The author's attitude toward George Eliot is best described as one of

(A) idolatrous devotion
(B) profound admiration
(C) feigned intimacy
(D) qualified enthusiasm
(E) reasoned objectivity

13. According to the speaker, George Eliot's heroines are "cloistered" (line 10) because they are

(A) in a church
(B) essentially alone
(C) in a monastery
(D) imprisoned in cloisters
(E) lost in prayer

14. In context, "the facts of human existence" (line 19)

(A) restrict both men and women
(B) restrict women only
(C) are applicable only to Eliot's heroines
(D) pertain to any literary character
(E) pertain to men only

15. "Save for" (line 22) most nearly means

(A) except for
(B) saving
(C) safe for
(D) guarding against
(E) keeping in mind

16. The "differences" mentioned in line 31 pertain to Eliot's

(A) profession
(B) class
(C) upbringing
(D) education
(E) gender

17. According to the speaker, Eliot

(A) enjoyed excellent health
(B) suffered from her independence and knowledge
(C) was prevented from attaining fame by men
(D) was very unlike the heroines of her books
(E) repudiated her feminine nature

GO ON TO THE NEXT PAGE.

18. In the sentence beginning "Thus we behold her" (lines 32–39), the speaker employs all of the following EXCEPT

   (A) apposition
   (B) hyperbole
   (C) personification
   (D) relative clauses
   (E) parallelism

19. It is reasonable to assume that the phrase "a fastidious yet hungry ambition" (lines 36–37)

   (A) is spoken by one of Eliot's heroines
   (B) comes from one of the speaker's literary works
   (C) is borrowed from one of Eliot's critics
   (D) is not to be taken seriously
   (E) does not represent the speaker's point of view

20. Generally, the style of the entire passage is best defined as

   (A) effusive and disorganized
   (B) pedantic and terse
   (C) sympathetic and concrete
   (D) abstract and metaphysical
   (E) intellectual and cynical

GO ON TO THE NEXT PAGE.

Questions 21–29. Read the following passage carefully before you choose your answers.

This passage is excerpted from a book of essays on race by renowned American sociologist W. E. B. Du Bois, published in 1903.

And yet, being a problem is a strange experience— peculiar even for one who has never been anything else, save perhaps in babyhood and in Europe. It is in the early
Line days of rollicking boyhood that the revelation first bursts
5 upon one, all in a day, as it were. I remember well when the shadow swept across me. I was a little thing, away up in the hills of New England, where the dark Housatonic winds between Hoosac and Taghkanic to the sea. In a wee wooden schoolhouse, something put it into the boys' and girls' heads
10 to buy gorgeous visiting-cards—ten cents a package—and exchange. The exchange was merry, till one girl, a tall newcomer, refused my card—refused it peremptorily, with a glance. Then it dawned upon me with a certain suddenness that I was different from the others; or like, mayhap, in heart
15 and life and longing, but shut out from their world by a vast veil. I had thereafter no desire to tear down that veil, to creep through; I held all beyond it in common contempt, and lived above it in a region of blue sky and great wandering shadows. That sky was bluest when I could beat my mates
20 at examination-time, or beat them at a foot-race, or even beat their stringy heads. Alas, with the years all this fine contempt began to fade; for the worlds I longed for, and all their dazzling opportunities, were theirs, not mine. But they should not keep these prizes, I said; some, all, I would wrest
25 from them. Just how I would do it I could never decide: by reading law, by healing the sick, by telling the wonderful tales that swam in my head—some way. With other black boys the strife was not so fiercely sunny: their youth shrunk into tasteless sycophancy, or into silent hatred of the pale
30 world about them and mocking distrust of everything white; or wasted itself in a bitter cry, Why did God make me an outcast and a stranger in mine own house? The shades of the prison-house closed round about us all: walls strait and stubborn to the whitest, but relentlessly narrow, tall, and
35 unscalable to sons of night who must plod darkly on in resignation, or beat unavailing palms against the stone, or steadily, half hopelessly, watch the streak of blue above.

21. The phrase "being a problem is a strange experience" (line 1) contributes to the unity of the passage in which of the following ways?

(A) As a contrast to the author's relationship with his schoolmates
(B) As a condemnation of racial prejudice
(C) As a parallel to the universal sense of black alienation
(D) As an indication of the author's own sense of racial disharmony
(E) As a satirical comment on the author's own shortcomings

22. In this passage, the anecdote of the visiting-cards serves as

(A) an epiphany for the speaker
(B) a moment of triumph for the speaker
(C) a revelation for the reader
(D) a turning point for the school
(E) a chance for redemption for the speaker

23. After presenting the incident of the visiting-cards, the speaker controls the rest of the passage by employing

(A) repeated appeals to authority
(B) a series of euphemisms
(C) a series of analogies
(D) two extended metaphors
(E) self-deprecating humor

24. In line 17, the word "it" refers to

(A) "world" (line 15)
(B) "veil" (line 16)
(C) "creep" (line 17)
(D) "contempt" (line 17)
(E) "sky" (line 18)

25. The speaker uses the word "beat" three times in lines 19–21 in order to

(A) appeal to the audience's moral sensibilities about race relations
(B) underscore his contempt of his peer group at that time
(C) establish a contrast between the first two uses of the word and the third use
(D) rely on a universal principle for future racial interactions
(E) analyze the power dynamics inherent in sociological interactions

GO ON TO THE NEXT PAGE.

26. The "sons of night" (line 35) are

    (A) evil young men
    (B) African American boys
    (C) sons of evil parents
    (D) lost souls
    (E) prisoners

27. One can infer from the passage all of the following EXCEPT that

    (A) the speaker considered himself inferior to his white peers
    (B) the speaker considered himself superior to his African American peers
    (C) the other African American boys treated their white peers with deference
    (D) the speaker was superior to his white peers in many ways
    (E) the speaker felt isolated from both white and African American peers

28. The speaker's contempt wanes and is replaced by

    (A) a commitment to become a famous professional
    (B) a pledge to beat his peers in athletic contests
    (C) a helpless rage against society
    (D) a spirit of revenge
    (E) actions that eventually lead him to prison

29. The tone of this passage would NOT be described as

    (A) self-aware
    (B) decisive
    (C) fervent
    (D) reflective
    (E) laudatory

GO ON TO THE NEXT PAGE.

Questions 30–40. Read the following passage carefully before you choose your answers.

This is from the Lincoln-Douglas Debates of 1858.

Now, I hold that Illinois had a right to abolish and prohibit slavery as she did, and I hold that Kentucky has the same right to continue and protect slavery that Illinois
Line had to abolish it. I hold that New York had as much right to
5   abolish slavery as Virginia has to continue it, and that each and every State of this Union is a sovereign power, with the right to do as it pleases upon this question of slavery, and upon all its domestic institutions. Slavery is not the only question which comes up in this controversy. There is a far
10   more important one to you, and that is, what shall be done with the free negro? We have settled the slavery question as far as we are concerned; we have prohibited it in Illinois forever, and in doing so, I think we have done wisely, and there is no man in the State who would be more strenuous in
15   his opposition to the introduction of slavery than I would; but when we settled it for our selves, we exhausted all our power over that subject. We have done our whole duty, and can do no more. We must leave each and every other State to decide for itself the same question. In relation to the policy to be
20   pursued toward the free negroes, we have said that they shall not vote; whilst Maine, on the other hand, has said that they shall vote. Maine is a sovereign State, and has the power to regulate the qualifications of voters within her limits. I would never consent to confer the right of voting and of citizenship
25   upon a negro, but still I am not going to quarrel with Maine for differing from me in opinion. Let Maine take care of her own negroes, and fix the qualifications of her own voters to suit herself, without interfering with Illinois, and Illinois will not interfere with Maine. So with the State of New York.
30   She allows the negro to vote provided he owns two hundred and fifty dollars' worth of property, but not otherwise. While I would not make any distinction whatever between a negro who held property and one who did not, yet if the sovereign State of New York chooses to make that distinction
35   it is her business and not mine, and I will not quarrel with her for it. She can do as she pleases on this question if she minds her own business, and we will do the same thing. Now, my friends, if we will only act conscientiously and rigidly upon this great principle of popular sovereignty,
40   which guarantees to each State and Territory the right to do as it pleases on all things, local and domestic, instead of Congress interfering, we will continue at peace one with another. Why should Illinois be at war with Missouri, or Kentucky with Ohio, or Virginia, with New York, merely
45   because their institutions differ? Our fathers intended that our institutions should differ. They knew that the North and the South, having different climates, productions, and interests, required different institutions. This doctrine of Mr. Lincoln, of uniformity among the institutions of the different
50   States, is a new doctrine, never dreamed of by Washington, Madison, or the framers of this government. Mr. Lincoln and the Republican party set themselves up as wiser than these

men who made this government, which has flourished for seventy years under the principle of popular sovereignty,
55   recognizing the right of each State to do as it pleased. Under that principle, we have grown from a nation of three or four millions to a nation of about thirty millions of people; we have crossed the Allegheny mountains and filled up the whole Northwest, turning the prairie into a garden, and
60   building up churches and schools, thus spreading civilization and Christianity where before there was nothing but savage barbarism. Under that principle we have become, from a feeble nation, the most powerful on the face of the earth, and if we only adhere to that principle, we can go forward
65   increasing in territory, in power, in strength, and in glory until the Republic of America shall be the north star that shall guide the friend of freedom throughout the civilized world. And why can we not adhere to the great principle of self-government upon which our institutions were originally
70   based? I believe that this new doctrine preached by Mr. Lincoln and his party will dissolve the Union if it succeeds. They are trying to array all the Northern States in one body against the South, to excite a sectional war between the free States and the slave States, in order that the one or the other
75   may be driven to the wall.

30. In this passage the speaker's purpose is to

   (A) analyze the causes of slavery
   (B) argue in favor of states' rights
   (C) criticize individual states
   (D) describe the advantages of a federal government
   (E) argue in favor of slavery

31. Which of the following best describes the tone of the passage?

   (A) Mock enthusiasm
   (B) Righteous indignation
   (C) Well-reasoned polemic
   (D) Objective rationalization
   (E) Ironic detachment

GO ON TO THE NEXT PAGE.

32. In the first two sentences (lines 1–8), the speaker grounds his central idea on which of the following rhetorical strategies?

    (A) Inductive reasoning
    (B) Deductive reasoning
    (C) Description
    (D) Classification
    (E) Appeal to ignorance

33. In line 36, the word "it" most closely refers to

    (A) "property" (line 33)
    (B) "State" (line 34)
    (C) "business" (line 35)
    (D) "distinction" (line 34)
    (E) "quarrel" (line 35)

34. The sentence that begins "Now, my friends, if we will..." (lines 38–43) contains all of the following EXCEPT

    (A) a classification
    (B) an appeal to a principle
    (C) a call to action
    (D) a definition
    (E) an accusation

35. The author suggests that which of the following is true of Maine, Illinois, and New York?

    (A) They have relatively liberal policies toward "negroes."
    (B) They prove that popular sovereignty has been generally successful.
    (C) They exemplify the principle of popular sovereignty.
    (D) They create inconsistent laws for both "negroes" and citizens.
    (E) They create laws concerned more with wealth than justice.

36. The speaker substantiates his central idea with

    (A) clever anecdotes
    (B) innovative symbols
    (C) unusual paradoxes
    (D) extended metaphors
    (E) appeal to authority

37. From the passage, it appears that the speaker's personal view is that African Americans

    (A) should be slaves and should not be allowed to hold property
    (B) should not be slaves and should be allowed to vote
    (C) should not be free but should be allowed to hold some property
    (D) should be free but not allowed to vote
    (E) should be allowed to hold property and to vote

38. The author implies that Abraham Lincoln's policies would have all of the following potential negative effects EXCEPT

    (A) consolidating power
    (B) hindering westward expansion
    (C) dissolving the Union
    (D) initiating war
    (E) hindering population growth

39. In the final lines of the passage, the speaker attempts to win over his audience by

    (A) inspiring confidence
    (B) shifting blame
    (C) instilling fear
    (D) reconciling differences
    (E) overstating a problem

40. The development of the passage can best be described as the

    (A) argument for a particular solution to a political problem
    (B) rebuttal of those who challenge the authority of Congress
    (C) explanation of the failings of a political opponent
    (D) exploration of the various meanings of a universal principle
    (E) comparison between two political entities

GO ON TO THE NEXT PAGE.

Questions 41–55. Read the following passage carefully before you choose your answers.

This passage is excerpted from a recent work that examines popular conceptions of the history of medieval Spain.

If you have read anything about medieval Spain, then you probably know about *convivencia*—the peaceful "coexistence" of Muslims, Christians, and Jews for nearly
Line eight hundred years on the Iberian peninsula. The story
5 is invariably told in the same way: "once upon a time,"[1] after the Muslim invasion of the Iberian peninsula in 711, a "culture of tolerance"[2] was created among Muslims, Christians, and Jews. Tolerant adherents of these three Abrahamic faiths shared philosophical and scientific
10 learning, translating previously unknown sources (especially the works of Aristotle) for the rest of Europe. "But," the author or narrator intones in his gravest voice, "this world too quickly vanished. Greed, fear, and intolerance swept it away. Puritanical judgments and absolutism snuffed out the
15 light of learning." Then the author or narrator laments the loss of this vanished world: "it was truly a bright light in what was largely a dark and ignorant medieval landscape. Its loss is one of the great tragedies in history."[3] This is almost always followed by a didactic—and dramatic—moral
20 about the relevance of medieval Spain for contemporary problems: "Humanity has never completely found the way back. Medieval Spain might help point the way."[4] This is a fairy tale for adults who, like children, know nothing about the actual (medieval) world it attempts to describe. The story
25 of *convivencia* fulfills the requirements of the genre, replete as it is with exotic journeys in faraway lands and epic battles between noble heroes and depraved villains. And like all fairy tales, this story of *convivencia* tells us much more about the world of storytelling in which it was created than about
30 the historical past or objective reality, on which it is only loosely based.
　While some of the recent books on *convivencia* have gestured in the direction of scholarly discourse, more often than not, they cannot resist the temptation to indulge
35 our basest tendencies to Orientalism and exoticism. In nearly every popular recounting of *convivencia,* images of an Islamic *locus amoenus* abound: we hear of gardens, bath-houses, exotic fruits, and enchanting mosques. Chris Lowney, in *A Vanished World,* emphasized that "daily life
40 was transformed as exotic new species like cotton, figs, spinach, and watermelon burgeoned in fields nourished by new irrigation techniques." The "luxury and sophistication" of the Islamic city of Cordoba "undoubtedly surpassed anything found elsewhere in Europe." Maria Rosa Menocal's
45 syrupy confection, *The Ornament of the World,* simmers

1　Maria Rosa Menocal, *Ornament of the World: How Muslims, Christians, and Jews Created a Culture of Tolerance in Medieval Spain* (New York: Little, Brown, 2002), 5.
2　The subtitle of Menocal's *Ornament of the World.*
3　Chris Lowney, *A Vanished World: Muslims, Christians, and Jews in Medieval Spain* (Oxford: Oxford University Press, 2005).
4　Lowney, *A Vanished World,* 14.

under a thick layer of Orientalized cheese. Some of her chapter titles themselves suffice to prove the point, "The Palaces of Memory," "The Mosque and the Palm Tree," "A Grand Vizier, A Grand City," "The Gardens of Memory,"
50 and "Sailing Away, Riding Away." And when these authors describe Islam, it is with the wonderment and delight of a tourist. We, their audience, are supposed to share in their surprise—and in the delicious irony—that Islam was a peaceful, tolerant religion, while Christianity was
55 persecutory, cruel, and violent.

41. One purpose of the first paragraph is to

　(A) discount the importance of medieval history
　(B) reinforce a popular perception of medieval Spain
　(C) suggest that historical research will need to explore new sources
　(D) define *convivencia* for non-specialists
　(E) distinguish among the various historical accounts of medieval Spain

42. The primary purpose of the quotes in the first paragraph is to

　(A) emphasize the author's bewilderment with the narrative of medieval history offered by most historians of medieval Spain
　(B) reinforce the author's position that proponents of *convivencia* misinterpret their evidence by quoting directly from their works
　(C) suggest an alternate interpretation of the historical record
　(D) recount the conventional narrative of *convivencia* in the words of its historians
　(E) provide a comprehensive survey of the history of medieval Spain

43. The footnotes serve to

　(A) demonstrate the range of sources he cites
　(B) reveal that all the quotes are from the same source
　(C) provide documentation for the sources of his quotes
　(D) impress the reader with the technical expertise of the author
　(E) explain the complexity of the argument at hand

GO ON TO THE NEXT PAGE.

44. The content of the second footnote

(A) undermines the claims made by Maria Rosa Menocal
(B) provides a citation for more information about the subject
(C) introduces information that will turn out to be essential to the main argument
(D) informs the reader of the whereabouts of a certain text
(E) clarifies the source of the expression used in the text

45. The word "contemporary" (line 20) most nearly means

(A) artistic
(B) current
(C) similar
(D) historical
(E) global

46. In line 25, the word "genre" refers to

(A) "fairy tale" (line 23)
(B) "*convivencia*" (line 25)
(C) "children" (line 23)
(D) "it" (line 26)
(E) "exotic journeys" (line 26)

47. Which of the following rhetorical devices is used in lines 22–24 ("This...describe")?

(A) Analogy
(B) Understatement
(C) Simile
(D) Classical allusion
(E) Hyperbole

48. Which one of the following characteristics of the scholarship on *convivencia* is most troublesome to the author?

(A) Its inherent lack of documentary evidence
(B) Its misleading emphasis on the importance of religion
(C) Its lack of methodological rigor or complexity
(D) Its preoccupation with Islamic historical trends
(E) Its tendency to exaggerate historical reality

49. All of the following accurately describe the tone of the second paragraph EXCEPT

(A) emphatic
(B) acerbic
(C) relieved
(D) comic
(E) vituperative

50. The word "gestured" (line 33) most nearly means

(A) addressed incompletely
(B) characterized dishonestly
(C) questioned fully
(D) transferred abruptly
(E) figured expressively

51. Which of the following sentences best represents the author's main point in the passage?

(A) "If you have read anything about medieval Spain, then you probably know about *convivencia*—the peaceful "coexistence" of Muslims, Christians, and Jews for nearly eight hundred years on the Iberian peninsula." (lines 1–4)
(B) "And like all fairy tales, this story of *convivencia* tells us much more about the world of storytelling in which it was created than about the historical past or objective reality, on which it is only loosely based." (lines 27–31)
(C) "While some of the recent books on *convivencia* have gestured in the direction of scholarly discourse, more often than not, they cannot resist the temptation to indulge our basest tendencies to Orientalism and exoticism." (lines 32–35)
(D) "And when these authors describe Islam, it is with the wonderment and delight of a tourist." (lines 50–52)
(E) "We, their audience, are supposed to share in their surprise—and in the delicious irony—that Islam was a peaceful, tolerant religion, while Christianity was persecutory, cruel, and violent." (lines 52–55)

52. The author's observation about Maria Rosa Menocal's *The Ornament of the World* (lines 44–46) is best described as an example of which of the following?

(A) Alliteration
(B) Metaphor
(C) Allegory
(D) Linguistic paradox
(E) Personification

GO ON TO THE NEXT PAGE.

53. The speaker mentions the chapter titles in lines 47–50 as examples of which of the following?

   (A) Islamic history
   (B) Poetic imagery
   (C) Hyperbolic language
   (D) Orientalist excess
   (E) Failed metaphors

54. Which of the following best describes the rhetorical function of the phrase "and in the delicious irony" (line 53)?

   (A) It raises a question the author answered at the beginning of the second paragraph.
   (B) It alludes to a contention made in the first paragraph.
   (C) It reiterates the thesis of the passage as stated in the first paragraph.
   (D) It critiques the scholarly discourse of *convivencia*.
   (E) It extends the metaphorical language of the second paragraph.

55. The passage as a whole is best characterized as

   (A) a treatise on history
   (B) an ironic attack
   (C) a qualified dismissal
   (D) an analysis of historical evidence
   (E) a vituperative comparison

END OF SECTION I

AP® English Language and Composition Exam

SECTION II: Free-Response Questions

DO NOT OPEN THIS BOOKLET UNTIL YOU ARE TOLD TO DO SO.

At a Glance

Total Time
2 hours, plus a 15-minute reading period

Number of Questions
3

Percent of Total Grade
55%

Writing Instrument
Pen required

Instructions

Section II of this examination requires answers in essay form. To help you use your time well, the coordinator will announce the time at which each question should be completed. If you finish any question before time is announced, you may go on to the following question. If you finish the examination in less than the time allotted, you may go back and work on any essay question you want.

Each essay will be judged on its clarity and effectiveness in dealing with the requirements of the topic assigned and on the quality of the writing. After completing each question, you should check your essay for accuracy of punctuation, spelling, and diction; you are advised, however, not to attempt many longer corrections. Remember that quality is far more important than quantity.

Write your essays with a pen, preferably in black or dark blue ink. Be sure to write CLEARLY and LEGIBLY. Cross out any errors you make.

The questions for Section II are printed in the green insert. You are encouraged to use the green insert to make notes and to plan your essays, but be sure to write your answers in the pink booklet. Number each answer as the question is numbered in the examination. Do not skip lines. Begin each answer on a new page in the pink booklet.

GO ON TO THE NEXT PAGE.

ENGLISH LANGUAGE AND COMPOSITION
SECTION II
Total Time—2 hours, 15 minutes

Question 1

Suggested reading and writing time—55 minutes.
It is suggested that you spend 15 minutes reading the question, analyzing and evaluating the sources,
and 40 minutes writing your response.
Note: You may begin writing your response before the reading period is over.

(This question counts for one-third of the total essay section score.)

Individuals have argued the concept of what it means to live a good life for thousands of years. Many have posited that happiness is an internal choice, a question of free will, and that it is something that can be reached every moment of every day. Others have pointed to external factors such as the slow accumulation of wealth and the construction of solid relationships—both of which require time and long-term strategy—as the primary drivers of a "life well-lived." More recently, some have even pointed to the role of genes in determining life satisfaction.

Carefully read the following seven sources, including the introductory information for each source. Then synthesize the information from at least three of the sources and incorporate it into a coherent, well-developed essay that argues a clear position on whether life satisfaction is better achieved by living in the moment or by working toward long-term goals.

Your argument should be the focus of your essay. Use the sources to develop your argument and explain the reasoning for it. Avoid merely summarizing the sources. Indicate clearly which sources you are drawing from, whether through direct quotation, paraphrase, or summary. You may cite the sources as Source A, Source B, and so forth, or by using the descriptions in parentheses.

Source A	(National Institute on Drug Abuse)
Source B	(Dixit)
Source C	(graph)
Source D	(Macdonald)
Source E	(chart)
Source F	(Ferriss)
Source G	(Department of Labor)

GO ON TO THE NEXT PAGE.

Source A

"Drugs, Brains, and Behavior: The Science of
Addiction." National Institute on Drug Abuse.
2014. Web. 2 Feb. 2017.

The following is excerpted from an article on the National Institute of Health's Web site.

How do drugs work in the brain to produce pleasure?

Most drugs of abuse directly or indirectly target the brain's reward system by flooding the circuit with dopamine. Dopamine is a neurotransmitter present in regions of the brain that regulate movement, emotion, motivation, and feelings of pleasure. When activated at normal levels, this system rewards our natural behaviors. Overstimulating the system with drugs, however, produces euphoric effects, which strongly reinforce the behavior of drug use—teaching the user to repeat it. Most drugs of abuse target the brain's reward system by flooding it with dopamine.

How does stimulation of the brain's pleasure circuit teach us to keep taking drugs?

Our brains are wired to ensure that we will repeat life-sustaining activities by associating those activities with pleasure or reward. Whenever this reward circuit is activated, the brain notes that something important is happening that needs to be remembered, and teaches us to do it again and again without thinking about it. Because drugs of abuse stimulate the same circuit, we learn to abuse drugs in the same way.

Why are drugs more addictive than natural rewards?

When some drugs of abuse are taken, they can release 2 to 10 times the amount of dopamine that natural rewards such as eating do. In some cases, this occurs almost immediately (as when drugs are smoked or injected), and the effects can last much longer than those produced by natural rewards. The resulting effects on the brain's pleasure circuit dwarf those produced by naturally rewarding behaviors. The effect of such a powerful reward strongly motivates people to take drugs again and again. This is why scientists sometimes say that drug abuse is something we learn to do very, very well.

What happens to your brain if you keep taking drugs?

For the brain, the difference between normal rewards and drug rewards can be described as the difference between someone whispering into your ear and someone shouting into a microphone. Just as we turn down the volume on a radio that is too loud, the brain adjusts to the overwhelming surges in dopamine (and other neurotransmitters) by producing less dopamine or by reducing the number of receptors that can receive signals. As a result, dopamine's impact on the reward circuit of the brain of someone who abuses drugs can become abnormally low, and that person's ability to experience *any* pleasure is reduced.

This is why a person who abuses drugs eventually feels flat, lifeless, and depressed, and is unable to enjoy things that were once pleasurable. Now, the person needs to keep taking drugs again and again just to try and bring his or her dopamine function back up to normal—which only makes the problem worse, like a vicious cycle. Also, the person will often need to take larger amounts of the drug to produce the familiar dopamine high—an effect known as tolerance.

GO ON TO THE NEXT PAGE.

Source B

Dixit, Jay. "The Art of Now: Six Steps to Living in the
Moment." *Psychology Today.* 1 Nov. 2008. Web.
2 Feb. 2017.

The following is excerpted from an article published by a Web site dedicated to current psychology topics and research.

Life unfolds in the present. But so often, we let the present slip away, allowing time to rush past unobserved and unseized, and squandering the precious seconds of our lives as we worry about the future and ruminate about what's past.

When we're at work, we fantasize about being on vacation; on vacation, we worry about the work piling up on our desks. We dwell on intrusive memories of the past or fret about what may or may not happen in the future. We don't appreciate the living present because our "monkey minds," as Buddhists call them, vault from thought to thought like monkeys swinging from tree to tree.

Most of us don't undertake our thoughts in awareness. Rather, our thoughts control us. "Ordinary thoughts course through our mind like a deafening waterfall," writes Jon Kabat-Zinn, the biomedical scientist who introduced meditation into mainstream medicine. In order to feel more in control of our minds and our lives, to find the sense of balance that eludes us, we need to step out of this current, to pause, and, as Kabat-Zinn puts it, to "rest in stillness—to stop doing and focus on just being."

We need to live more in the moment. Living in the moment—also called mindfulness—is a state of active, open, intentional attention on the present. When you become mindful, you realize that you are not your thoughts; you become an observer of your thoughts from moment to moment without judging them. Mindfulness involves being with your thoughts as they are, neither grasping at them nor pushing them away. Instead of letting your life go by without living it, you awaken to experience.

Cultivating a nonjudgmental awareness of the present bestows a host of benefits. Mindfulness reduces stress, boosts immune functioning, reduces chronic pain, lowers blood pressure, and helps patients cope with cancer. By alleviating stress, spending a few minutes a day actively focusing on living in the moment reduces the risk of heart disease. Mindfulness may even slow the progression of HIV.

Mindful people are happier, more exuberant, more empathetic, and more secure. They have higher self-esteem and are more accepting of their own weaknesses. Anchoring awareness in the here and now reduces the kinds of impulsivity and reactivity that underlie depression, binge eating, and attention problems. Mindful people can hear negative feedback without feeling threatened. They fight less with their romantic partners and are more accommodating and less defensive. As a result, mindful couples have more satisfying relationships.

Mindfulness is at the root of Buddhism, Taoism, and many Native-American traditions, not to mention yoga. It's why Thoreau went to Walden Pond; it's what Emerson and Whitman wrote about in their essays and poems.

"Everyone agrees it's important to live in the moment, but the problem is how," says Ellen Langer, a psychologist at Harvard and author of *Mindfulness.* "When people are not in the moment, they're not there to know that they're not there." Overriding the distraction reflex and awakening to the present takes intentionality and practice.

Living in the moment involves a profound paradox: You can't pursue it for its benefits. That's because the expectation of reward launches a future-oriented mindset, which subverts the entire process. Instead, you just have to trust that the rewards will come.

GO ON TO THE NEXT PAGE.

Source C

Desilver, Drew. "The Bipartisan Federal Debt Limit."
Pew Research Center. 27 Sept 2013. Web. 2 Feb
2018.

The following chart shows the growth of national debt between 1980 and 2013.

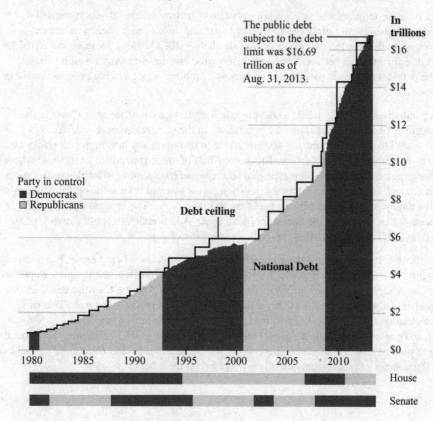

Source: Pew Research Center, "The Bipartisan Federal Debt Limit."

GO ON TO THE NEXT PAGE.

Source D

Macdonald, Donald E. "Climate Change Strategies 101." *Earth Common Journal*, a publication of MacEwan University. Vol. 3, No. 1. 2013.

The following is excerpted from an academic journal focused on environmental issues.

Climate change is a long-term decadal issue, while western-style democracies are short-term (2-4 year). Rising GHG emissions are tightly linked to energy use and development, with our current heavy reliance on fossil fuels as the root cause of climate change (IPCC, 2007). Hofmeister (2010) has argued that this timing mismatch between long-term energy use and development, resulting climate changes, and the political process is part of our fundamental problem in not making progress on these intertwined issues.

Bold new policy initiatives generally need to take place before the term of office is half over as this is generally thought to be a high-risk venture by politicians. In the second half of the elected term, politicians tend to shift to pre-electioneering and are averse to taking on any new high-risk policy or fiscal actions that may affect their electability. This second half of the term tends to be the time wherein new climate change policies that have been approved and announced can move to implementation—a politically quiet activity. However, this raises the question…how can you review the performance or effectiveness of a policy in the limited time frame of the political cycle? The results of strong policy may not be evident for years beyond the normal political cycle. Additionally, the policy review phase is often hammered by GHG data that is often two or more years out of date.

This makes it difficult for policy makers to assess whether or not progress is being made. For relatively stable governments, who tend to stay in power for long periods of time (such as the People's Republic of China or the conservative-dominated government in the province of Alberta, Canada) this does not pose a great problem. However, most democracies have a great deal of political turnover. This can lead to constantly changing climate policy positions and strategies with few policy actions moving to implementation and consequently, little progress being made in reducing GHG emissions. The United States is a case in point; Democrat administrations try to put climate change and environmental policies in place while Republican administrations usually attempt to roll them back.

GO ON TO THE NEXT PAGE.

Source E

"8-channel model of flow," a concept in psychology based on the research of psychologist Mihály Csíkszentmihályi.

In positive psychology, flow, also known as the zone, is the mental state of operation in which a person performing an activity is fully immersed in a feeling of energized focus, full involvement, and enjoyment in the process of the activity. The chart below describes the balance that a person encounters, when doing an activity, between how much challenge the task presents and how much skill that person already possesses for the activity. Experts such as Mihály Csíkszentmihályi have suggested that happiness can be found by entering the upper right quadrant of this chart.

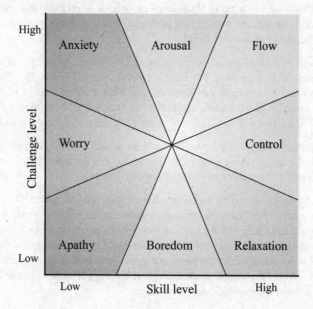

GO ON TO THE NEXT PAGE.

Source F

Ferriss, Timothy. *The 4-Hour Work Week.* 2007.

The following is excerpted from a book about redesigning your lifestyle in order to work less and increase your income.

To do or not to do? To try or not to try? Most people will vote no, whether they consider themselves brave or not. Uncertainty and the prospect of failure can be very scary noises in the shadows. Most people will choose unhappiness over uncertainty. For years, I set goals, made resolutions to change direction, and nothing came of either. I was just as insecure and scared as the rest of the world.

The simple solution came to me accidentally four years ago. At that time, I had more money than I knew what to do with—I was making $70K or so per month—and I was completely miserable, worse than ever. I had no time and was working myself to death. I had started my own company, only to realize it would be nearly impossible to sell.

Critical mistakes in its infancy would never let me sell it. I could hire magic elves and connect my brain to a supercomputer—it didn't matter. My little baby had some serious birth defects. The question then became, How do I free myself from this Frankenstein while making it self-sustaining? How do I pry myself from the tentacles of workaholism and the fear that it would fall to pieces without my 15-hour days? How do I escape this self-made prison? A trip, I decided. A sabbatical year around the world.

So I took the trip, right? First, I felt it prudent to dance around with my shame, embarrassment, and anger for six months, all the while playing an endless loop of reasons why my cop-out fantasy trip could never work. One of my more productive periods, for sure.

Then a funny thing happened. In my undying quest to make myself miserable, I accidentally began to backpedal. As soon as I cut through the vague unease and ambiguous anxiety by defining my nightmare, the worst-case scenario, I wasn't as worried about taking a trip. I could always take a temporary bartending job to pay the rent if I had to. I could sell some furniture and cut back on eating out. I could steal lunch money from the kindergarteners who passed by my apartment every morning. The options were many. I realized it wouldn't be that hard to get back to where I was, let alone survive. None of these things would be fatal—not even close.

I realized that on a scale of 1–10, 1 being nothing and 10 being permanently life-changing, my so-called worst-case scenario might have a temporary impact of 3 or 4. On the other hand, if I realized my best-case scenario, or even a probable-case scenario, it would easily have a permanent 9 or 10 positive life-changing effect.

In other words, I was risking an unlikely and temporary 3 or 4 for a probable and permanent 9 or 10, and I could easily recover my baseline workaholic prison with a bit of extra work if I wanted to. This all equated to a significant realization: There was practically no risk, only huge life-changing upside potential.

That is when I made the decision to take the trip and bought a one-way ticket to Europe. I started planning my adventures and eliminating my physical and psychological baggage. None of my disasters came to pass, and my life has been a near fairy tale since.

GO ON TO THE NEXT PAGE.

Source G

"Top 10 Ways to Prepare for Retirement." *Employee Benefits Security Administration/United States Department of Labor.* Web. 2 Feb. 2017.

The following is excerpted from a pamphlet on retirement savings.

Fewer than half of Americans have calculated how much they need to save for retirement.

In 2014, 30 percent of private industry workers with access to a defined contribution plan (such as a 401(k) plan) did not participate.

The average American spends roughly 20 years in retirement. Putting money away for retirement is a habit we can all live with. Remember…saving matters!

Start saving, keep saving, and stick to your goals. If you are already saving, whether for retirement or another goal, keep going! You know that saving is a rewarding habit. If you're not saving, it's time to get started. Start small if you have to and try to increase the amount you save each month. The sooner you start saving, the more time your money has to grow. Make saving for retirement a priority. Devise a plan, stick to it, and set goals. Remember, it's never too early or too late to start saving.

Know your retirement needs. Retirement is expensive. Experts estimate that you will need at least 70 percent of your preretirement income—lower earners, 90 percent or more—to maintain your standard of living when you stop working. Take charge of your financial future. The key to a secure retirement is to plan ahead.

Contribute to your employer's retirement savings plan. If your employer offers a retirement savings plan, such as a 401(k) plan, sign up and contribute all you can. Your taxes will be lower, your company may kick in more, and automatic deductions make it easy. Over time, compound interest and tax deferrals make a big difference in the amount you will accumulate. Find out about your plan. For example, how much would you need to contribute to get the full employer contribution and how long you would need to stay in the plan to get that money?

Learn about your employer's pension plan. If your employer has a traditional pension plan, check to see if you are covered by the plan and understand how it works. Ask for an individual benefit statement to see what your benefit is worth. Before you change jobs, find out what will happen to your pension benefit. Learn what benefits you may have from a previous employer. Find out if you will be entitled to benefits from your spouse's plan.

Consider basic investment principles. How you save can be as important as how much you save. Inflation and the type of investments you make play important roles in how much you'll have saved at retirement. Know how your savings or pension plan is invested. Learn about your plan's investment options and ask questions. Put your savings in different types of investments. By diversifying this way, you are more likely to reduce risks and improve return. Your investment mix may change over time depending on a number of factors such as your age, goals, and financial circumstances. Financial security and knowledge go hand in hand.

Don't touch your retirement savings. If you withdraw your retirement savings now, you'll lose principal and interest and you may lose tax benefits or have to pay withdrawal penalties. If you change jobs, leave your savings invested in your current retirement plan, or roll them over to an IRA or your new employer's plan.

GO ON TO THE NEXT PAGE.

Question 2

Suggested time—40 minutes.

(This question counts for one-third of the total essay section score.)

The passage below is excerpted from one of Mark Twain's most famous essays, "Fenimore Cooper's Literary Offenses." At the time Twain wrote his essay, Cooper's novels were generally well liked and respected. Read the passage carefully. Then, in a well-developed essay, analyze the rhetorical strategies Twain uses to convey his attitude.

If Cooper had been an observer his inventive faculty would have worked better; not more interestingly, but more rationally, more plausibly. Cooper's proudest creations in
Line the way of "situations" suffer noticeably from the absence of
5 the observer's protecting gift. Cooper's eye was splendidly inaccurate. Cooper seldom saw anything correctly. He saw nearly all things as through a glass eye, darkly. Of course a man who cannot see the commonest little every-day matters accurately is working at a disadvantage when he is
10 constructing a "situation." In the *Deerslayer* tale Cooper has a stream which is fifty feet wide where it flows out of a lake; it presently narrows to twenty as it meanders along for no given reason, and yet when a stream acts like that it ought to be required to explain itself. Fourteen pages later the width
15 of the brook's outlet from the lake has suddenly shrunk thirty feet, and become "the narrowest part of the stream." This shrinkage is not accounted for. The stream has bends in it, a sure indication that it has alluvial banks and cuts them; yet these bends are only thirty and fifty feet long. If Cooper had
20 been a nice and punctilious observer he would have noticed that the bends were often nine hundred feet long than short of it.

Cooper made the exit of that stream fifty feet wide, in the first place, for no particular reason; in the second place,
25 he narrowed it to less than twenty to accommodate some Indians. He bends a "sapling" to form an arch over this narrow passage, and conceals six Indians in its foliage. They are "laying" for a settler's scow or ark which is coming up the stream on its way to the lake; it is being hauled against
30 the stiff current by rope whose stationary end is anchored in the lake; its rate of progress cannot be more than a mile an hour. Cooper describes the ark, but pretty obscurely. In the matter of dimensions "it was little more than a modern canal boat." Let us guess, then, that it was about one hundred and
35 forty feet long. It was of "greater breadth than common." Let us guess then that it was about sixteen feet wide. This leviathan had been prowling down bends which were but a third as long as itself, and scraping between banks where it only had two feet of space to spare on each side. We
40 cannot too much admire this miracle. A low-roofed dwelling occupies "two-thirds of the ark's length"—a dwelling ninety feet long and sixteen feet wide, let us say—a kind of

vestibule train. The dwelling has two rooms—each forty-five feet long and sixteen feet wide, let us guess. One of
45 them is the bedroom of the Hutter girls, Judith and Hetty; the other is the parlor in the daytime, at night it is papa's bedchamber. The ark is arriving at the stream's exit now, whose width has been reduced to less than twenty feet to accommodate the Indians—say to eighteen. There is a foot
50 to spare on each side of the boat. Did the Indians notice that there was going to be a tight squeeze there? Did they notice that they could make money by climbing down out of that arched sapling and just stepping aboard when the ark scraped by? No, other Indians would have noticed these things, but
55 Cooper's Indians never notice anything. Cooper thinks they are marvelous creatures for noticing, but he was almost always in error about his Indians. There was seldom a sane one among them.

The ark is one hundred and forty-feet long; the dwelling
60 is ninety feet long. The idea of the Indians is to drop softly and secretly from the arched sapling to the dwelling as the ark creeps along under it at the rate of a mile an hour, and butcher the family. It will take the ark a minute and a half to pass under. It will take the ninety-foot dwelling a minute to
65 pass under. Now, then, what did the six Indians do? It would take you thirty years to guess, and even then you would have to give it up, I believe. Therefore, I will tell you what the Indians did. Their chief, a person of quite extraordinary intellect for a Cooper Indian, warily watched the canal-boat
70 as it squeezed along under him and when he had got his calculations fined down to exactly the right shade, as he judged, he let go and dropped. And missed the boat! That is actually what he did. He missed the house, and landed in the stern of the scow. It was not much of a fall, yet it knocked
75 him silly. He lay there unconscious. If the house had been ninety-seven feet long he would have made the trip. The error lay in the construction of the house. Cooper was no architect.

There still remained in the roost five Indians. The boat
80 has passed under and is now out of their reach. Let me explain what the five did—you would not be able to reason it out for yourself. No. 1 jumped for the boat, but fell in the water astern of it. Then No. 2 jumped for the boat, but fell in the water still further astern of it. Then No. 3 jumped for

GO ON TO THE NEXT PAGE.

85 the boat, and fell a good way astern of it. Then No. 4 jumped
for the boat, and fell in the water away astern. Then even No. 5
made a jump for the boat—for he was a Cooper Indian. In that
matter of intellect, the difference between a Cooper Indian and
the Indian that stands in front of the cigar-shop is not spacious.

90 The scow episode is really a sublime burst of invention; but it
does not thrill, because the inaccuracy of details throw a sort
of air of fictitiousness and general improbability over it. This
comes of Cooper's inadequacy as observer.

GO ON TO THE NEXT PAGE.

Question 3

Suggested time—40 minutes.

(This question counts for one-third of the total essay section score.)

The French Enlightenment writer Voltaire wrote, "It is dangerous to be right in matters about which the established authorities are wrong."

In a well-written essay, develop your position on Voltaire's claim. Use appropriate evidence from your reading, experience, or observations to support your argument.

STOP

END OF EXAM

_____

Practice Test 2:
Answers and
Explanations

PRACTICE TEST 2 ANSWER KEY

1. C	29. E
2. B	30. B
3. C	31. C
4. A	32. A
5. A	33. D
6. A	34. A
7. D	35. C
8. E	36. E
9. A	37. D
10. A	38. E
11. B	39. C
12. B	40. A
13. B	41. D
14. B	42. D
15. A	43. C
16. E	44. E
17. B	45. B
18. D	46. A
19. A	47. C
20. C	48. E
21. D	49. C
22. A	50. A
23. D	51. B
24. B	52. B
25. C	53. D
26. B	54. E
27. A	55. B
28. A	

PRACTICE TEST 2 EXPLANATIONS

Multiple-Choice Questions

1. **C**   Often AP questions will ask you to infer—to draw a conclusion based on what is said in the text. The best course of action to take when approaching this question is POE. Choice (B) is the only one that posits a positive answer (to "laud" means to praise), and it can be eliminated easily because of the word "linear." The final sentence of the first paragraph does laud Browne's writing, but the author suggests that the reading process is like going through a series of mazes. This is anything but straightforward—or linear. Later in the text, there is an indirect allusion to William Shakespeare ("the time of Elizabeth"), but there is nothing resembling a comparison between Browne and Shakespeare; eliminate (D). There is even less reason to suspect that there is any suggestion of a comparison between the author of the passage (Samuel Johnson) and Browne; so you can eliminate (E). Now you're down to two choices. The author criticizes the exuberance and lack of clarity that makes it difficult to understand his reasoning; he does not suggest that Browne reasons poorly (or not at all); thus, (A) is incorrect. You're left with (C), which fits: the author complains about Browne's lack of clarity.

2. **B**   This question also requires you to use POE. The first answer should be suspect—it would be far too easy if they just expected you to equate "poesy" and "poetry." Remember that the author applies the poesy to Browne's style, which the author qualifies with a combination of positive and negative attributes. In essence, you must match the positive qualities ("excellencies") and negative ones ("faults") with one of the answer choices. None of the last three answers—all of which are tied to "poetry" to keep you leaning toward a simplistic answer—is appropriate. Browne says that greatness is connected to certain extremes (both good and bad) in an individual's character; the author of the passage suggests that the extremes of Browne's character help explain the eccentricities of his style. More often than not, the correct answer will be similar, but not identical, to the answer that you come up with from reading the passage. Your goal is to identify the best answer, and (B) is the only plausible one.

3. **C**   You don't need to know Latin to answer this question! Check the context around it: "To have great excellencies and great faults...is the poesy of the best natures" (lines 12–14). So, the "best" people (with the best natures) have both "great excellencies and great faults." Choices (A) and (D) are traps, since the quote is about human nature, not poetry or poesy. The quote cannot refer only to Browne, so rule out (E). Choice (B) is very close, but is far more extreme than (C). Choice (C) is the best answer because it says "often."

4. **A**   Here's another example for which POE comes in handy. At first glance, (B) seems plausible, but the problem lies in the word "hints." The author does not hint; rather, he says outright that the style is pedantic. The author describes, but does not justify or argue, so (C) and (D) are out. Choice (E) can't be correct; Browne's style is many things (including complex), but it is definitely not facile (easy). It is true that there are some positive elements in the author's evaluation, but these are outweighed by the negative epithets: rugged, pedantic (overly bookish), obscure, harsh, and uncouth. This appears to be open criticism, so (A) is the best answer.

5. **A**   The key to answering this question correctly is to recognize that the author establishes a clear parallel pattern: a sequence of positive qualifiers contrasted with related negative ones (this, but that). At the end of the sentence, however, the author combines two pejorative statements (this and that). This parallelism tips the balance toward the negative, revealing the author's point of view. Remember

that the passage begins with Browne's own comment that suggests greatness originates in a sort of balance between the great qualities and great faults. By adding on only faults at the end of the sentence describing Browne's style, the author shows that he sees more faults than "excellencies." Some of the answer choices are deliberately misleading. Both (B) and (C) pertain to "balance," although each has nothing to do with your answer. Choice (D) appears to function only as "filler." (If you chose this answer, review the definition of parallelism!) Choice (E) is the exact opposite of the correct answer; "obfuscate" means to intentionally mislead.

6. **A**   The first sentence of the third paragraph allows you to use POE to begin eliminating incorrect answer choices: "He fell into an age in which our language began to lose the stability…." Right away, you can eliminate (B), (C), and (E). You should be suspicious of (D) because of the word "metaphorical." Where does "metaphorical" come in? It doesn't, which is why (D) is not the correct answer. Browne lived in a time of linguistic experimentation, and the author of the passage takes the time to discuss this to put some of Browne's excesses in context.

7. **D**   The author at first classifies Browne's use of vocabulary as "useful" and then goes on to describe some of it as "superfluous" and "obscure." You can use POE to eliminate the incorrect answer choices. The last word in the correct answer, "deleterious," may have given you problems; this word means "harmful." The idea that some of his vocabulary is, in fact, harmful to his writing is given in the lines that say that some words "conceal his meaning rather than explain it."

8. **E**   For this question, all of the answer choices probably seem plausible. Your first step should be to find the appropriate part of the text. In the next-to-last paragraph, the author writes, "in defence of his uncommon words and expressions, we must consider, that he had uncommon sentiments, and was not content to express, in many words, that idea for which any language could supply a single term." Thus, the author attributes Browne's unusual diction (word choice) to his desire to find the exact word that expresses his uncommon thoughts or feelings, instead of circuitously expressing them through the use of many words.

9. **A**   This question does not ask anything new; in essence, it addresses the same content as the preceding question, but in a slightly different way while indirectly testing your knowledge of a couple of words. If you understand that "heteroclite diction" signifies the use of words that are unusual or unusually varied, you can probably pick out the correct answer. If not, use POE. You can eliminate (D) right away. You may be familiar with the word "homogeneous," which would allow you to eliminate (B). Even if you aren't sure about the meaning of "mundane" (ordinary, usual, worldly) or "trope" (similar in meaning to a rhetorical figure, for example, metaphor), you will have narrowed your choices to three options and should guess and move on.

10. **A**   This question is relatively straightforward; using POE would enable you to eliminate (B) and (D) since Milton is solely mentioned in line 23 and the author employs an appraisal tone towards Browne's work.. You may have been tempted by (C), but you should have noticed that the author of the passage discusses Browne as though he were writing in the past; for example, the third paragraph begins, "He fell into an age in which our language began to lose the stability which it had obtained in the time of Elizabeth." Finally, if you know that "polemic" means "debate" and that "virulent polemic" means something like a "heated debate," then you can eliminate (E).

11. **B**   Remember that with this type of question, if you can determine that half of the answer is untrue, then you can eliminate the entire answer. Thus, the fact that "sarcastic" seems way off-base allows you to eliminate (A), the inappropriateness of "harsh" allows you to get rid of (C), and the use of

"sentimental" (or "capricious") disqualifies (E). It may not seem unreasonable to claim that the author of the passage is somewhat condescending, but it would be inaccurate to say that he is indulgent; the author appears to genuinely appreciate and admire certain aspects of Browne's style. In fact, he analyzes the style in a scholarly manner, which is why (B) is the best answer.

12. **B**   In the very last line, the author, Virginia Woolf, says that we should "bestow laurel and rose" upon George Eliot. This would have a positive connotation, so rule out "feigned," (C), and "reasoned objectivity," (E). "Qualified" means "with some possible exceptions or reservations," so (D) is too negative. That leaves (A) and (B). Choice (B) is less extreme, so it is therefore the best answer.

13. **B**   This question digs deeper into the relevance of the discussion of religion as it applies to the speaker's view of Eliot as a feminist writer (or as a writer about the feminine condition). Don't let the simile ("like a place of worship") mislead you. The speaker claims that at the heart of Eliot's novels the reader finds a young woman's struggle "in aspiration and agony" for "something that is perhaps incompatible with the facts of human existence." There is no statement about where the heroine might be physically, so (A), (C), and (D) should be eliminated right away. Choice (E) may seem plausible, but in fact, the heroine, as a woman in a world dominated by men, is shut off from "the real world" and forced into herself, not necessarily "lost in prayer." She is more precisely "essentially alone."

14. **B**   The great fact of human existence in the context of this passage is that it's a man's world (remember that Eliot wrote in 19th-century England). The entire passage is about women and their place in "the human condition." Choice (C) may have tempted you, but "the facts of human existence" cannot be limited to these female protagonists. You may have felt that (A) was correct because human existence restricts both men and women in some way; however, the aspirations of the heroines are incompatible only with "the facts of human existence." In this context, the incompatibility pertains only to women.

15. **A**   Every once in a while, the exam will surprise you with a straightforward question like this one. "Save for," which you may have seen written before, is sometimes substituted for the phrase "except for." Choice (A) is correct.

16. **E**   "The difference of [point of] view" and "the difference of standard" are Eliot's "inheritance." Like men, Eliot sought and achieved a significant grasp of art and culture, but according to the speaker, she did not renounce the feminine qualities—the results of her gender—that made her different.

17. **B**   At the end of the passage, the speaker calls Eliot's knowledge and freedom a "double burden" and suggests that the burden led directly to Eliot's death, in the phrase "sank worn out." Clearly, Eliot was not in good health (see lines 41–42, for example, which state "with every obstacle against her—sex and health and convention"), so (A) can be eliminated. Choice (C) is incorrect because Eliot was in fact famous. Choice (D) is also untrue according to the passage, and (E) is the opposite of what is stated in the passage. Choice (B) is the best answer.

18. **D**   The best way to approach this type of question is to use POE. The apposition ("her, a memorable figure") appears almost at the beginning of the sentence, so (A) is not the correct answer. The claim that Eliot reached out "for all that life could offer" may be intended literally, but the statement is hyperbolic (an overstatement). As for (C), there is a clear example of personification when Eliot shrinks "back into the arms of love." One could also argue that there are multiple examples of not very noteworthy parallelism, but perhaps the most obvious one is the construction "reaching out with… confronting her feminine aspirations with." You may expect to find a relative clause in such a long periodic sentence; however, there is none, and the correct answer is (D).

19. **A** The question boils down to this: who is speaking? Use POE. The speaker put the phrase in quotation marks to show that it is not hers; therefore, (B) is incorrect. If the speaker borrowed it from one of Eliot's critics, she would need to identify the citation somehow; (C), therefore, does not seem plausible. From context, it is clear that the reader should take the phrase seriously, and the phrase does represent the speaker's point of view, which is why it is there in the first place. Therefore, (D) and (E) can be eliminated. The entire text centers on Eliot's relationship to her feminine protagonists, and so it seems very probable (in this case, certain) that the speaker would integrate a phrase from one of Eliot's heroines. Choice (A) is the best answer.

20. **C** It would be difficult to accept either qualifier in (A), but "disorganized" is far too pejorative and not appropriate for this passage. Choice (B) is far off the mark too, especially if you can discern between "scholarship" and "pedantry." "Pedantic" means to be characterized by a narrow, often ostentatious concern for book learning and formal rules. You can also eliminate (D), as this passage cannot accurately be described as "metaphysical." Choice (E) is half right; the style could be called "intellectual," but there is no cynicism here. POE leaves you with (C).

21. **D** The passage is from *The Souls of Black Folk*, written by African American author W. E. B. Du Bois, and deals with racism and its psychological effects on him. This is apparent in lines 13–16 and the author's reference to "other black boys" in lines 27–28. Both the author and the other black boys feel estranged from the white society around them. The sense of "being a problem" is not a contrast, (A); it is a comparison. There is no satire in this passage, so rule out (E). The author is not directly condemning racial prejudice, (B); he is simply relating his own psychological perspective. Choice (C) is very tempting, but "universal" makes this answer too extreme. Choice (D) is the best answer.

22. **A** An epiphany is a sudden realization; in this passage, there is a rhetorical statement that announces the moment of epiphany: "Then it dawned upon me with a certain suddenness…." Even if you didn't know the meaning of epiphany, you could use POE to arrive at the correct answer. The author is definitely not describing the incident as a moment of triumph (B). Choice (C) is partly true because the moment is a revelation, but the epiphany is for the boy, not for the reader. The remaining answer choices are not supported by the passage.

23. **D** The most obvious of the metaphors is the sky, which is extended by "dazzling," "sunny," and "streak of blue." The blue, dazzling, and sunny sky represents the world of opportunity that shines above the white children and, for a while, the author. As the child matures, he realizes the narrowness of his opportunities (the blue is reduced to a streak). The other metaphor is the house/prison with its straight, narrow, tall, and unscalable walls of stone; of course, this edifice is not a real prison, but the limiting restrictions of racism. You may have noticed that the walls of the prison are white. You can eliminate the other answers unless you are not familiar with "euphemism," which is a word or phrase that replaces a crass, crude, or simply inappropriate word or phrase.

24. **B** Questions like this can be challenging, but take your time to find out what the word "it" is actually referring to. In this case, the correct answer is (B), "veil." When Du Bois talks about holding "all beyond it in common contempt," he is not talking about a verb, so eliminate "creep" in (C). Similarly, "contempt" and "sky" come after the word "it," so (D) and (E) can be eliminated.

25. **C**   Du Bois does appeal to moral sensibilities about race at various points in the text, but he does not specifically rely on the use of the "beat" to accomplish this goal, so eliminate (A). "Contempt" for his peer group never becomes a dominant emotion for him, even though he says he wants to "beat their stringy heads" (line 21), so (B) can be eliminated as well. Because (D) and (E) both reference abstract concepts not really mentioned in this passage, those answers are not correct and can be eliminated. Thus, (C) is correct. Du Bois uses "beat" in the first two instances to mean "to defeat, overcome" and in the third instance "to hit, strike," which is a clever play on words. Watch how the authors of the AP exam test this particular feature of good writing.

26. **B**   This is a common AP exam phenomenon: two questions so closely linked that you are more likely to get both right or both wrong. "Night" is used metonymically to suggest the color of the boys' skin. (In metonymy, one term is substituted for another term with which it is closely associated.) Therefore, (B) is the correct answer.

27. **A**   You can eliminate (C), (D), and (E) with certainty. The author states that his comrades shrank into "sycophancy"; he implies that he had moments of intellectual and physical triumph over his white peers; he also sets himself somewhat apart from his African American comrades ("other black boys"). Choosing between (A) and (B) is the tricky part. On the one hand, even though the author does finally include himself ("the shades of the prison-house closed around us all"), the author places himself above them by accusing the other black boys of being sycophants, and saying that only he wrested his share of opportunity. By saying that he could win his share of prizes and contests at school, he suggests that he could at least hold his own in professional life (law, medicine, literature), if given the opportunity. Choice (A) is the correct answer.

28. **A**   The previous explanation hints at the answer to this question. The author's first reaction was to remain aloof and "above" the racism at school; however, he realizes that this attitude will do nothing to change one stark reality: that he would not be able to remain apart if he were to somehow "wrest from them" the opportunities open to white boys. He vows to succeed in a field restricted almost exclusively to white men: law, medicine, or literature. The answer is (A).

29. **E**   *Laudatory* means "praiseworthy or congratulatory," and if you know this, the question is not too difficult. If you didn't know this, then POE will enable you to eliminate all of the answers except (E). Watch out for questions that say "EXCEPT" or "NOT"—in these questions, you're looking for the opposite of what you'd usually look for.

30. **B**   This passage is from one of the famous Lincoln-Douglas debates; here, Douglas argues in favor of states' rights. You should note that it is possible to eliminate several of the choices based on the verb used. The speaker presents an argument; he does not analyze, (A); criticize, (C); or describe, (D). Douglas says directly that he is vehemently opposed to the idea of slavery in his home state of Illinois; he argues in favor of letting each state decide the issue for itself and goes on to claim that the greatness of the country rests on the sovereignty of the states to do so.

31. **C**   You might not agree with what Douglas is saying in this passage, but he controls his tone carefully; remember, he is engaged in a debate at a time when people turned out in droves, expecting not colossal home runs, spectacular slam-dunks, hockey fights, or touchdown passes, but brilliantly conceived, expertly delivered rhetoric.

If you use POE, you can narrow it down to three choices by eliminating (A) and (E). Choice (D) may be tempting, but be careful not to apply a 21st-century point of view to 19th-century reality. It may be tempting to see Douglas's defense of states' rights as a mask for his true feelings on slavery or, at least, as a poor veil for a racist bias. However, none of that is appropriate to the task at hand. The tone is best described as the tone of a debate; in other words, the speaker attempts to step back and let the force of his words (the voice of reason, if you will) carry the day. Also, remember that a polemic is a controversial argument.

32. **A**   The speaker uses inductive reasoning (reasoning derived from detailed facts to form general principles) that goes something like this: you all agree that it was right for Illinois to vote as it chose and abolish slavery; thus, every state should be able to make its own choice on this issue. Moreover, every state should be able to make its own choices on just about everything.

33. **D**   In this instance, the word "it" is referring to the choice of New York to make the distinction between "a negro who held property and one who did not" (line 33), so (D) is the best answer. Each of the other answer choices points to a different antecedent and is therefore not correct.

34. **A**   The long sentence in lines 38–43 accomplishes many of Douglas's goals at once. It appeals to the principle of "popular sovereignty" (line 39), defines the term (lines 39–41), accuses Congress of "interfering" (line 42), and encourages his readers to "act conscientiously and rigidly" (lines 38–39). Thus, (A) is the correct answer because this question highlights the word "EXCEPT" in capital letters. There is no evidence of a classification taking place in this sentence.

35. **C**   Check lines 18–37. The author shows that Maine and New York have very different laws regarding African Americans, and that Maine and Illinois are not "interfering" with each other. Lines 39–42 define popular sovereignty as a guarantee "to each State and Territory the right to do as it pleases on all things, local and domestic." This supports either (B) or (C). Choice (B) is too strong, since it uses the word "prove," and the author has not necessarily shown that the laws are "successful." Therefore, (C) is the best answer.

36. **E**   The correct answer may not have been readily apparent, but using POE allows you to eliminate (A) through (D). Douglas uses no anecdotes, much less clever ones; likewise, there are no symbols, paradoxes, or metaphors. The authorities in this case are not only the other states (meaning the voters in the other states), but also the founding fathers: "Washington, Madison, or the framers of this government."

37. **D**   Douglas states his own opinion on slavery (his official opinion, at least) at the beginning of the passage ("there is no man in the State who would be more strenuous in his opposition to the introduction of slavery than I would"). Douglas also presents a clear position on voting: "I would never consent to confer the right of voting and of citizenship upon a negro...." Finally, there is a clear position on property: "I would not make any distinction whatever between a negro who held property and one who did not...." Of course, this implies that he would allow African Americans to have property, but he states that, propertied or not, they should not be able to vote. With this information, it is possible to answer the question with certainty; the correct answer is (D).

38. **E**   Use POE! The last paragraph claims that Abraham Lincoln's policies will bring about the end of America's greatness and plunge the nation into Civil War. The "new doctrine" (line 70) is in opposition to "popular sovereignty" (line 54) and thus would lead to a consolidation of power, (A). Westward expansion, (B), is suggested in lines 57–59, and the author states that popular sovereignty enabled such expansion (line 65–66), so Lincoln's "new doctrine" may hinder that. Choice (C) is explicitly stated in line 71. Choice (D) is also stated directly in line 73. Population, (E), is mentioned in lines 56–57, but there is no direct link between Lincoln's policies and population growth.

39. **C**   In a way, this is simply a reprise of question 36, but here Douglas pushes his scare tactic even further by saying that Lincoln and his party are deliberately infringing on states' rights to incite a civil war. Hopefully you were not fooled by (B). While it is true that Douglas is blaming the war (that hadn't yet begun) on Lincoln and his political party, he is not shifting any blame; nowhere does he imply that anyone was blaming or accusing Douglas and his party of trying to provoke a war, and to shift blame, Douglas would have to have had blame at some point.

40. **A**   In this passage, Douglas is arguing for the application of the doctrine of "popular sovereignty" against the claims of Abraham Lincoln, which is why (A) is correct. He does not spend his time talking at length about Lincoln's failings, so (C) is incorrect. Douglas offers a nuanced argument, but he does not spend his time exploring "the various meanings" of a "universal principle," so (D) is out as well. Because Douglas actively criticizes Congress (in lines 41–42, for example), (B) can also not be correct. Finally, (E) may be referring to the comparison of different states at the beginning of the passage, but this does not describe "the development of the passage as a whole," so eliminate (E).

41. **D**   The first paragraph lays out the definition of *convivencia* ("coexistence" among Muslims, Christians, and Jews in medieval Spain), so (D) is correct. Choices (A) and (B) are incorrect because the author does not want to say that medieval history is unimportant, just that it is portrayed incorrectly in popular histories, which he hardly wants to "reinforce." Notice the way the test writers used words and phrases that sounded correct ("discount the importance of..." and "the popular perception of..."), but were not part of complete, correct answer choices. Remember that if an answer is slightly wrong, it is entirely wrong on the AP English Language and Composition Exam. Choices (C) and (E) don't appear in the passage, which does not discuss historical sources or have "various historical accounts."

42. **D**   The author strings together quotes from various authors in order to retell the traditional "fairy tale" of medieval *convivencia*, which he then goes on to attack. This is why (D) is correct. While the author is frustrated with the "narrative of medieval history offered by most historians of medieval Spain," he is not confused by the narrative, so eliminate (A). Though the author criticizes the works of others, he does not offer his own interpretation in this excerpt, so eliminate (C). Choice (E) may be appealing in that the author does survey the story told by many scholars, but his account is hardly "comprehensive" in describing the entire "history of medieval Spain," so (E) can be eliminated. Choice (B) is also incorrect; although the author is interested in how the "proponents of *convivencia* misinterpret" history, he is less concerned with their understanding of evidence. Besides, that's not the primary reason he used quotes in this paragraph.

43. **C**   The primary purpose of the footnotes in the first paragraph is to document the sources for the expressions in quotes, so (C) is correct. While footnotes can "demonstrate the range of sources" in a work, this is not the case here, so (A) can be eliminated. Choice (D) is not likely to be true because that is a relatively shallow reason for including footnotes and not one that can be easily detected. In fact, most of the wrong answers are too subjective and judgmental to be correct.

44. **E**   The second footnote clarifies that the expression "culture of tolerance" originates in the subtitle of Maria Rosa Menocal's book. While the author is interested in undermining the claims of Menocal, (A) is not correct. Neither are the other choices, which do not accurately portray the author's purposes for including this information here.

45. **B**   The word "contemporary" can have many meanings. If two people live at the same time, then they are considered contemporaries of one another. Contemporary art refers to the art scene of the past decade or so. In this case, the author uses "contemporary" to refer to current problems, so (B) is correct.

46. **A** "Genre" refers in this case directly to "fairy tale," so (A) is correct. The AP exam writers love to embed these grammatical/vocabulary questions into the multiple-choice section. Remember to take your time rereading a few lines above and a few lines below the sentence in which "genre" appears. Then, begin eliminating every word that you know does not relate to "genre" directly, such as "exotic journeys," (E), and "children," (C).

47. **C** The author claims that the proponents of *convivencia* are promoting a fairy tale to a largely ignorant audience: "This is a fairy tale for adults who, like children, know nothing about the actual (medieval) world it attempts to describe." The phrase "like children" is a clear example of a simile—a metaphor that contains the words "like" or "as," so (C) is correct.

48. **E** The author does not mention documentary evidence or methodology, so eliminate (A) and (C) right away. He does claim that some scholars have distorted the relationship between Islam and Christianity during this period, but he does not do so in terms of (B) or (D), which are not precise. The author believes that *convivencia* exaggerates historical reality and distorts the history of medieval Spain into a fairy tale, so (E) is the correct answer.

49. **C** Don't forget the word "EXCEPT" (printed entirely in capital letters) or you will have trouble with this kind of question. Four of these answer choices will be accurate in describing the tone of the second paragraph and one will not. The author shifts his tone between sharp criticism of academic works and elaborate metaphors and humorous insults. He certainly does insist on some of his claims, so (A) is accurate and can be eliminated. "Acerbic," (B), means sharp or bitter, and accurately describes much of this paragraph, as does "vituperative," (E), which means harsh and abusive in its criticism. Eliminate these answer choices as well. At no point does the author express a distinct feeling of relief, so (C) must be correct.

50. **A** When we normally think of "gesture," we think of motions we make with our hands when we speak. This author is going beyond this literal sense to emphasize that the proponents of *convivencia* are only halfheartedly committed to scholarship on the subject. This is why "addressed incompletely" in (A) is correct. When you try each of the other answer choices in the sentence, they either make no sense ("transferred abruptly in the direction of scholarship") or change the meaning of the passage ("characterized dishonestly in the direction of scholarship"). Choice (E) draws from the literal meaning of "gesture" as we normally understand it.

51. **B** This question asks you to identify the author's main point in this passage, which is that the proponents of *convivencia* have encouraged people to believe a "fairy tale" about medieval Spain rather than its real history. Choice (A) is merely the author's introduction of the concept of *convivencia*, while (D) and (E) are more like asides than the main point. While (C) is appealing, it is making a specific point about "Orientalism and exoticism" that the author sustains throughout the second paragraph, not the entire passage. Choice (B) emphasizes the disconnect the author identifies between *convivencia* as a myth and the historical record, which he does not believe supports this view of *convivencia*.

52. **B** By calling *The Ornament of the World* a "syrupy confection" that "simmers under a thick layer of Orientalized cheese," the author uses a metaphor built around food imagery to attack the book as unserious. Thus (B) is correct. Remember that alliteration, (A), is the repetition of the same sound at the beginning of a word; and allegory, (C), is an extended series of symbols in a story. There is not a directly paradoxical (contradictory) claim in the sentence, so eliminate (D). Finally, the author does not ascribe human characteristics to a nonhuman subject, so eliminate (E).

53. **D** As you saw in the previous question, the author directly states that the chapter titles of the *The Ornament of the World* emphasize the extent to which the book "simmers under a thick layer of Orientalized cheese," so (D) is correct. While the titles do refer to Islamic history, (A), and use poetic images, (B), the titles are not included to demonstrate either of these features. The author makes many accusations in this excerpt, but he does not accuse Menocal of hyperbole or failed metaphors, so eliminate (C) and (E) as well.

54. **E** This is a challenging question. The author inserts "and in the delicious irony" as an aside in the final sentence of the second paragraph. Throughout the paragraph, he alluded to sickly sweet food products in the overly dramatic characterizations of *convivencia*: he criticizes "Menocal's syrupy confection" and says that it "simmers under a thick layer of Orientalized cheese." This metaphorical language is extended by his choice of the word "delicious" here, so (E) is correct. The phrase is too short and too unimportant to do any of the tasks mentioned in the other four answer choices.

55. **B** This is a critique of a particular historical perspective, but it is hardly comprehensive or complete enough to be considered a "treatise," so eliminate (A). And while the author is certainly writing a "dismissal," he is not qualifying it in the sense of limiting or restricting a critique, so eliminate (C) because it is only partially correct. (Remember that when "qualified" appears on the exam, it rarely refers to qualifications or credentials.) Because there is no "analysis" of evidence or "comparison" at work in the passage, both (D) and (E) can be eliminated as well. Choice (B) is correct because the author sustains an aggressive attack on a position while employing humor and irony throughout.

Free-Response Questions

Question 1—Synthesis Essay

This sample essay is above average. The student does a good job defining the two sides of the question, choosing one, and defending it. However, it could be argued that the student spends too much time attacking the counterargument, and not enough time supporting his or her own side. Also, the analysis of Source A is very thin—it's not enough to merely recast the source in different words. The student should have added original analysis. The conclusion is well structured and makes a salient point. Overall, this essay would likely earn an 8.

> It seems that there are as many approaches to life as there are people. However, in general, these approaches can be divided into two categories: living for the moment and living for the future. People who live for the moment are often spiritual and artistic personalities, individuals who feel that they may have reached the perfect way to live but who sometimes fail to take care of some of the more mundane parts of life. Those who live for the future, however, have usually made concrete plans that yield benefits over the course of one's life, allowing them to find their happiness later, once the material comforts are taken care of. Of these two ways of living, the future-oriented style produces a better life overall, even though it may be seen as boring or nonspontaneous by some.

> While not all of those who "live in the present" use drugs, of course, generally people who use drugs are not focused on the future. The problem with that approach, as shown in Source A, is that drug use changes your dopamine levels (which are responsible for happiness), resulting in a reduced "ability to experience any pleasure." Then, not only is that person unable to live in the moment, but life begins to seem more pointless.

The hazards of living solely in the moment may also be seen in examples taken from economic and financial areas. In Source G, the Department of Labor urges all people to begin saving for their retirement, noting that "30 percent of private industry workers with access to a defined contribution plan (such as a 401(k) plan) did not participate." That means that those workers, even if they're living in the blissful moment by taking expensive vacations and buying the latest trendy technology, will most likely find themselves in hard economic times come retirement. If those people would begin to save just a few hundred dollars per month, with the power of compounding interest, they could guarantee a better material future for themselves. Our nation has committed similar stupidity on a grand scale. According to Source C, the national debt has gone from $1 trillion to almost $17 trillion in about 35 years. Why did the federal government think it was okay to borrow that kind of money? Didn't it realize that it would someday have to pay it back—and that the youngest taxpayers would be responsible for that?

The happiest people have usually been the ones who have put aside their short-term needs to build a good long-term life. This means making lifelong friends, studying many hours to get a high-paying job, and avoiding momentary distractions like drugs that can derail these goals. It's very possible that, after many years, a future-oriented person can "relax" and have some short-term fun. There are dangers to this approach, of course; a person can become burdened by stress, leading to poor health, or forget how to have fun. But this is still an often safer and more prudent approach than the alternative.

Question 2—Rhetorical Analysis Essay

The following sample is a slightly better than adequate response; the strong writing would probably carry it to a 7 or 8, despite the tenuous grasp of rhetorical strategies. It would be possible to question the student's assertion that Mark Twain's comment that "the scow episode is really a sublime burst of invention" proves that "he is a reasonable critic and not bent on purely insulting the popular author." Most likely, this represents more of Twain's sarcasm.

Mark Twain's well-known essay "Fenimore Cooper's Literary Offenses" seeks to mock both the work itself and its devoted readers. Though Twain's piece has a decidedly ironic tone and is not meant to be serious literary criticism, he employs a variety of rhetorical tactics to argue his point and persuade the audience that not only is Cooper's work flawed and ridiculous, but also that they are misled in having enjoyed Cooper's writing. Twain uses rhetorical devices rooted in both language and content to convince the reader of the validity of his scathing conclusion about Cooper.

By subtle choices of persuasive writing, Twain conveys his meaning through his language. He uses the first person plural as his point of view to connect with the reader and to give an impression of a sympathetic guide alerting the reader to literary inadequacy. Instead of always presenting his evidence outright, Twain uses rhetorical questions to intensify his essay and to catch the reader's attention. By demanding "Did the Indians notice [...]?" he highlights the unrealistic nature of Cooper's work. In the final paragraph, he employs an anaphora, beginning several successive sentences with "Then No...." This repetitive wording emphasizes his message of Cooper's inadequacy. His phrasing plays a key role in convincing the reader of his point.

In addition, Twain's choice of evidence is clearly intended to strengthen his argument. He uses a simile, "He saw nearly all things as through a glass eye, darkly" to help the audience visualize and better comprehend his meaning. To dramatize his critique, Twain writes "It would take you thirty years to guess," an obvious hyperbole that vividly depicts the ridiculousness of Cooper's work. Throughout the essay, Twain relies on mathematical computations and logic to undermine Cooper's credibility, hoping that objective reasoning will sway his readers. Finally, in a concession to Cooper's competency, Twain admits that "the scow episode is really a sublime burst of invention" to illustrate that he is a reasonable critic and not bent on purely insulting the popular author.

Twain's wide range of rhetorical techniques serve to convince his audience in as many different ways as possible that he is a logical, credible critic and that his argument is valid.

Question 3—Argument Essay

The sample essay below serves as a great model, for it exudes an ease that can come only with great practice with the art of writing. There is a clear thesis and organizational structure. Quality replaces quantity, and the clarity is pristine. Remember that above all else, the AP reader craves clarity. The work might not earn a 9, but it would definitely receive an 8.

For as long as authority has existed, there have been those who have challenged it, rebelled against it, and even refused to acknowledge it. Institutions that hold great power—the government, the church, public opinion—have dictated what is right and wrong to those under their control. However, when an individual's personal convictions come into conflict with authority's established morality, persecution, isolation, and other such punishments often follow. Voltaire was correct in his assertion that "it is dangerous to be right" in opposition to the status quo, as demonstrated in history and literature.

As science developed during the Renaissance and humans began to have a more objective understanding of the world, the church held vehemently to its tenets and persecuted those who contradicted its teachings. Italian astronomer Galileo Galilei, whose observations played a pivotal role in our model for the solar system, was one such man who suffered greatly for his non-Christian hypotheses. Though Galileo's theories were indeed correct, the Church nonetheless suppressed his work and placed him under house arrest. Similarly, during the 1950s, McCarthyism swept America, as the government tried to root out "Communists." For the few who condemned the inherent immorality of McCarthy's campaign and tactics, the result was that they too would be blacklisted and effectively ruined. In contradicting the Church and the government, independent thinkers have suffered greatly for "being right" throughout history.

The dangers of questioning authority have not been neglected in world literature. In Milan Kundera's The Joke, the protagonist Ludvik is expelled from the university and the Communist Party for making comments derogatory to the Party. Though his criticisms would certainly be deemed valid by later generations, his correct thinking is rewarded with isolation and prison-like punishment in the military. Fighting against both the establishment and the majority, Arthur Miller's character John Proctor is indeed "right" that the Salem witch trials depicted in The Crucible are madness, and ruining the lives of innocent people. However, his unpopular beliefs only cause him danger as he, too, is soon labeled as a witch. These two protagonists, whose lone voices of reason decry the authorities' "wrong" stance, suffer great dangers as a result of their challenges to the establishment. Voltaire's claim has been continually confirmed by history and literature.

HOW TO SCORE PRACTICE TEST 2

Section I: Multiple-Choice

_____ × 1.2500 = _____
Number of Correct   Weighted
(out of 55)   Section I Score
                                 (Do not round)

Section II: Free Response

(See if you can find a teacher or classmate to score your essays using the guidelines in Chapter 4.)

Question 1   _____ × 3.0556 = _____
                 (out of 9)   (Do not round)

Question 2   _____ × 3.0556 = _____
                 (out of 9)   (Do not round)

Question 3   _____ × 3.0556 = _____
                 (out of 9)   (Do not round)

Sum = _____
        Weighted Section II
        Score (Do not round)

AP Score Conversion Chart English Language and Composition	
Composite Score Range	AP Score
112–150	5
98–111	4
80–97	3
55–79	2
0–54	1

Composite Score

_____ + _____ = _____
    Weighted   Weighted   Composite Score
 Section I Score   Section II Score   (Round to nearest
                                         whole number)

Completely darken bubbles with a No. 2 pencil. If you make a mistake, be sure to erase mark completely. Erase all stray marks.

1. YOUR NAME: _____
(Print)   Last   First   M.I.

SIGNATURE: _____ DATE: ____ / ____ / ____

HOME ADDRESS: _____
(Print)   Number and Street
_____
           City   State   Zip Code

PHONE NO. : _____
(Print)

IMPORTANT: Please fill in these boxes exactly as shown on the back cover of your test book.

2. TEST FORM
_____

6. DATE OF BIRTH

Month		Day		Year	
○ JAN					
○ FEB					
○ MAR	⓪	⓪	⓪	⓪	
○ APR	①	①	①	①	
○ MAY	②	②	②	②	
○ JUN	③	③	③	③	
○ JUL		④	④	④	
○ AUG		⑤	⑤	⑤	
○ SEP		⑥	⑥	⑥	
○ OCT		⑦	⑦	⑦	
○ NOV		⑧	⑧	⑧	
○ DEC		⑨	⑨	⑨	

3. TEST CODE   4. REGISTRATION NUMBER

⓪ Ⓐ ⓪ ⓪ ⓪ ⓪ ⓪ ⓪ ⓪ ⓪ ⓪ ⓪
① Ⓑ ① ① ① ① ① ① ① ① ① ①
② Ⓒ ② ② ② ② ② ② ② ② ② ②
③ Ⓓ ③ ③ ③ ③ ③ ③ ③ ③ ③ ③
④ Ⓔ ④ ④ ④ ④ ④ ④ ④ ④ ④ ④
⑤ Ⓕ ⑤ ⑤ ⑤ ⑤ ⑤ ⑤ ⑤ ⑤ ⑤ ⑤
⑥ Ⓖ ⑥ ⑥ ⑥ ⑥ ⑥ ⑥ ⑥ ⑥ ⑥ ⑥
⑦ ⑦ ⑦ ⑦ ⑦ ⑦ ⑦ ⑦ ⑦ ⑦ ⑦
⑧ ⑧ ⑧ ⑧ ⑧ ⑧ ⑧ ⑧ ⑧ ⑧ ⑧
⑨ ⑨ ⑨ ⑨ ⑨ ⑨ ⑨ ⑨ ⑨ ⑨ ⑨

7. SEX
○ MALE
○ FEMALE

The **Princeton Review**®
© TPR Education IP Holdings, LLC
FORM NO. 00001-PR

5. YOUR NAME

First 4 letters of last name					FIRST INIT	MID INIT
Ⓐ	Ⓐ	Ⓐ	Ⓐ		Ⓐ	Ⓐ
Ⓑ	Ⓑ	Ⓑ	Ⓑ		Ⓑ	Ⓑ
Ⓒ	Ⓒ	Ⓒ	Ⓒ		Ⓒ	Ⓒ
Ⓓ	Ⓓ	Ⓓ	Ⓓ		Ⓓ	Ⓓ
Ⓔ	Ⓔ	Ⓔ	Ⓔ		Ⓔ	Ⓔ
Ⓕ	Ⓕ	Ⓕ	Ⓕ		Ⓕ	Ⓕ
Ⓖ	Ⓖ	Ⓖ	Ⓖ		Ⓖ	Ⓖ
Ⓗ	Ⓗ	Ⓗ	Ⓗ		Ⓗ	Ⓗ
Ⓘ	Ⓘ	Ⓘ	Ⓘ		Ⓘ	Ⓘ
Ⓙ	Ⓙ	Ⓙ	Ⓙ		Ⓙ	Ⓙ
Ⓚ	Ⓚ	Ⓚ	Ⓚ		Ⓚ	Ⓚ
Ⓛ	Ⓛ	Ⓛ	Ⓛ		Ⓛ	Ⓛ
Ⓜ	Ⓜ	Ⓜ	Ⓜ		Ⓜ	Ⓜ
Ⓝ	Ⓝ	Ⓝ	Ⓝ		Ⓝ	Ⓝ
Ⓞ	Ⓞ	Ⓞ	Ⓞ		Ⓞ	Ⓞ
Ⓟ	Ⓟ	Ⓟ	Ⓟ		Ⓟ	Ⓟ
Ⓠ	Ⓠ	Ⓠ	Ⓠ		Ⓠ	Ⓠ
Ⓡ	Ⓡ	Ⓡ	Ⓡ		Ⓡ	Ⓡ
Ⓢ	Ⓢ	Ⓢ	Ⓢ		Ⓢ	Ⓢ
Ⓣ	Ⓣ	Ⓣ	Ⓣ		Ⓣ	Ⓣ
Ⓤ	Ⓤ	Ⓤ	Ⓤ		Ⓤ	Ⓤ
Ⓥ	Ⓥ	Ⓥ	Ⓥ		Ⓥ	Ⓥ
Ⓦ	Ⓦ	Ⓦ	Ⓦ		Ⓦ	Ⓦ
Ⓧ	Ⓧ	Ⓧ	Ⓧ		Ⓧ	Ⓧ
Ⓨ	Ⓨ	Ⓨ	Ⓨ		Ⓨ	Ⓨ
Ⓩ	Ⓩ	Ⓩ	Ⓩ		Ⓩ	Ⓩ

Section ①

Start with number 1 for each new section.
If a section has fewer questions than answer spaces, leave the extra answer spaces blank.

1. Ⓐ Ⓑ Ⓒ Ⓓ Ⓔ   31. Ⓐ Ⓑ Ⓒ Ⓓ Ⓔ   61. Ⓐ Ⓑ Ⓒ Ⓓ Ⓔ   91. Ⓐ Ⓑ Ⓒ Ⓓ Ⓔ
2. Ⓐ Ⓑ Ⓒ Ⓓ Ⓔ   32. Ⓐ Ⓑ Ⓒ Ⓓ Ⓔ   62. Ⓐ Ⓑ Ⓒ Ⓓ Ⓔ   92. Ⓐ Ⓑ Ⓒ Ⓓ Ⓔ
3. Ⓐ Ⓑ Ⓒ Ⓓ Ⓔ   33. Ⓐ Ⓑ Ⓒ Ⓓ Ⓔ   63. Ⓐ Ⓑ Ⓒ Ⓓ Ⓔ   93. Ⓐ Ⓑ Ⓒ Ⓓ Ⓔ
4. Ⓐ Ⓑ Ⓒ Ⓓ Ⓔ   34. Ⓐ Ⓑ Ⓒ Ⓓ Ⓔ   64. Ⓐ Ⓑ Ⓒ Ⓓ Ⓔ   94. Ⓐ Ⓑ Ⓒ Ⓓ Ⓔ
5. Ⓐ Ⓑ Ⓒ Ⓓ Ⓔ   35. Ⓐ Ⓑ Ⓒ Ⓓ Ⓔ   65. Ⓐ Ⓑ Ⓒ Ⓓ Ⓔ   95. Ⓐ Ⓑ Ⓒ Ⓓ Ⓔ
6. Ⓐ Ⓑ Ⓒ Ⓓ Ⓔ   36. Ⓐ Ⓑ Ⓒ Ⓓ Ⓔ   66. Ⓐ Ⓑ Ⓒ Ⓓ Ⓔ   96. Ⓐ Ⓑ Ⓒ Ⓓ Ⓔ
7. Ⓐ Ⓑ Ⓒ Ⓓ Ⓔ   37. Ⓐ Ⓑ Ⓒ Ⓓ Ⓔ   67. Ⓐ Ⓑ Ⓒ Ⓓ Ⓔ   97. Ⓐ Ⓑ Ⓒ Ⓓ Ⓔ
8. Ⓐ Ⓑ Ⓒ Ⓓ Ⓔ   38. Ⓐ Ⓑ Ⓒ Ⓓ Ⓔ   68. Ⓐ Ⓑ Ⓒ Ⓓ Ⓔ   98. Ⓐ Ⓑ Ⓒ Ⓓ Ⓔ
9. Ⓐ Ⓑ Ⓒ Ⓓ Ⓔ   39. Ⓐ Ⓑ Ⓒ Ⓓ Ⓔ   69. Ⓐ Ⓑ Ⓒ Ⓓ Ⓔ   99. Ⓐ Ⓑ Ⓒ Ⓓ Ⓔ
10. Ⓐ Ⓑ Ⓒ Ⓓ Ⓔ   40. Ⓐ Ⓑ Ⓒ Ⓓ Ⓔ   70. Ⓐ Ⓑ Ⓒ Ⓓ Ⓔ   100. Ⓐ Ⓑ Ⓒ Ⓓ Ⓔ
11. Ⓐ Ⓑ Ⓒ Ⓓ Ⓔ   41. Ⓐ Ⓑ Ⓒ Ⓓ Ⓔ   71. Ⓐ Ⓑ Ⓒ Ⓓ Ⓔ   101. Ⓐ Ⓑ Ⓒ Ⓓ Ⓔ
12. Ⓐ Ⓑ Ⓒ Ⓓ Ⓔ   42. Ⓐ Ⓑ Ⓒ Ⓓ Ⓔ   72. Ⓐ Ⓑ Ⓒ Ⓓ Ⓔ   102. Ⓐ Ⓑ Ⓒ Ⓓ Ⓔ
13. Ⓐ Ⓑ Ⓒ Ⓓ Ⓔ   43. Ⓐ Ⓑ Ⓒ Ⓓ Ⓔ   73. Ⓐ Ⓑ Ⓒ Ⓓ Ⓔ   103. Ⓐ Ⓑ Ⓒ Ⓓ Ⓔ
14. Ⓐ Ⓑ Ⓒ Ⓓ Ⓔ   44. Ⓐ Ⓑ Ⓒ Ⓓ Ⓔ   74. Ⓐ Ⓑ Ⓒ Ⓓ Ⓔ   104. Ⓐ Ⓑ Ⓒ Ⓓ Ⓔ
15. Ⓐ Ⓑ Ⓒ Ⓓ Ⓔ   45. Ⓐ Ⓑ Ⓒ Ⓓ Ⓔ   75. Ⓐ Ⓑ Ⓒ Ⓓ Ⓔ   105. Ⓐ Ⓑ Ⓒ Ⓓ Ⓔ
16. Ⓐ Ⓑ Ⓒ Ⓓ Ⓔ   46. Ⓐ Ⓑ Ⓒ Ⓓ Ⓔ   76. Ⓐ Ⓑ Ⓒ Ⓓ Ⓔ   106. Ⓐ Ⓑ Ⓒ Ⓓ Ⓔ
17. Ⓐ Ⓑ Ⓒ Ⓓ Ⓔ   47. Ⓐ Ⓑ Ⓒ Ⓓ Ⓔ   77. Ⓐ Ⓑ Ⓒ Ⓓ Ⓔ   107. Ⓐ Ⓑ Ⓒ Ⓓ Ⓔ
18. Ⓐ Ⓑ Ⓒ Ⓓ Ⓔ   48. Ⓐ Ⓑ Ⓒ Ⓓ Ⓔ   78. Ⓐ Ⓑ Ⓒ Ⓓ Ⓔ   108. Ⓐ Ⓑ Ⓒ Ⓓ Ⓔ
19. Ⓐ Ⓑ Ⓒ Ⓓ Ⓔ   49. Ⓐ Ⓑ Ⓒ Ⓓ Ⓔ   79. Ⓐ Ⓑ Ⓒ Ⓓ Ⓔ   109. Ⓐ Ⓑ Ⓒ Ⓓ Ⓔ
20. Ⓐ Ⓑ Ⓒ Ⓓ Ⓔ   50. Ⓐ Ⓑ Ⓒ Ⓓ Ⓔ   80. Ⓐ Ⓑ Ⓒ Ⓓ Ⓔ   110. Ⓐ Ⓑ Ⓒ Ⓓ Ⓔ
21. Ⓐ Ⓑ Ⓒ Ⓓ Ⓔ   51. Ⓐ Ⓑ Ⓒ Ⓓ Ⓔ   81. Ⓐ Ⓑ Ⓒ Ⓓ Ⓔ   111. Ⓐ Ⓑ Ⓒ Ⓓ Ⓔ
22. Ⓐ Ⓑ Ⓒ Ⓓ Ⓔ   52. Ⓐ Ⓑ Ⓒ Ⓓ Ⓔ   82. Ⓐ Ⓑ Ⓒ Ⓓ Ⓔ   112. Ⓐ Ⓑ Ⓒ Ⓓ Ⓔ
23. Ⓐ Ⓑ Ⓒ Ⓓ Ⓔ   53. Ⓐ Ⓑ Ⓒ Ⓓ Ⓔ   83. Ⓐ Ⓑ Ⓒ Ⓓ Ⓔ   113. Ⓐ Ⓑ Ⓒ Ⓓ Ⓔ
24. Ⓐ Ⓑ Ⓒ Ⓓ Ⓔ   54. Ⓐ Ⓑ Ⓒ Ⓓ Ⓔ   84. Ⓐ Ⓑ Ⓒ Ⓓ Ⓔ   114. Ⓐ Ⓑ Ⓒ Ⓓ Ⓔ
25. Ⓐ Ⓑ Ⓒ Ⓓ Ⓔ   55. Ⓐ Ⓑ Ⓒ Ⓓ Ⓔ   85. Ⓐ Ⓑ Ⓒ Ⓓ Ⓔ   115. Ⓐ Ⓑ Ⓒ Ⓓ Ⓔ
26. Ⓐ Ⓑ Ⓒ Ⓓ Ⓔ   56. Ⓐ Ⓑ Ⓒ Ⓓ Ⓔ   86. Ⓐ Ⓑ Ⓒ Ⓓ Ⓔ   116. Ⓐ Ⓑ Ⓒ Ⓓ Ⓔ
27. Ⓐ Ⓑ Ⓒ Ⓓ Ⓔ   57. Ⓐ Ⓑ Ⓒ Ⓓ Ⓔ   87. Ⓐ Ⓑ Ⓒ Ⓓ Ⓔ   117. Ⓐ Ⓑ Ⓒ Ⓓ Ⓔ
28. Ⓐ Ⓑ Ⓒ Ⓓ Ⓔ   58. Ⓐ Ⓑ Ⓒ Ⓓ Ⓔ   88. Ⓐ Ⓑ Ⓒ Ⓓ Ⓔ   118. Ⓐ Ⓑ Ⓒ Ⓓ Ⓔ
29. Ⓐ Ⓑ Ⓒ Ⓓ Ⓔ   59. Ⓐ Ⓑ Ⓒ Ⓓ Ⓔ   89. Ⓐ Ⓑ Ⓒ Ⓓ Ⓔ   119. Ⓐ Ⓑ Ⓒ Ⓓ Ⓔ
30. Ⓐ Ⓑ Ⓒ Ⓓ Ⓔ   60. Ⓐ Ⓑ Ⓒ Ⓓ Ⓔ   90. Ⓐ Ⓑ Ⓒ Ⓓ Ⓔ   120. Ⓐ Ⓑ Ⓒ Ⓓ Ⓔ

1. YOUR NAME: _____
(Print)   Last   First   M.I.

SIGNATURE: _____   **DATE:** _____ / _____ / _____

HOME ADDRESS: _____
(Print)
                         Number and Street
_____
              City   State   Zip Code

PHONE NO. : _____
(Print)

5. YOUR NAME

First 4 letters of last name				FIRST INIT	MID INIT
Ⓐ	Ⓐ	Ⓐ	Ⓐ	Ⓐ	Ⓐ
Ⓑ	Ⓑ	Ⓑ	Ⓑ	Ⓑ	Ⓑ
Ⓒ	Ⓒ	Ⓒ	Ⓒ	Ⓒ	Ⓒ
Ⓓ	Ⓓ	Ⓓ	Ⓓ	Ⓓ	Ⓓ
Ⓔ	Ⓔ	Ⓔ	Ⓔ	Ⓔ	Ⓔ
Ⓕ	Ⓕ	Ⓕ	Ⓕ	Ⓕ	Ⓕ
Ⓖ	Ⓖ	Ⓖ	Ⓖ	Ⓖ	Ⓖ
Ⓗ	Ⓗ	Ⓗ	Ⓗ	Ⓗ	Ⓗ
Ⓘ	Ⓘ	Ⓘ	Ⓘ	Ⓘ	Ⓘ
Ⓙ	Ⓙ	Ⓙ	Ⓙ	Ⓙ	Ⓙ
Ⓚ	Ⓚ	Ⓚ	Ⓚ	Ⓚ	Ⓚ
Ⓛ	Ⓛ	Ⓛ	Ⓛ	Ⓛ	Ⓛ
Ⓜ	Ⓜ	Ⓜ	Ⓜ	Ⓜ	Ⓜ
Ⓝ	Ⓝ	Ⓝ	Ⓝ	Ⓝ	Ⓝ
Ⓞ	Ⓞ	Ⓞ	Ⓞ	Ⓞ	Ⓞ
Ⓟ	Ⓟ	Ⓟ	Ⓟ	Ⓟ	Ⓟ
Ⓠ	Ⓠ	Ⓠ	Ⓠ	Ⓠ	Ⓠ
Ⓡ	Ⓡ	Ⓡ	Ⓡ	Ⓡ	Ⓡ
Ⓢ	Ⓢ	Ⓢ	Ⓢ	Ⓢ	Ⓢ
Ⓣ	Ⓣ	Ⓣ	Ⓣ	Ⓣ	Ⓣ
Ⓤ	Ⓤ	Ⓤ	Ⓤ	Ⓤ	Ⓤ
Ⓥ	Ⓥ	Ⓥ	Ⓥ	Ⓥ	Ⓥ
Ⓦ	Ⓦ	Ⓦ	Ⓦ	Ⓦ	Ⓦ
Ⓧ	Ⓧ	Ⓧ	Ⓧ	Ⓧ	Ⓧ
Ⓨ	Ⓨ	Ⓨ	Ⓨ	Ⓨ	Ⓨ
Ⓩ	Ⓩ	Ⓩ	Ⓩ	Ⓩ	Ⓩ

IMPORTANT: Please fill in these boxes exactly as shown on the back cover of your test book.

2. TEST FORM

3. TEST CODE   **4. REGISTRATION NUMBER**

⓪	Ⓐ	⓪	⓪	⓪	⓪	⓪	⓪	⓪	⓪	⓪	⓪
①	Ⓑ	①	①	①	①	①	①	①	①	①	①
②	Ⓒ	②	②	②	②	②	②	②	②	②	②
③	Ⓓ	③	③	③	③	③	③	③	③	③	③
④	Ⓔ	④	④	④	④	④	④	④	④	④	④
⑤	Ⓕ	⑤	⑤	⑤	⑤	⑤	⑤	⑤	⑤	⑤	⑤
⑥	Ⓖ	⑥	⑥	⑥	⑥	⑥	⑥	⑥	⑥	⑥	⑥
⑦		⑦	⑦	⑦	⑦	⑦	⑦	⑦	⑦	⑦	⑦
⑧		⑧	⑧	⑧	⑧	⑧	⑧	⑧	⑧	⑧	⑧
⑨		⑨	⑨	⑨	⑨	⑨	⑨	⑨	⑨	⑨	⑨

6. DATE OF BIRTH

Month		Day		Year	
◯ JAN					
◯ FEB					
◯ MAR	⓪	⓪	⓪	⓪	
◯ APR	①	①	①	①	
◯ MAY	②	②	②	②	
◯ JUN	③	③	③	③	
◯ JUL		④	④	④	
◯ AUG		⑤	⑤	⑤	
◯ SEP		⑥	⑥	⑥	
◯ OCT		⑦	⑦	⑦	
◯ NOV		⑧	⑧	⑧	
◯ DEC		⑨	⑨	⑨	

7. SEX
◯ MALE
◯ FEMALE

The Princeton Review®
© TPR Education IP Holdings, LLC
FORM NO. 00001-PR

Section ① Start with number 1 for each new section.
If a section has fewer questions than answer spaces, leave the extra answer spaces blank.

1. Ⓐ Ⓑ Ⓒ Ⓓ Ⓔ
2. Ⓐ Ⓑ Ⓒ Ⓓ Ⓔ
3. Ⓐ Ⓑ Ⓒ Ⓓ Ⓔ
4. Ⓐ Ⓑ Ⓒ Ⓓ Ⓔ
5. Ⓐ Ⓑ Ⓒ Ⓓ Ⓔ
6. Ⓐ Ⓑ Ⓒ Ⓓ Ⓔ
7. Ⓐ Ⓑ Ⓒ Ⓓ Ⓔ
8. Ⓐ Ⓑ Ⓒ Ⓓ Ⓔ
9. Ⓐ Ⓑ Ⓒ Ⓓ Ⓔ
10. Ⓐ Ⓑ Ⓒ Ⓓ Ⓔ
11. Ⓐ Ⓑ Ⓒ Ⓓ Ⓔ
12. Ⓐ Ⓑ Ⓒ Ⓓ Ⓔ
13. Ⓐ Ⓑ Ⓒ Ⓓ Ⓔ
14. Ⓐ Ⓑ Ⓒ Ⓓ Ⓔ
15. Ⓐ Ⓑ Ⓒ Ⓓ Ⓔ
16. Ⓐ Ⓑ Ⓒ Ⓓ Ⓔ
17. Ⓐ Ⓑ Ⓒ Ⓓ Ⓔ
18. Ⓐ Ⓑ Ⓒ Ⓓ Ⓔ
19. Ⓐ Ⓑ Ⓒ Ⓓ Ⓔ
20. Ⓐ Ⓑ Ⓒ Ⓓ Ⓔ
21. Ⓐ Ⓑ Ⓒ Ⓓ Ⓔ
22. Ⓐ Ⓑ Ⓒ Ⓓ Ⓔ
23. Ⓐ Ⓑ Ⓒ Ⓓ Ⓔ
24. Ⓐ Ⓑ Ⓒ Ⓓ Ⓔ
25. Ⓐ Ⓑ Ⓒ Ⓓ Ⓔ
26. Ⓐ Ⓑ Ⓒ Ⓓ Ⓔ
27. Ⓐ Ⓑ Ⓒ Ⓓ Ⓔ
28. Ⓐ Ⓑ Ⓒ Ⓓ Ⓔ
29. Ⓐ Ⓑ Ⓒ Ⓓ Ⓔ
30. Ⓐ Ⓑ Ⓒ Ⓓ Ⓔ

31. Ⓐ Ⓑ Ⓒ Ⓓ Ⓔ
32. Ⓐ Ⓑ Ⓒ Ⓓ Ⓔ
33. Ⓐ Ⓑ Ⓒ Ⓓ Ⓔ
34. Ⓐ Ⓑ Ⓒ Ⓓ Ⓔ
35. Ⓐ Ⓑ Ⓒ Ⓓ Ⓔ
36. Ⓐ Ⓑ Ⓒ Ⓓ Ⓔ
37. Ⓐ Ⓑ Ⓒ Ⓓ Ⓔ
38. Ⓐ Ⓑ Ⓒ Ⓓ Ⓔ
39. Ⓐ Ⓑ Ⓒ Ⓓ Ⓔ
40. Ⓐ Ⓑ Ⓒ Ⓓ Ⓔ
41. Ⓐ Ⓑ Ⓒ Ⓓ Ⓔ
42. Ⓐ Ⓑ Ⓒ Ⓓ Ⓔ
43. Ⓐ Ⓑ Ⓒ Ⓓ Ⓔ
44. Ⓐ Ⓑ Ⓒ Ⓓ Ⓔ
45. Ⓐ Ⓑ Ⓒ Ⓓ Ⓔ
46. Ⓐ Ⓑ Ⓒ Ⓓ Ⓔ
47. Ⓐ Ⓑ Ⓒ Ⓓ Ⓔ
48. Ⓐ Ⓑ Ⓒ Ⓓ Ⓔ
49. Ⓐ Ⓑ Ⓒ Ⓓ Ⓔ
50. Ⓐ Ⓑ Ⓒ Ⓓ Ⓔ
51. Ⓐ Ⓑ Ⓒ Ⓓ Ⓔ
52. Ⓐ Ⓑ Ⓒ Ⓓ Ⓔ
53. Ⓐ Ⓑ Ⓒ Ⓓ Ⓔ
54. Ⓐ Ⓑ Ⓒ Ⓓ Ⓔ
55. Ⓐ Ⓑ Ⓒ Ⓓ Ⓔ
56. Ⓐ Ⓑ Ⓒ Ⓓ Ⓔ
57. Ⓐ Ⓑ Ⓒ Ⓓ Ⓔ
58. Ⓐ Ⓑ Ⓒ Ⓓ Ⓔ
59. Ⓐ Ⓑ Ⓒ Ⓓ Ⓔ
60. Ⓐ Ⓑ Ⓒ Ⓓ Ⓔ

61. Ⓐ Ⓑ Ⓒ Ⓓ Ⓔ
62. Ⓐ Ⓑ Ⓒ Ⓓ Ⓔ
63. Ⓐ Ⓑ Ⓒ Ⓓ Ⓔ
64. Ⓐ Ⓑ Ⓒ Ⓓ Ⓔ
65. Ⓐ Ⓑ Ⓒ Ⓓ Ⓔ
66. Ⓐ Ⓑ Ⓒ Ⓓ Ⓔ
67. Ⓐ Ⓑ Ⓒ Ⓓ Ⓔ
68. Ⓐ Ⓑ Ⓒ Ⓓ Ⓔ
69. Ⓐ Ⓑ Ⓒ Ⓓ Ⓔ
70. Ⓐ Ⓑ Ⓒ Ⓓ Ⓔ
71. Ⓐ Ⓑ Ⓒ Ⓓ Ⓔ
72. Ⓐ Ⓑ Ⓒ Ⓓ Ⓔ
73. Ⓐ Ⓑ Ⓒ Ⓓ Ⓔ
74. Ⓐ Ⓑ Ⓒ Ⓓ Ⓔ
75. Ⓐ Ⓑ Ⓒ Ⓓ Ⓔ
76. Ⓐ Ⓑ Ⓒ Ⓓ Ⓔ
77. Ⓐ Ⓑ Ⓒ Ⓓ Ⓔ
78. Ⓐ Ⓑ Ⓒ Ⓓ Ⓔ
79. Ⓐ Ⓑ Ⓒ Ⓓ Ⓔ
80. Ⓐ Ⓑ Ⓒ Ⓓ Ⓔ
81. Ⓐ Ⓑ Ⓒ Ⓓ Ⓔ
82. Ⓐ Ⓑ Ⓒ Ⓓ Ⓔ
83. Ⓐ Ⓑ Ⓒ Ⓓ Ⓔ
84. Ⓐ Ⓑ Ⓒ Ⓓ Ⓔ
85. Ⓐ Ⓑ Ⓒ Ⓓ Ⓔ
86. Ⓐ Ⓑ Ⓒ Ⓓ Ⓔ
87. Ⓐ Ⓑ Ⓒ Ⓓ Ⓔ
88. Ⓐ Ⓑ Ⓒ Ⓓ Ⓔ
89. Ⓐ Ⓑ Ⓒ Ⓓ Ⓔ
90. Ⓐ Ⓑ Ⓒ Ⓓ Ⓔ

91. Ⓐ Ⓑ Ⓒ Ⓓ Ⓔ
92. Ⓐ Ⓑ Ⓒ Ⓓ Ⓔ
93. Ⓐ Ⓑ Ⓒ Ⓓ Ⓔ
94. Ⓐ Ⓑ Ⓒ Ⓓ Ⓔ
95. Ⓐ Ⓑ Ⓒ Ⓓ Ⓔ
96. Ⓐ Ⓑ Ⓒ Ⓓ Ⓔ
97. Ⓐ Ⓑ Ⓒ Ⓓ Ⓔ
98. Ⓐ Ⓑ Ⓒ Ⓓ Ⓔ
99. Ⓐ Ⓑ Ⓒ Ⓓ Ⓔ
100. Ⓐ Ⓑ Ⓒ Ⓓ Ⓔ
101. Ⓐ Ⓑ Ⓒ Ⓓ Ⓔ
102. Ⓐ Ⓑ Ⓒ Ⓓ Ⓔ
103. Ⓐ Ⓑ Ⓒ Ⓓ Ⓔ
104. Ⓐ Ⓑ Ⓒ Ⓓ Ⓔ
105. Ⓐ Ⓑ Ⓒ Ⓓ Ⓔ
106. Ⓐ Ⓑ Ⓒ Ⓓ Ⓔ
107. Ⓐ Ⓑ Ⓒ Ⓓ Ⓔ
108. Ⓐ Ⓑ Ⓒ Ⓓ Ⓔ
109. Ⓐ Ⓑ Ⓒ Ⓓ Ⓔ
110. Ⓐ Ⓑ Ⓒ Ⓓ Ⓔ
111. Ⓐ Ⓑ Ⓒ Ⓓ Ⓔ
112. Ⓐ Ⓑ Ⓒ Ⓓ Ⓔ
113. Ⓐ Ⓑ Ⓒ Ⓓ Ⓔ
114. Ⓐ Ⓑ Ⓒ Ⓓ Ⓔ
115. Ⓐ Ⓑ Ⓒ Ⓓ Ⓔ
116. Ⓐ Ⓑ Ⓒ Ⓓ Ⓔ
117. Ⓐ Ⓑ Ⓒ Ⓓ Ⓔ
118. Ⓐ Ⓑ Ⓒ Ⓓ Ⓔ
119. Ⓐ Ⓑ Ⓒ Ⓓ Ⓔ
120. Ⓐ Ⓑ Ⓒ Ⓓ Ⓔ

International Offices Listing

China (Beijing)
1501 Building A,
Disanji Creative Zone,
No.66 West Section of North 4th Ring Road Beijing
Tel: +86-10-62684481/2/3
Email: tprkor01@chol.com
Website: www.tprbeijing.com

China (Shanghai)
1010 Kaixuan Road
Building B, 5/F
Changning District, Shanghai, China 200052
Sara Beattie, Owner: Email: tprenquiry.sha@sarabeattie.com
Tel: +86-21-5108-2798
Fax: +86-21-6386-1039
Website: www.princetonreviewshanghai.com

Hong Kong
5th Floor, Yardley Commercial Building
1–6 Connaught Road West, Sheung Wan, Hong Kong
(MTR Exit C)
Sara Beattie, Owner: Email: tprenquiry.sha@sarabeattie.com
Tel: +852-2507-9380
Fax: +852-2827-4630
Website: www.princetonreviewhk.com

India (Mumbai)
Score Plus Academy
Office No.15, Fifth Floor
Manek Mahal 90
Veer Nariman Road
Next to Hotel Ambassador
Churchgate, Mumbai 400020
Maharashtra, India
Ritu Kalwani: Email: director@score-plus.com
Tel: + 91 22 22846801 / 39 / 41
Website: www.scoreplusindia.com

India (New Delhi)
South Extension
K–16, Upper Ground Floor
South Extension Part–1,
New Delhi-110049
Aradhana Mahna: aradhana@manyagroup.com
Monisha Banerjee: monisha@manyagroup.com
Ruchi Tomar: ruchi.tomar@manyagroup.com
Rishi Josan: Rishi.josan@manyagroup.com
Vishal Goswamy: vishal.goswamy@manyagroup.com
Tel: +91-11-64501603/ 4, +91-11-65028379
Website: www.manyagroup.com

Lebanon
463 Bliss Street
AlFarra Building–2nd floor
Ras Beirut
Beirut, Lebanon
Hassan Coudsi: Email: hassan.coudsi@review.com
Tel: +961-1-367-688
Website: www.princetonreviewlebanon.com

Korea
945-25 Young Shin Building
25 Daechi-Dong, Kangnam-gu
Seoul, Korea 135-280
Yong-Hoon Lee: Email: TPRKor01@chollian.net
In-Woo Kim: Email: iwkim@tpr.co.kr
Tel: + 82-2-554-7762
Fax: +82-2-453-9466
Website: www.tpr.co.kr

Kuwait
ScorePlus Learning Center
Salmiyah Block 3, Street 2 Building 14
Post Box: 559, Zip 1306, Safat, Kuwait
Email: infokuwait@score-plus.com
Tel: +965-25-75-48-02 / 8
Fax: +965-25-75-46-02
Website: www.scorepluseducation.com

Malaysia
Sara Beattie MDC Sdn Bhd
Suites 18E & 18F
18th Floor
Gurney Tower, Persiaran Gurney
Penang, Malaysia
Email: tprkl.my@sarabeattie.com
Sara Beattie, Owner: Email: tprenquiry.sha@sarabeattie.com
Tel: +604-2104 333
Fax: +604-2104 330
Website: www.princetonreviewKL.com

Mexico
TPR México
Guanajuato No. 242 Piso 1 Interior 1
Col. Roma Norte
México D.F., C.P.06700
registro@princetonreviewmexico.com
Tel: +52-55-5255-4495
+52-55-5255-4440
+52-55-5255-4442
Website: www.princetonreviewmexico.com

Qatar
Score Plus
Villa No. 49, Al Waab Street
Opp Al Waab Petrol Station
Post Box: 39068, Doha, Qatar
Email: infoqatar@score-plus.com
Tel: +974 44 36 8580, +974 526 5032
Fax: +974 44 13 1995
Website: www.scorepluseducation.com

Taiwan
The Princeton Review Taiwan
2F, 169 Zhong Xiao East Road, Section 4
Taipei, Taiwan 10690
Lisa Bartle (Owner): lbartle@princetonreview.com.tw
Tel: +886-2-2751-1293
Fax: +886-2-2776-3201
Website: www.PrincetonReview.com.tw

Thailand
The Princeton Review Thailand
Sathorn Nakorn Tower, 28th floor
100 North Sathorn Road
Bangkok, Thailand 10500
Thavida Bijayendrayodhin (Chairman)
Email: thavida@princetonreviewthailand.com
Mitsara Bijayendrayodhin (Managing Director)
Email: mitsara@princetonreviewthailand.com
Tel: +662-636-6770
Fax: +662-636-6776
Website: www.princetonreviewthailand.com

Turkey
Yeni Sülün Sokak No. 28
Levent, Istanbul, 34330, Turkey
Nuri Ozgur: nuri@tprturkey.com
Rona Ozgur: rona@tprturkey.com
Iren Ozgur: iren@tprturkey.com
Tel: +90-212-324-4747
Fax: +90-212-324-3347
Website: www.tprturkey.com

UAE
Emirates Score Plus
Office No: 506, Fifth Floor
Sultan Business Center
Near Lamcy Plaza, 21 Oud Metha Road
Post Box: 44098, Dubai
United Arab Emirates
Hukumat Kalwani: skoreplus@gmail.com
Ritu Kalwani: director@score-plus.com
Email: info@score-plus.com
Tel: +971-4-334-0004
Fax: +971-4-334-0222
Website: www.scorepluseducation.com

Our International Partners

The Princeton Review also runs courses with a variety of partners in Africa, Asia, Europe, and South America.

Georgia
LEAF American-Georgian Education Center
www.leaf.ge

Mongolia
English Academy of Mongolia
www.nyescm.org

Nigeria
The Know Place
www.knowplace.com.ng

Panama
Academia Interamericana de Panama
http://aip.edu.pa/

Switzerland
Institut Le Rosey
http://www.rosey.ch/

All other inquiries, please email us at
internationalsupport@review.com